CHILD POVERTY IN AMERICA TODAY

CHILD POVERTY IN AMERICA TODAY

Volume 2: Health and Medical Care

Edited by Barbara A. Arrighi and David J. Maume

Praeger Perspectives

Westport, Connecticut
London

Library of Congress Cataloging-in-Publication Data

Child poverty in America today / edited by Barbara A. Arrighi and David J. Maume.
    p. cm.
    Includes bibliographical references and index.
    ISBN 978–0–275–98926–2 (set : alk. paper)—ISBN 978–0–275–98927–9 (v. 1 : alk. paper)—
    ISBN 978–0–275–98928–6 (v. 2 : alk. paper)—ISBN 978–0–275–98929–3 (v. 3 : alk. paper)—
    ISBN 978–0–275–98930–9 (v. 4 : alk. paper)
    1. Poor children—United States.   2. Poor families—United States.   3. Poverty—United States.
    4. Child welfare—United States.   5. Children—United States—Social conditions.
    6. Children—Government policy—United States.   I. Arrighi, Barbara A.   II. Maume, David J.
  HV741.C4875   2007
  362.7086′9420973–dc22   2007003046

British Library Cataloguing in Publication Data is available.

Library of Congress Catalog Card Number: 2007003046
ISBN-10: 0–275–98926–7 (set)   ISBN-13: 978–0–275–98926–2 (set)
         0–275–98927–5 (vol. 1)   978–0–275–98927–9 (vol. 1)
         0–275–98928–3 (vol. 2)   978–0–275–98928–6 (vol. 2)
         0–275–98929–1 (vol. 3)   978–0–275–98929–3 (vol. 3)
         0–275–98930–5 (vol. 4)   978–0–275–98930–9 (vol. 4)

First published in 2007

Praeger Publishers, 88 Post Road West, Westport, CT 06881
An imprint of Greenwood Publishing Group, Inc.
www.praeger.com

Printed in the United States of America

The paper used in this book complies with the
Permanent Paper Standard issued by the National
Information Standards Organization (Z39.48–1984).

10 9 8 7 6 5 4 3 2 1

To our children
Eiler, Elena, and Megan
and
Meghan and Allison
Our concern for their welfare piqued our interest in the
welfare of all children

CONTENTS

ACKNOWLEDGMENTS

First, we wish to thank all of the contributors to the four volumes for the exceptional caliber of their research. Their dedication and commitment to understanding the causes of child and family poverty is remarkable. It has been a pleasure to work with such a fine group of scholars. It is noteworthy, too, that more than a few of the contributors endured family emergencies and/or experienced personal crises during the research and writing phase, yet remained committed to the project. For that, we are grateful.

We are honored that Diana Pearce is the author of the Introduction for Volume 1: Families and Children. Professor Pearce has written a thoughtful essay weaving common threads among diverse chapters. She is a tireless researcher who has been a pioneer in examining the causes and effects of poverty in the lives of women and children. Not only has Professor Pearce illuminated the way for other researchers in explaining the complex factors influencing women's poverty, she has been an ardent advocate for ending the feminization of poverty.

Thanks to Rachel Sebastian, graduate student at the University of Cincinnati, who assisted with the project. We appreciate, too, the guidance of Elizabeth Potenza, editor at Praeger, throughout the editorial process, Anne Rehill who assisted early on in the project, Nicole Azze, production manager, Vivek Sood, and Saloni Jain who oversaw the copyediting. Finally, thanks to Marie Ellen Larcada, who first approached Barbara about editing the four-volume set.

INTRODUCTION

Barbara A. Arrighi

"Access to quality care is necessary, but not sufficient to eliminate children's health disparities. We cannot narrow the gap in health without addressing disparities in educational
opportunity, employment, economic security, and housing."

Marian Wright Edelman, President and Founder of the Children's Defense Fund

A recent report from the Children's Defense Fund offers a disturbing estimate: "For
the first time in the nation's history, the projected life expectancy for children may
be *less* than that of their parents."[1] However, not all children have an equal chance of
dying younger. Children who live in poverty are at greater risk.

The health disparities among different segments of the population begin to show
up within the first year of life. For example, the infant mortality rate for blacks is
more than twice that of whites (13.9 for blacks and 5.8 for whites, respectively) and
maternal mortality rate for mothers who are black is four times that of whites (24.9
and 6 respectively).[2] In fact, the United States—the wealthiest nation in the world
with the most advanced medical technology—is ranked 25th in infant mortality,[3]
in part, because not all citizens have equal access to health care from the time of
conception.

Healthy infants begin with healthy parents, especially healthy mothers. However,
young girl children living in poverty are at risk for growing up to be women living
in poverty. Prenatal care would be best thought of as care that occurs years before
the nine months of pregnancy. When a life begins in the womb of a woman who
has experienced a matrix of long-term unhealthy physical and emotional conditions
prior to pregnancy—food insecurity, spotty or nonexistent health and dental care,
neighborhood violence, dilapidated living spaces, exposure to lead poisoning, perhaps
homelessness, asthma—can it be said that the life developing within her has an equal

start in life? Can the cumulative physical and psychological stressors that children in poverty experience well into adulthood be neutralized by prenatal care in the first trimester? That the majority of women now seek medical care within the first trimester of pregnancy[4] is laudable, but is it enough? That the wealthiest nation, with the most advanced medical technology, can do better for its youngest and most vulnerable citizens is indisputable? Does it have the will to do so is the question. Other nations that have less do more.

Food insecurity is one of the many issues that children living in poverty face and is addressed in Alaimo's Chapter. About 14 million households suffered food insecurity during 2004,[5] meaning people didn't know if they would be able to provide enough food for all members of their families. If children do not have consistent and sufficient caloric intake, their physical and mental development can be irreversibly compromised. Will the young child who consistently suffers food insecurity during her formative years mature into a healthy young woman whose body is capable of providing the nourishing environment vital for a developing embryo?

The harmful effects of poverty extend beyond infancy. Lead poisoning is a silent threat to children that can and does cause irreversible brain damage. There is mounting evidence that children with lead poisoning have lower IQs, more behavior problems, difficulty learning, and are more likely to engage in criminal behavior.[6] National statistics suggest children receiving Medicaid and children in poverty seem to be disproportionately affected—Medicaid represents 60 percent of children with elevated lead levels in their blood.[7] One reason poor kids are more likely to be affected is because they are more likely to live in older, dilapidated housing with peeling paint that contains lead. In fact, they are more than five times likely to have higher levels of lead in their blood than are children from higher-income families.[8]

There is an expectation that public health organizations will be dogged in tracking harmful conditions. Recently, the Cincinnati Department of Health was ordered by the Ohio Supreme Court to open its records concerning lead paint in rental properties. Five hundred seventy kids suffered lead poisoning in Cincinnati since 2002—250; kids age 6 and younger suffered dangerously high levels of lead in their blood in 2004.[9] The records revealed that although about 300 homes and apartments in Cincinnati were cited for lead paint, the City did nothing to enforce corrective measures. Although jail time was added for offenders in 1994, Cincinnati took less than 1 percent of the cases to court. In fact, of the 300 open cases, 250 exceeded the statute of limitations and require re-filing. The Cincinnati Enquirer (noted for its conservative leanings) reported that a property owner living in Cincinnati is thousands of times more likely to be cited for litter (17,000 property owners were cited) than for renting property with lead paint (only five taken to court). Cincinnati failed to follow through on remedies, even when given federal dollars to do so. For instance, in 1994 Cincinnati received $6 million dollars in Federal funding for lead abatement but not even half of the properties were abated.

Dental care is yet another health issue that separates the rich and the poor. Poor oral health care disproportionately affects children in low-income families. They are more than two times as likely as kids in higher-income families to have untreated cavities and almost a quarter have not been to a dentist within the last year.[10] Not only can poor dental hygiene lead to gum disease, poor eating, and digestive issues, but there is some evidence that, if untreated, poor dental hygiene can lead to heart disease. The thinking is that the bacteria that collects around the gums gets into the bloodstream increasing the risk of blood clots and damaging heart tissue[11] Despite the fact that a connection exists between dental health and overall health, dental health is woefully lacking for children living in poverty. Only about 10 percent of dentists are willing to treat Medicaid patients and only about 20 percent of children covered by Medicaid were seen by a dentist.[12] The dental care statistics indicate that the lack of oral health care for poor children is just one more factor that puts them at increased risk for not being healthy adults.

The universal health care provided by other industrialized countries for their children through age 12 (or older) demonstrates a commitment to proactive preventive care that fosters healthier children and thus, healthier adult citizens. In the United States, federal/state health care for children is means tested, meaning it is available only to low-income children and families. Even at that, despite public health insurance programs like Medicaid and the State Children's Health Insurance Program (SCHIP), over 9 million children in the United States do not have health insurance. Rather than exhausting resources to expand coverage to all children, the federal government, in the last few years, has been shifting fiscal responsibility (but dwindling dollars) from the federal budget to state budgets.[13] Strapped under the increased burden and facing their own fiscal crises, states, in some instances, have shifted Medicaid dollars to other programs. In 1996, Medicaid state spending was 3 percent of state budgets. In 2003, it was approximately 12.7 percent, but in 2006 it declined to 5.5 percent. States are being forced to do more with less.[14]

Unfortunately, things are about to get worse for both state budgets and families living in poverty. The current administration recently proposed to ". . . reduce Medicaid payments to . . . public hospitals . . . by reducing allowable costs.[15] The administration claims "stricter limits" were necessary because federal payments were more than state costs. However, the fear for some is it will simply mean access to health care for the poor will be even more limited. In some areas, such as Los Angeles County, about a third of residents are uninsured and most likely use public hospitals for health care. Reductions in payments could spell disaster for public health in that County. The cuts don't stop at hospitals. The administration plans to tighten Medicaid for school-based health services, expecting to save more than $12.2 billion in the next five years.[16]

The proposed cuts are striking because public health initiatives play a crucial role in reducing health risks for the general population as well as costs. For example, the Centers for Disease Control estimate that a dollar spent on preventive immunization saves $16 in medical treatment for the diseases.[17] And public health immunization programs like Vaccines for Children (VFC) have been instrumental in children starting school with the required immunizations. Immunization programs check the spread of disease and decreases school and work absenteeism. Even at that children of color living in poverty lag behind in their immunizations. As Medicaid increasingly limits coverage for families, what entities have the capacity to carry the fiscal burden and produce the health care results for millions of people?

Federal safety nets are dismantled and states face increasing fiscal challenges, families and children in poverty, underserved by government, are cast off to the private sector. For example, as food stamps become scarce for families and the issue of food insecurity increases for school-age children, backpack clubs have emerged around the country.[18] To ensure school children do not go without a meal over the weekend, kids are given a backpack filled with food items that don't require can openers or cooking. The children return the bag for a refill the next week. The question is what is the nutritional value of the food items in the bag? Do the foods contain higher levels of sodium as most processed foods do? Although the intent of backpack club is positive, there are two issues: (1) School usurps family as the source of nourishment; (2) Family voice is weakened in what the child consumes. A better solution would be for parents to have decent paying jobs so their families do not suffer food insecurity?

One entrepreneur, Gary Davis, used lobbyists and former Senators Dole and McGovern to chase federal dollars (two billion dollars) for his "grab-and-go" Breakfast Breaks for eligible children in poverty. In courting schools to accept his program "He aligned with nonprofits Share our Strength and the Alliance to End Hunger and donates a portion of his sales to those and other groups; for 2006, he expects donations to total about $1 million."[19] Not to be outdone, Kellogg Cereal giant created Morning Jump Starts a box that contains Froot Loops, Pop-Tarts or Graham crackers, and fruit juice.[20] In response to concerns about the healthiness of Froot Loops and Pop Tarts for breakfast, Ruth Jonen, past president of the School Nutrition Association said: "If it improves participation in the breakfast program, we'll take it and hopefully improve on it over time."[21] Do not poor children deserve the highest standard of breakfast now? Should poor children have to wait for *possible* improvements to a bureaucratic program *over time*? Time is not on their side. Should poor children have to settle for complacency from those who ought to be their most potent advocates?

Other nongovernmental aid is coming from nonprofits and corporate partnerships in an attempt to improve the odds for moms and their newborns. For example, Proctor and Gamble partnered with a nonprofit group to form Every Child Succeeds, a program that targets at-risk, low-income pregnant woman and new mothers, usually single.[22] The program is designed to improve both the health of the mothers prenatally and the infants postnatally, thereby decreasing the infant mortality rate. A relatively small and narrowly focused program in existence since 1999, it has served almost 2,000 women and infants. Can it be expanded to hundreds of thousands? Evidence indicates a number of positive outcomes: A majority of mothers quit smoking, more women chose to breastfeed their infants, many women reported eating healthfully, and women were returning to school or obtaining a job."[23]

The chapters in this text examine the struggles that families and children living in poverty endure from the moment of birth. Oberg and Rinaldi's analysis of infant mortality rates illustrates the intersection of poverty and race, ethnicity, and the infant mortality rate. It is a tribute to the health care in the United States that the infant mortality rate (IMR) dropped from 21.8 in 1968 to 7.2 in 1998 as the authors report and that by 2010, the expectation is that it will be at 4.5. However, the authors note that an IMR of 4.5 has been achieved by non-Hispanic whites in some states. Yet the rate for black infants was 13.3 in 2001. Then, too, it is higher for infants born into poverty. Oberg and Rinaldi examine the campaigns to decrease sudden infant death (SIDs) by advancing the Back-to-Sleep (BTS) campaign (having infants sleep on their backs to reduce the risk of SIDs) and the campaign to reduce neural tube defects (NTD) by using a folic acid supplement. Oberg and Rinaldi consider the Diffusion of Innovation (DOI) theory as a guide to advance public health initiatives like Back-to-Sleep and folic acid intake to combat Neural Tube Defects.

Alaimo's chapter is especially timely because it exemplifies life in paradoxical America. While the United States has the highest rate of obesity in the world, it also has one of the highest rates of food insecurity among industrialized nations. The author presents a comprehensive analysis of food insecurity, linking it to multiple variables, including poor health, delayed motor skill, cognitive deficits, decreased school performance, increased rates of infection, as well as depression.

Alaimo notes that the United States has not ratified and signed the Convention on the Rights of the Child, a document signed by all other industrial countries and adopted by the UN in 1990. The document simply states, in part, the "right of the child to the enjoyment of the highest attainable standard of health." The wealthiest nation in the world can ensure a decent standard for its young citizens who represent the nation's future? Can the wealthiest nation—that cares for its children—be satisfied that 13 million children within its borders are impoverished? Alaimo reminds readers that rights must be "socially negotiated and necessitate enforcement by societal institutions."

In a concise yet comprehensive examination of the interaction of race, poverty, and illness, Clark analyzes asthma, a chronic and potentially fatal condition for children. Asthma triggers can be found in the physical and psychological environments in which children of impoverished families live. Potential dangers exist, too often, in the lack of effective communication not only because of social class differences but because of perceived sociocultural differences. Although anxiety can trigger asthma, anxiety can be a consequence of asthma—asthma can increase a child's feeling of vulnerability, especially when it interrupts children's daily lives.

Using ethnographic research Skinner, Lachicotte, and Burton, interviewed 42 families who live in poverty and have at least one child with a disability (seizures, Down's syndrome, autism, pervasive development disorder, asthma). Using interviews over a matter of several years the researchers determine if changes occurred in the families' status—economically, health, as well as in terms of support networks. The authors provide a detailed analysis of the enormous task of a family's daily physical care routine, advocacy, coordination of medical and therapeutic (physical and psychological) services, transportation, and constant mounds of bureaucratic paperwork—the task of a caregiver who is too often not in good health. The research provides an understanding of why families with children who have a disabling condition are almost twice as likely as others to be in poverty.

Similar to Skinner, Lachicotte, and Burton's study, Fletcher and Winter's qualitative research presents a descriptive analysis of 35 families living in poverty who have at least one child who suffers from chronic health conditions (autism, developmental delays, seizure, ADHD, mental retardation). What complicates each family's daily situation is the fact that they live in a rural area, with limited medical resources readily accessible. Treatment for the children, then, in addition to the coordination that Skinner's research delineates, requires an inordinate amount of travel time. For example, one child suffers from a seizure disorder and requires frequent airlifts or 8-hour ambulance rides for treatment. The research illustrates how family life revolves around one child's needs. It is a full-time job that prevents caregivers from taking a job. A constant concern of caregivers is loss of health insurance for their children and, of course, lack of adequate financial resources. Therein is the catch-22. If caregivers take a job, they risk losing insurance for their child's condition. On the other hand, not having a job means lower income and precludes obtaining additional needed therapies. Living in a rural area exacerbates the family's constraints: fewer job opportunities and disallows access to health care. Overall, Fletcher and Winter's study provides an important examination of the difficulty of maneuvering the health care system with limited resources over long distances.

Eiraldi and Mazzuca's research examines a segment of the population that continues to be understudied despite the fact Latinos represent the largest minority group in the United States. Children of Latino backgrounds represent the fastest growing minority group. First, the researchers argue for the disaggregation of the Latino population into appropriate subgroups rather than analyzing all—because of a common language—with a broad monolithic brush. The researchers note, too, the intersection of ethnicity and poverty. In their study of children with ADHD, Eiraldi and Mazzuca are interested in why Latino children are less likely to receive mental health services. Building on prior help-seeking models, they construct a model using multiple variables that influence the process Latino parents tend to follow in seeking health care assistance for their children.

In a study somewhat similar to Eiraldi and Mazzuca, Spencer et al examine the parental perceptions of preschool mental health services. The study focuses on low-income African Americans because although the use of mental health services has doubled in the last two decades, that has not been the case for minorities. Although prior research has targeted adult services, the present study is interested in children's services. The authors discuss the themes that emerge as well as the constraints perceived by parents that impede access to services.

Two studies examine immigrant families and health services. First, using data from the *National Health Interview Survey*, Szaflarski and Ying examine the intersection of child immigrant status, poverty, indicators of child's health, and access to health care (such as health insurance). The researchers found that immigrant children were less likely to have access to health care and they were less likely to have health problems. The study found that the effects of poverty varied by immigrant status, race, and ethnicity.

In an exploratory study Segal, Segal, and Diwakaran compare perceptions of low-income immigrant families with perceptions of low-income native born families on a variety of economic, social, physical, psychological, and health variables. The researchers used a Likert-type questionnaire administered to families as they waited in the examination room at a hospital. Two hundred thirty-five responded (170 native born, 17 second generation, 30 immigrants). Using factor analysis four underlying perceptual dimensions were identified: antisocial behavior; helplessness; low levels of belonging; poor financial resources.

NOTES

1. "Improving Children's Health: Understanding Children's Health Disparities and Promising Approaches to Address Them," *State of America's Children 2006* (Washington, D.C.: Children's Defense Fund), 31.

2. Ibid., 36.

3. Ibid., 31.

4. Ibid., 35.

5. Ibid., 18.

6. Sharon Coolidge, "Lead's Dangerous Legacy," *Cincinnati Enquirer*, June 25, 2006, 1, E1-5; Richard L. Canfield, et al., "Intellectual Impairment in Children with Blood Lead Concentrations Below 10mg per Deciliter," *The New England Journal of Medicine* 348(16) (2003): 1517–1526.

7. "Improving Children's Health," 39; U.S. General Accounting Office, *Medicaid: Elevated Blood Lead Levels in Children*, GAO/HEHS-98–78 (Washington, DC: U.S. General Accounting Office, 1998).

8. "Improving Children's Health," 39.

9. Sharon Coolidge, "Lead's Dangerous Legacy."

10. American Academy of Periodontology, "Levels of Bacteria in Plaque Beneath the Gum Line May Increase Risk for Hearth Attacks," 1–3, available at www.perio.org/consumer/plaque-risk; Denise Grady, "Linking Infection to Heart Disease, *The New Times*, February 17 1998, 1–4. Available at www.nytimes.com/specials/women/warchive/980217

11. Ibid.

12. "Improving Children's Health," 42–43.

13. Ibid., 46–47; Cindy Mann and Samantha Artiga, "Kaiser Commission on Medicaid and the Uninsured," *Kaiser Commission*, June 2006, 1–20.

14. Ibid., 8

15. Robert Pear, "Planned Medicaid Cuts Cause Rift with States," *The New York Times*, August 13, 2006, 16.

16. Ibid.

17. "Improving Children's Health," 50; Terry White, Suzanne Lavoie, and Mary D. Nettleman, "Potential Cost Savings Attributable to Influenza Vaccination of School-aged Children," *Pediatrics* 103(6) (1999): 73–77.

18. Roger Thurow, "Meal Plan: For Hungry Kids 'Backpack Clubs' Try to Fill a Gap," *The Wall Street Journal*, August 31, 2006, 1, A10.

19. Roger Thurow, "Wake-Up Call: Entrepreneur Finds Millions Are Left on Breakfast Table," *The Wall Street Journal*, August 31, 2006, 1, A10.

20. Ibid.

21. Ibid.

22. Gautam Naik, "Baby Steps: Cincinnati Applies a Corporate Model to Saving Infants," *The Wall Street Journal*, June 20, 2006, 1, A14.

23. Ibid.

CHAPTER 1

UNDERSTANDING POVERTY, RACE, AND INFANT MORTALITY*

Charles N. Oberg and Maria C. Rinaldi

The national health objective for 2010 targets an infant mortality rate (IMR) of 4.5 infant deaths per 1,000 live births. In addition, an overarching goal calls for eliminating disparities by income, race, and/or ethnicity. The IMR is defined as the number of infants per 1,000 live births who die prior to the age of 1. Infant deaths are categorized as either neonatal deaths (those which occur from birth through 28 days of life) or postneonatal deaths (those occurring from 29 days to age 1). Over the course of the twentieth century, the United States has made remarkable strides in reducing the infant mortality rate. In the 30 years between 1968 and 1998, the IMR dropped from 21.8 to 7.2 deaths per 1,000 live births.

A report from the Centers for Disease Control and Prevention (CDC) shows that the 2001 infant mortality rate in the United States reached a record low of 6.8 per 1,000 live births.[1] However, data that linked birth/infant death data sets for 1995–2002, which was analyzed from the National Vital Statistics System and maintained by CDC's National Center for Health, indicates that the overall IMR in the United States declined from 7.6 infant deaths per 1,000 live births in 1995 to 6.8 in 2001, and then increased to 7.0 in 2002.[2]

These data further indicate that the national target of 4.5 infant deaths per 1,000 live births was achieved for a select few racial/ethnic populations and in few states. The IMR data for the years of 1995–2002 indicates that the 2010 target of 4.5 infant deaths per 1,000 live births was achieved among infants of non-Hispanic white mothers in Washington DC, Massachusetts, New Hampshire, and New Jersey. Additionally, this target was reached for infants of Asian/Pacific Islander mothers in eight states (Connecticut, Massachusetts, Missouri, New Jersey, New York, Oregon, Pennsylvania, and Texas). However, the target was not achieved in any state for infants of non-Hispanic black, Hispanic, or American Indian/Alaska Native mothers. A further decline of 36 percent overall is needed to reach the target IMR of 4.5 infant deaths per 1,000 live births in 2010, and even greater declines are required for certain racial/ethnic populations to reach the target.

The next section of this chapter will provide an overview of child health disparities and the complex interface between poverty, race, and ethnicity. The paper will then go on to explore infant mortality with an examination of two recent public health interventions to improve birth outcomes; the "Back to Sleep" campaign to address Sudden Infant Death Syndrome (SIDS) and the supplementation of folic acid to reduce neural tube defects. Finally, the Diffusion of Innovation (DOI) theory will be applied to examine the effectiveness of these interventions across poverty, race, and ethnicity.

UNRAVELING HEALTH DISPARITIES—THE INTERFACE OF POVERTY AND RACE/ETHNICITY

The interface of poverty, race, and ethnicity in unraveling and understanding persistent health disparities for children is a "complex" issue and cannot be treated as a one-dimensional phenomenon.[3] It is influenced by the ability of families with children to meet basic needs and secure a basic level of shelter, nutrition, and health care. It is also influenced by the increased risk of detrimental influences faced by families living in poverty such as marital conflict, psychological distress, depression, and loss of self-esteem. Brofenbrenner's ecological approach mandates a contextual view that incorporates the attributes of the child in a home environment duly placed in a community striving to meet unmet needs and the need to obtain long-term resources.[4] Therefore, the impact of childhood poverty needs to be examined epidemiologically from the perspective of adverse health outcomes and the disproportionate burden it places on minority families.

A seminal study from the early 1970s demonstrated the effect of both family characteristics and income on infant and child well-being. The National Collaborative Perinatal Project (NCPP) was conducted as an in-depth follow-up of 26,700 infants. The two factors most predictive of intellectual performance at 4 years of age were family income, represented by socioeconomic status (SES), and maternal education.[5] In addition, Duncan and his colleagues at the University of Michigan two decades later found that children born at low birthweight, or less than 2500 grams, who lived in poverty for their first 5 years of life had IQs that were 9.1 points lower than low birthweight infants never subjected to poverty.[6]

Werner and her colleagues conducted one of the longest longitudinal works comparing perinatal and environmental factors in the developmental outcomes of children. The study was initiated in 1955 and followed 6,987 children born on the island of Kauai, Hawaii. These children, who were exposed to significant perinatal stress, experienced an increased incident of neonatal health problems, learning disabilities, mental retardation, and increased rates of delinquency and teen pregnancy. However, the effects of the family environment and the long-term impact of the care were actually more powerful than the residual effect of perinatal compilations with the risks blunted by an enriched environment in a family with high SES.[7]

It is also well documented that the escalation of childhood poverty witnessed over the past three decades and the burden it places on families has been disproportionately carried by children of color. Whereas the poverty rate in 2003 for white non-Hispanic children is at 10 percent, the rate for black children is 34 percent and 30 percent for Hispanic children. In addition, the number of black children living in extreme poverty, as defined as living in families with incomes less than 50 percent of the Federal Poverty Threshold, is at its highest level in 23 years and is more than four times the rate for white children.[8]

A study by Bazargan and colleagues in 2005 provided a physical and mental health profile of African American and Latino children aged 18 years and younger in public housing communities in Los Angeles County. Results of the study suggest that publicly housed minority children are a particularly vulnerable subgroup in underserved communities. Results indicate that children of poor families living in public housing suffer from chronic physical and mental conditions such as asthma, dental and vision problems, ADHD, and depression, at two to four times the rate of the children in the general population.[9]

Pediatric health disparities are defined as differences in health indicators that exist across subgroups of a population. Just as it has been demonstrated that children of color are disproportionately poor, it has also been demonstrated repeatedly that minority children face greater health disparities.[10] This interplay between income and race/ethnicity though well established has not been adequately explored on the contribution each makes to adverse health outcomes experienced by children of color. Whereas, the socioeconomic disparities in health indicators and utilizations have been well documented for adults, the interface is less clear for infants and children.[11]

Chen, Martin, and Mathews conducted a study to determine whether childhood health disparities are best understood as effects of race, socioeconomic status, or a synergistic effect of the two. The study utilized data provided by the National Health Interview Survey of children aged 0 through 18 years old. The researchers analyzed race by socioeconomic status, which was based on parental education, to predict health outcomes in a large, nationally representative sample of U.S. children.

Results of the analysis indicated that the effects of race and SES are best understood when analyzed together. The study revealed that SES had a significant effect on health outcomes as children from less educated families were more likely to be in fair/poor health. Significant effects of race on health outcomes were evident for black, Hispanic, and Asian children such that children from each minority group were more likely to be rated in fair/poor health than were white children. Lastly, the education by race interaction effect was not significant for black compared to white children, indicating that both white and black children had similar education gradients for fair/poor health. However, the interaction effect was significant for Hispanic compared to white children ($p < 0.001$) and for Asian compared to white children ($p = 0.08$) indicating that education gradients for Hispanics and Asians were less steep for fair/poor health than for white children.[12]

As the Institute of Medicine's report on *Unequal Treatment* states: "Attempts to control for SES differences are inconsistent, with some researchers employing patient income or education as sole indicators of SES, and others using proxy variables such as estimates of income on the basis of patients' zip code information."[13] We are left with this interface where it is evident that poverty contributes substantially to the heath disparities and yet when income and class are controlled for, disparities persist though less striking than when both poverty and race/ethnicity are evident. The next section will provide an overview of infant mortality and epidemiological trends by income, race, and ethnicity.

OVERVIEW OF INFANT MORTALITY TRENDS

While the IMR for most racial/ethnic populations declined over the past several years, major disparities in the rates by race and ethnicity exist. In 2001, rates ranged from 3.2 per 1,000 live births for Chinese mothers to 13.3 for black mothers. Between 1995 and 2001, the overall infant mortality rate declined by 10.5 percent, but rates were down 9 percent for black infants and 14 percent for infants of Hispanic mothers. Infant mortality rates were higher for infants whose mothers were poor, had no prenatal care, were teenagers, had less education, and were unmarried or smoked during pregnancy. Infant mortality rates are higher for infants of U.S.-born women compared to women born outside the United States. Infant mortality rates are higher for male infants, multiple births, and infants born preterm or at low birthweight. Infant mortality also varied greatly by state. Rates are generally higher for states in the South and lowest for states in the West and Northeast. Infant mortality rates among states ranged from 10.4 for Mississippi to 4.9 for Massachusetts.[1]

In addition to the disparities in IMR among most racial/ethnic groups, little improvement has been noted in the relative differences in IMRs among the different racial and ethnic populations. Blacks and American Indian/Alaska Natives continue to have higher rates than whites, Hispanics, and Asian/Pacific Islanders as well as rates above the national average.

Examination of the IMR stratified by race further emphasizes the impressive racial disparity. Analysis of these data, which are expressed as black/white IMR ratios, reveals a number of significant trends. First, the IMR decreased substantially for both whites and black infants over the last 50 years, which most likely reflects improvements in both the medical and public health systems. However, the rate of decline has been less significant for black infants. Figure 1.1, depicts this differential rate of deceleration and the disparities are even more striking when visualized graphically. As can be seen in the diagram, the IMR black/white ratio increased from 1.89 to 2.50 between 1970 and 2000 respectively. These results highlight the powerful influence of race on health disparities. These observations are by no means new, and the effect of both racial and financial income differences on health outcomes has been the focus of study.

A recent study by Shen and colleagues demonstrated that African American women had more pregnancy and childbirth complications, which contribute to this widening disparity in infant deaths. Compared to white women, African American women

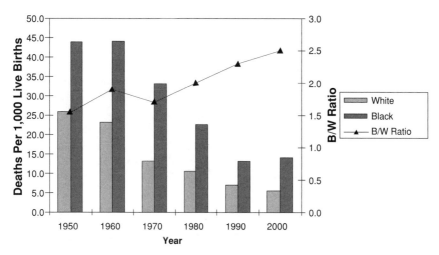

Figure 1.1
Comparison of Black/White Ratio of IMR, 1950–2000

had higher rates of preterm labor, preeclampsia, transient and pregnancy-inducted hypertension, diabetes, placenta previa, placental abruption, premature rupture of membrane (PROM), infection, and cesarean section, all of which can contribute to low birthweight and preterm infants who are a great risk for infant mortality.[14]

Examination of the distribution and frequency of causes of infant death provides insight into the source of the differential IMRs. A recent study linked birth and infant death records of over 23 million singletons belonging to six birth cohorts (1989–1991 and 1995–1997). The results highlight racial differences in the overall and cause-specific infant mortality rates across time in the United States. Infant deaths were predominately attributable to congenital anomalies, short gestation/low birthweight, sudden infant death syndrome, respiratory distress syndrome, and maternal complications. The comparative data between 1989–1991 and 1995–1997 reveal that the overall IMR declined 19.9 percent in the 1995–1997 cohorts compared to the 1989–1991 cohorts. In each birth cohort, non-Hispanic whites, Asian/Pacific Islanders, and Hispanics had lower IMRs than the non-Hispanic blacks and American Indians. In addition, the smallest gains over time were found in the non-Hispanic black population.[15]

Sudden Infant Death Syndrome

One of the major causes of infant death is Sudden Infant Death Syndrome (SIDS). SIDS is the leading diagnosis of infant death in babies who survive past the first month of life and accounts for nearly one third of postneonatal deaths. Despite recent changes in the epidemiology of sudden unexpected death in infancy, it remains one of the most significant causes of infant death in developed countries.

A systematic review of fifty-two studies, undertaken in 16 countries and including over 10,000 sudden unexpected infant deaths during the period 1956 to 1998 was conducted on the relationship between SIDS and socioeconomic status.[16] Socioeconomic status represents a constellation of factors reflecting social position and social circumstances including income, occupation, education, and ownership of resources such as housing. For the purposes of this study, marital status and maternal age, which are not strictly socioeconomic status variables, but have been consistently shown to be strongly associated with measures of social status especially in studies of pregnancy and infant outcome, were used as proxy for economic status.[16] The results of the review show an increased risk of sudden unexpected infant death associated with low socioeconomic status, measured by a range of indicators, which is consistent over time and between countries.

Another recent study from New Zealand also examined the relationship between economic deprivation and one's geographic area of residence and SIDS. The results again confirmed that the risk of SIDS increases significantly as one's residential area of residence becomes more deprived. Specifically, the infants living in the most economically disadvantaged locations were 5.9 times more likely to die of SIDS as compared with infants living in the most affluent areas.[17] The findings of this study suggest that socioeconomic factors have an important role in the pathways leading to SIDS.

Congenital Anomalies: Neural Tube Defects

Congenital anomalies are responsible for a significant proportion of infant deaths during the first year of life. Opportunities to reduce infant mortality and/or morbidity associated with congenital anomalies exist from preconception through the postneonatal period. Interventions may be directed to both the prevention of congenital anomalies and prevention of death from these birth defects. Neural tube defects (NTDs), a term which encompasses a spectrum of disorders from Spina Bifida Occulta to Anencephaly, represent a major preventable source for infant mortality and morbidity.

Table 1.1 reveals that the aggregated NTD-specific IMR for the years 1996–1998 varied by race and ethnicity. While black infants with a NTD were 27 percent less likely than white infants with NTD to die in the first year of life, there was a marked disparity in the high NTD-specific IMR among Hispanics. Hispanic infants had a 50 percent higher NTD-specific IMR when compared to non-Hispanic white infants and this risk was even higher for infants of Mexican descent. Genetics, cultural differences, dietary preferences, and attitudes toward multivitamin use all likely contribute to the disparities. Importantly, the figures underscore the need to focus prevention programs on the Hispanic population.[18]

THE THEORY OF DIFFUSION OF INNOVATION (DOI)

The Diffusion of Innovation theory initially emerged in the early twentieth century from the fields of sociology and communication theory. Everett Rogers formalized the

Table 1.1
NTD-Specific IMR by Maternal Race and Ethnicity, United States, 1996–1998

	Total U.S. Live births	NTD Deaths	NTD IMR[a]	Relative risk (95% CI)
Maternal race				
White	9,284,424	1,081	11.6	–
Black	1,804,596	154	8.6	0.73 (0.62–0.87)
Native American	116,724	13	11.5	0.96 (0.55–1.65)
Asian/Pacific Islander	508,197	50	9.8	0.85 (0.64–1.12)
Ethnicity				
Non-Hispanic white	7,053,814	729	10.3	–
Non-Hispanic black	1,752,657	151	8.6	0.83 (0.70–0.99)
Total Hispanic	2,145,767	330	15.4	1.49 (1.31–1.69)
Mexican	1,504,701	255	17.0	1.64 (1.42–1.89)
Puerto Rican	167,662	17	10.4	0.98 (0.61–1.59)
Central/South American	293,519	35	11.9	1.15 (0.82–1.62)
Total	11,713,941[b]	1.299[b]	11.1	

[a] Per 1000,000 live births.
[b] Sum of categories may not equal total due to missing values.

constructs and broadened its applicability to public health.[19] Diffusion is defined as the process through which an innovation perceived as new, spreads via certain communication channels over time among members of a particular social system. Thus, the theory has four main elements; the innovation, communication channels, time, and a social system. Application of DOI theory into practice has the potential to expand the number of people reached by successful interventions thereby strengthening the public health impact.

In regard to the topic of examining the issue of infant deaths, the first element is innovation and would consist of the new strategies to reduce the IMR for selected populations. The second element is the channels of communication. The innovation transitions through the channels of knowledge, persuasion, decision, implementation, and confirmation. Awareness of these channels of communication create the opportunity for public health professionals to target intervention activities toward influential stages of communication, such as the knowledge and persuasion stages, to create behavior change more effectively.[20] For instance, in the knowledge stage, the target population is learning about the intervention. During this stage, the professional focuses on spreading information by means of mass media to introduce the innovation to the community. During persuasion, when people form an opinion of the program, the public health professional must focus on interpersonal channels of communication and leverage influential capacities of change agents, influential people in the community. The final two elements of DOI are the variables of time and social systems which indicate that adoption varies over time for selected populations that contribute to economic and racial disparities.

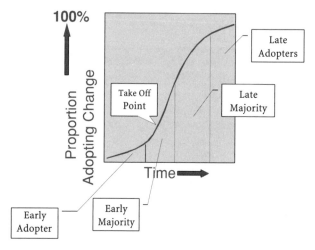

Figure 1.2
The "Classic" Diffusion Cure

The Diffusion of Innovation (DOI) theory also allows us to quantitate and measure change. The theory states that behavior change is contextual thus consistent with Brofenbrenner's work mentioned earlier. Human behavior is formed in the context of multiple factors (e.g., social, political, economic, and individual). Secondly, we presume that the factors that influence our behavior are modifiable and amenable to intervention. This axiom makes the diffusion perspective a more complex theory. Third, change can be measured, not only at the individual level, but also at the organizational, community, and societal level. Fourth, change is continuous. Finally, the rate of change can be influenced.

Diffusion theory states that the percentage of the population that adopts a new behavior follows a predictable pattern over time. Researchers have found that the adoption process is most often described by a curve that resembles an "S-shaped" curve. Figure 1.2, provides a schematic of the classic diffusion curve. On the "Y" axis is the percent of the population adopting a certain intervention with the goal of 100 percent adoption for any particular intervention. The "X" axis is time. All interventions have a very similar pattern for the diffusion curve in the beginning. Research indicates that a program must reach approximately 25 percent, the takeoff point, to ensure a successful intervention in a significant percentage of the population. If an intervention is able to reach this take-off point it has a chance of broad acceptance and the incorporation of the desired behavioral change.

The exact shape of the diffusion curve varies from innovation to innovation. The innovation adoption curve or diffusion curve is a model that classifies adopters of innovations into various categories based on the idea that certain individuals are inevitably more open to adaptation than others. The process begins with the Early Adopters (frequently, innovators and opinion leaders) who will take the lead and incorporate a change into their behavior. The Early Adopters are the first 16 percent to adopt the behavior change. The next class of adopters is the early majority, who comprise the next 34 percent. Behavior change by the early adopters achieves the 50 percent point of adoption of an intervention by a community. At the 50 percent point, the slope of the curve changes and creates a mirror image, with the next 34 percent representing the Late Majority and the last 16 percent representing the Late Adopters.[21] The total of 100 percent does not mean that 100 percent of the population adopts the change but rather the total of 100 percent of those who choose to change. The number represents a cumulative percentage. When an innovation is introduced the majority of the population has intervention adoption rates that fall in between the Early Adopters and the Late Adopters. By identifying the characteristics of people in each adopter category, professionals are able to more effectively plan and implement strategies customized to their needs.

APPLICATION OF DOI TO TWO SELECTED PUBLIC HEALTH INTERVENTION STRATEGIES

The Diffusion of Innovation (DOI) theory has been used successfully for forty years in health, education, and the social sciences. Examples include the expansion of nutrition interventions, tobacco control, and the initiation of family planning and prevention of HIV/AIDS.[22,23] The generalizability of the diffusion model allows the theoretical framework to be applied to a variety of problems.

In a review of the literature on DOI, a discussion was not found on how diffusion theory relates to the two interventions mentioned in the previous section, the "Back-to-Sleep" campaign and folic acid supplementation. While both campaigns achieved some success, an understanding of the Diffusion of Innovation theory clarifies why the interventions were not as successful in certain segments of our population. If applied successfully, the Diffusion of Innovation theory has the potential to help reduce racial/ethnic disparities in IMRs. The campaigns were not as effective initially in the first two channels of DOI, increasing knowledge and persuading communities of color to adopt the changes or in addressing the characteristics of an innovation.

The Back-to-Sleep Campaign and SIDS

The National Institute of Child Health and Human Development (NICHD) and the Maternal and Child Health Bureau (MCHB) developed a national health education campaign in 1994 to encourage parents to put their infants "Back to Sleep." The campaign was based on research showing that a supine sleeping position (infants sleeping on their backs rather than abdomens) greatly decreases the risk of SIDS among full-term, healthy infants.[24,25] The campaign was launched through primary health providers and was embraced by the American Academy of Pediatrics (AAP). As indicated in Figure 1.3, a significant reduction in prone sleeping following the initiation of the "Back to Sleep" campaign was associated with a concomitant decrease in the incidence of SIDS.[26]

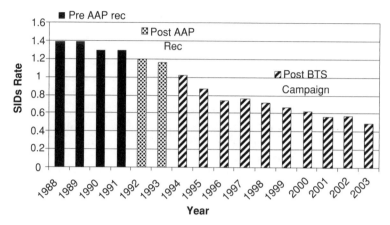

Figure 1.3
SIDs Rate, 1998–2003 (Deaths per 1,000 Live Births)

Figure 1.4 reveals that the substantial drop in sudden infant death syndrome (SIDS) was not shared by all racial and ethnic groups. The figure reflects the "S" shape of the classic diffusion curve with the highest rate of adoption by non-Hispanic whites and Asian families. It is evident that the Back-to-Sleep intervention was less effective in the African American community, in which the SIDS rate remained significantly higher among African American as compared to whites. In 2001 the SIDS rate for infants of black and American Indian mothers was more than double that of non-Hispanic white mothers.

A study conducted by Pickett, Lou, and Lauderdale examined social inequalities in risk of SIDS before and after the introduction of the Back-to-Sleep campaign. The study utilized a cohort of data from the U.S. National Center for Health Statistics

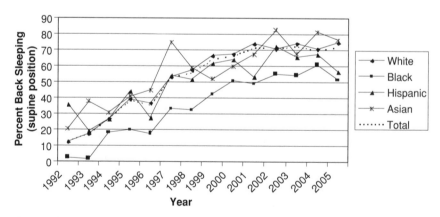

Figure 1.4
Percent of Children Sleeping on Their Back by Year and Race

linked birth and death certificate data on all infants born in the United States and those who die in the first year of life. Data analysis compared birth outcomes in pre-campaign years (1989–1990) and post-campaign years (1996–1998).

The results indicate that infants born in the post-campaign cohort were significantly less likely to die from SIDS ($p. < 0.001$) than infants born in the pre-campaign cohort. The decline was more pronounced for infants born to Hispanic women ($OR = 0.51$) and less pronounced for infants born to black women ($OR = 0.63$) as compared to white women ($OR = 0.58$).[27] In addition, rates declined within each education and race/ethnicity category. In all education groups and in both birth cohorts, infants born to black mothers were at higher risk of death than those born to white mothers, and infants born to Hispanic mothers were at lower risk of death than those born to white mothers.[27]

In sum, the study found that social class inequities in SIDS, as measured by maternal education, did not narrow after the Back-to-Sleep campaign compared with the pre-campaign era. Although the absolute risk of SIDS was reduced for all social class groups, a widening social class inequality was evident as mothers with more education experienced a greater decline than women with less education.

Pickett and colleagues examined the effectiveness of the Back-to-Sleep campaign as a function of social class. Social class was measured by maternal educational achievement. The researchers used data sets of all infant deaths caused by SIDS for the years 1989–1991 and 1996–1998 from the U.S. National Center for Health Statistics linked birth and death certificate data on all infants born in the United States and those who died in the first year. In sum, the study found that social class inequities in SIDS, measured by maternal education, did not narrow after the Back-to-Sleep campaign compared with the pre-campaign era. Absolute risk of SIDS was reduced for all social class groups, though a widening social class inequity was evident as women with more education experienced a greater decline than women with less education.[27]

Following the initial success of the "Back-to-Sleep" campaign and because of the persistent disparity in its adoption, the educational efforts were expanded to include additional community organizations so as to achieve greater penetration into the black community. For example, the U.S. Department of Health and Human Services' Office of Minority Health launched a new public education campaign in 2005 to reduce infant mortality in African American communities entitled "Know What to Do for Life". The campaign uses health prevention messages aimed at fathers, caretakers, and expectant mothers to encourage early prenatal care, abstinence from alcohol and tobacco, proper nutrition, and adoption of a prone sleeping position for infants.[28] This effort will increase knowledge; an important facet of a successful intervention.

It is always important to remember that health professionals, researchers, and public health educators need to continue to assess the environment and identity changes in populations that may be at risk. A recent study in the United Kingdom analyzed five years of case control data to highlight the changing etiology of SIDS. The results indicated that the Back-to-Sleep campaign had been successful in the United Kingdom in reducing the rate of SIDS. However the epidemiology of SIDS has shifted to with SIDS occurring increasingly from low SES families that also included an increase in single parents, younger mothers, and low birthweight infants.[29]

However, as mentioned, it is evident that in addition to increasing knowledge, the second channel, persuasion, and the characteristics of an innovation, relative advantage, compatibility, complexity, trialability, and observability need to be addressed in order to achieve successful adoption in the African American community. Incorporating elements of the Diffusion of Innovation theory into the "Know What to Do for Life" campaign may enhance adoption of behaviors in this segment of the population that will reduce IMR.

Folic Acid Supplementation and Neural Tube Defects

It is well recognized that inadequate intake of folic acid prior to conception and during early pregnancy contributes to the development of NTDs. Nutritional supplementation with the recommended 400 micrograms of folic acid per day not only is associated with a significant reduction in NTDs but also seems to confer a protective effect against low birthweight deliveries.[30–32] Unfortunately, results from the 1991 to 1994 National Health and Nutrition Examination Survey (NHANES) revealed that only 21 percent of non-pregnant women aged 15 to 44 years consumed the recommended daily 400 micrograms of folic acid from any source, including diet, fortified foods, or dietary supplements. As closure of the embryonic neural tube occurs in the first 4–8 weeks of fetal development, pre-pregnancy nutrition is critical as women often are unaware of the conception by this early stage. With improper closure of the neural tube, a spectrum of disorders from Spina Bifida Occulta to Anencephaly may arise. It has been estimated that approximately 50 percent of NTDs may have been prevented with adequate consumption of folic acid from 1 month prior to conception through the end of the first trimester of pregnancy.[33,34]

Naturally occurring dietary sources of folic acid, a synthetic form of the B-vitamin folate, are limited and occur primarily in foods such as beans, legumes, spinach, orange juice, and various meats. As a result, in 1998, the Food and Drug Administration (FDA) mandated that 100 micrograms of folic acid be added to a variety of grain products including breads, rice, and cereals.[35] Despite this dietary fortification, a 2003 March of Dimes/Gallup poll demonstrated that two-thirds of American women of childbearing age still were not receiving the daily-recommended 400 micrograms of folic acid.[36] Successful strategies to further reduce the 2,000 children born each year in the United States with NTDs might include an increase in the folic acid supplementation from the current 100 up to 200 micrograms.[37]

A recent study looked at the initiation of folic acid supplementation based on income and/or SES. Relton and colleagues assessed the use of folic acid supplementations in a small sample of pregnant women suing a social derivation measurement in the United Kingdom. The measure used was the Townsend deprivation index, which is a geographic based measure of social deprivation and poverty. A striking finding was that as the level of deprivation increased there was a concomitant reduction in the correct use of folic acid supplementation. Younger women and/or women who

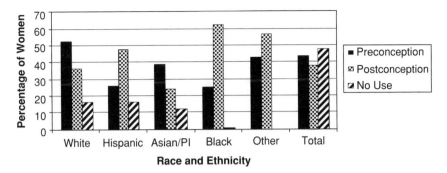

Figure 1.5
Use of Folic Acid Containing Supplements in the Current Pregnancy by Race and Ethnicity (2003–2004)

were more SES disadvantaged were less likely to use folic acid during the critical preconception period.[38]

Further evidence of disparities in consumption were revealed in a 2002 retrospective study using period linked infant birth/death data from the National Center for Health Statistics (NCHS). Figure 1.5 demonstrates the use of consumption of folic acid by race and initiation of supplementation. As can be seen whites and blacks have the highest consumption in the pre-pregnancy and prenatal periods with the lowest in the Hispanic and Asian communities.

The fortification of food with folic acid campaign may also benefit from application of the Diffusion of Innovation theory. To be effective, the increase in folic acid consumption has to occur in the pre-pregnancy period due to the fact that the neural tube closes in the first eight weeks of gestation (during the germinal and embryonic periods) prior to when many women are aware of the pregnancy. For instance, based on DOI theory, an intervention should focus on knowledge of this fact followed by a persuasion campaign to increase the intake of folic acid either through a diet more rich in folic acid or through greater consumption of folic acid fortified grains for all women of childbearing age. To that extent, if the public health intervention is focused toward a shifting of prenatal supplementation for the Hispanic and non-Hispanic black to the pre-pregnancy period, a concomitant reduction in neural tube defects would be realized.

A recent national folic acid campaign was launched in the Netherlands to boost the early and appropriate consumption of folic acid prior to pregnancy. The goal was to reach women from low SES due to the documentation that women from low SES situations had a greater risk of NTDs than higher SES women. The intervention was the use of a mass media campaign to educate women on the importance of folic acid. The results were mixed, showing that once information reached women, it was equally well understood by all groups irrespective of SES and educational backgrounds. However, they did document that the media campaign was not as effective as reaching the women of lower SES status. The conclusion was that to enhance the effectiveness of a media campaign strategies must utilize new effective channels of communications that not only include a focus on income but also address the normative expectations of the woman as well as her partner, friends, and extended family would be to explore in the future.[39]

CONCLUSION

As we continue to work toward reaching the 2010 goals for infant mortality with the elimination of disparities across income, race, and ethnicity, it will be necessary to transform our interventions from a one size fits all to interventions that address unique characteristics of all segments of the population. Once this is achieved, the United States will then realize equity in that all children will be able to live and reach their full potential. It is becoming increasingly important to address both poverty and social class and how it contributes to the health disparities experience by children of color. As Chen and colleagues have recently demonstrated, to better understand and address childhood health disparities we must examine the synergy between both race and socioeconomic status and how each contributes to unmet health-care needs.[12]

The diffusion model provides valuable insights into why some interventions are effective in changing behavior and others are not as successful. The theory's components may serve as a guide for those who work to promote adoption of best evidence practice. Application of the diffusion of innovation theory concepts to public health interventions has the potential to expand the number of people exposed to the program and strengthen the public health impact.

However, developing effective programs is not enough. There are numerous examples of interventions that research has shown to be efficacious but which have failed to translate the research into public health adoption and action. The efficacy of public health interventions is determined in part by the extent to which it is implemented and adopted by individuals, groups of individuals, larger segments of a community and, ultimately, the population at large. Diffusion theory offers a plausible explanation as to why some behaviors are adopted rapidly and others not, despite strong evidence of their potential benefits. Some clinical behaviors may be adopted relatively easily because of the nature of the behavior itself, while others may involve a complex interplay between social systems, communication style, and the decision-making process. Intervention is the process of taking research and translating and disseminating it into communities to effect change. We must disseminate and diffuse the programs effectively in order to reach their full potential for improving population health among all racial and ethnic populations.

NOTES

* Supported in part by Project #T76 MC0005 from the Maternal and Child Health Bureau (Title V, Social Security Act), Health Resources and Services Administration, Department of Health and Human Services.

1. T Mathews and KG Keppel. Racial/ethnic disparities in infant mortality—United States, 1995–2002. *MMWR: Morbidity & Mortality Weekly Report* 2003;54(22):553.

2. TJ Mathews, F Menacker, and MF MacDorman. Infant mortality statistics from the 2001 period linked birth/infant death data set. *Natl Vital Stat Rep* 2003;52(2):1–28.

3. AC Huston, VC McLoyd, CG Coll. Children and poverty: Issues in contemporary research. *Child Dev* 1994;65(2 Spec No):275–282.

4. U Brofenbrenner. Toward an experimental psychology of human development. *Am Psychol* 1977;32:513–531.

5. S Broman, PL Nichols, W Kennedy. *Preschool IQ-Early Prenatal and Early Developmental Correlates.* New York: Wiley, 1975, pp. 1–2.

6. GJ Duncan, J Brooks-Gunn, PK Klebanov. Economic deprivation and early childhood development. *Child Dev* 1994;65(2 Spec No):296–318.

7. E Werner. Risk and resilience in individual with learning disabilities: Lessons learned from the Kauai Longitudinal Study. *Learn Disabil Res Pract* 1993;8:28–34.

8. *America's Children: Key National Indicators of Well-Being 2005*, Federal Interagency Forum on Child and Family Statistics, Editor. 2005, U.S. Government Printing Office.

9. M Bazargan. A profile of chronic mental and physical conditions among African-American and Latino children in urban public housing. *Ethn Dis* 2005;15(4 Suppl 5): S5-3–9.

10. CN Oberg, M Rinaldi. Pediatric health disparities. *Curr Probl Pediatr Adolesc Health Care* 2006;36(7):251–268.

11. G Flores, H Bauchner, AR Feinstein, UT Nyguyen. The impact of ethnicity, family income, and parental education on children's health and use of health services. *Am J Public Health* 1999;89(7):1066–1071.

12. E Chen, AD Martin, KA Matthews. Understanding health disparities: The role of race and socioeconomic status in children's health. *Am J Public Health* 2006;96(4):702–708.

13. Institute of Medicine, *Unequal treatment-confronting racial and ethnic disparities in healthcare.* U.S. Government Printing Office, 2001, p. 75.

14. JJ Shen, C Tymkow, N MacMullen. Disparities in maternal outcomes among four ethnic populations. *Ethn Dis* 2005;15(3):492–497.

15. PK Muhuri, MF MacDorman, TM Ezzati-Rice. Racial differences in leading causes of infant death in the United States. *Paediatr Perinat Epidemiol* 2004;18(1):51–60.

16. N Spencer, S Logan. Sudden unexpected death in infancy and socioeconomic status: A systematic review. *J Epidemiol Community Health* 2004;58(5):366–373.

17. EA Mitchell, AW Stewart, P Crampton, C Salmond. Deprivation and sudden infant death syndrome. *Soc Sci Med* 2000; 51(1):147–150.

18. MJ Davidoff, J Petrini, K Damus, RB Russell, D Mattison. Neural tube defect-specific infant mortality in the United States. *Teratology* 2002;66(Suppl 1):S17–22.

19. E Rogers. *Diffusion of Innovation.* New York: Free Press, 2003.

20. M Haider, GL Kreps. Forty years of diffusion of innovations: Utility and value in public health. *J Health Commun* 2004;9(Suppl 1):3–11.

21. LB Snyder, MA Hamilton, EW Mitchell, J Kiwanuka-Tondo, F Fleming-Milici, D Proctor. A meta-analysis of the effect of mediated health communication campaigns on behavior change in the United States. *J Health Commun* 2004;9:71–96.

22. J Bertrand. Diffusion of Innovation and HIV/AIDS. *J Health Commun* 2004;9:113–121.

23. E Murphy. Diffusion of innovation: Family planning in developing countries. *J Health Commun* 2004;9:123–129.

24. M Willinger, HJ Hoffman, KT Wu, JR Hou, RC Kessler, SL Ward, TG Keens, MJ Corwin. Factors associated with the transition to nonprone sleep positions of infants in the United States: The National Infant Sleep Position Study. *JAMA: The Journal of the American Medical Association* 1998;280(4):329–335.

25. N Oyen, T Markestad, R Skjaerve, LM Irgens, K Helweg-Larsen, B Alm, G Norvenius, G Wennergren. Combined effects of sleeping position and prenatal risk factors in sudden infant death syndrome: The Nordic Epidemiological SIDS Study. *Pediatrics* 1997;100(4):613–621.

26. American Academy of Pediatrics Task Force on Infant Sleep Position and Sudden Infant Death Syndrome. Changing concepts of sudden infant death syndrome: Implications for infant sleeping environment and sleep position. *Pediatrics* 2000;105(3 Pt 1):650–656.

27. KE Pickett, Y Luo, DS Lauderdale. Widening social inequalities in risk for sudden infant death syndrome. *Am J Public Health* 2005;95(11):1976–1981.

28. USDHHS. *Minority Health and Health Disparities.* 2005 [cited August 20, 2006]; Available from URL: http://www.hrsa.gov/OMH/

29. PS Blair, P Sidebotham, PJ Berry, M Evans, PJ Fleming. Major epidemiological changes in sudden infant death syndrome: A 20-year population-based study in the UK. *Lancet* 2006;367(9507):314–319.

30. YH Neggers, RL Goldenberg, T Tamura, SP Cliver, HJ Hoffman. The relationship between maternal dietary intake and infant birthweight. *Acta Obstet Gynecol Scand Suppl* 1997;165:71–75.

31. GM Shaw, RF Librman, K Todoroff, CR Wasserman. Low birth weight, preterm delivery, and periconceptional vitamin use. *J Pediatr* 1997;130(6):1013–1014.

32. TO Scholl, WG Johnson. Folic acid: Influence on the outcome of pregnancy. *Am J Clin Nutr* 2000;71(5 Suppl):1295S–303S.

33. WF Rayburn, JR Stanley, ME Garrett. Periconceptional folate intake and neural tube defects. *J Am Coll Nutr* 1996;15(2):121–125.

34. TO Scholl, ML Hediger, JI Schall, C-S Khoo, RL Fischer. Dietary and serum folate: Their influence on the outcome of pregnancy. *Am J Clin Nutr* 1996;63(4):520–525.

35. LJ Williams, SA Rasmussen, A Flores, RS Kirby, Edmonds LD. Decline in the prevalence of spina bifida and anencephaly by race/ethnicity: 1995–2002. *Pediatrics* 2005;116(3):580–586.

36. March of Dimes. 2004. *Folic Acid,* [cited August 20, 2006]; Available from URL: http://www.marchofdimes.com/professionals/681_1151.asp

37. RL Brent, GP Oakley, Jr. The Food and Drug Administration must require the addition of more folic acid in "enriched" flour and other grains. *Pediatrics* 2005;116(3): 753–755.

38. CL Relton, DM Hammal, J Rankin, L Parker. Folic acid supplementation and social deprivation. *Public Health Nutr* 2005;8(3):338–340.

39. KM Van der Pal-de Bruin, HEK De Walle, CM de Rover, W Jeeninga, MC Comel, LTW de Jong-van den Berg, SE Buitendijk, TGWM Paulussen. Influence of educational level on determinants of folic acid use. *Pediatr Perinat Epidemiol* 2003;17:256–263.

CHAPTER 2

CHILD HUNGER IN THE UNITED STATES: AN OVERVIEW

Katherine Alaimo

I cried only once. I was in a soup kitchen one night, trying but failing to appear incon-spicuous, when a young mother rushed in with three children—an infant and twin boys. She was running from something, but no one seemed to care. Her boys were about 4, dressed in rags and bone thin, and they attacked a tray of peanut butter sandwiches as if they hadn't seen food in a month. A volunteer fixed them a place with cookies, an apple, a cup of vegetable soup and more sandwiches. They ate furiously, their eyes darting in all directions as if someone might stop them. They stuffed themselves, because they knew the uncertainties of tomorrow. Little street soldiers, preparing for the coming battles. Is this the Third World, I asked myself? Or is this America?

        —John Grisham, on his experiences researching his novel, *The Street Lawyer*[1]

Although the United States is one of the wealthiest nations in the world, a significant segment of U.S. population do not reap the benefits, including children. According to a recent UNICEF report, the United States has the second highest relative child poverty rate (percentage of children below 50% of the median household income) of 24 other rich countries.[2] Absolute poverty levels are also comparatively high; almost 20 percent of U.S. children are poor, when using the U.S. poverty line as a measure-ment standard, in contrast to less than 10 percent in 11 other countries, including Canada, France, and Germany.[3] This translates into over 13 million children currently growing up in poverty the United States.[4]

For many, the issue of poverty in America is intertwined with images of hunger. As the opening quote illustrates, the immediacy of a hungry child has a strong psychological impact, and the extraordinary network of feeding programs available—food banks and soup kitchens, government food assistance, such as the Food Stamp Program and School Lunch Program, food drives and donations by corporations and religious and service institutions, and the community food security movement are a testament to our collective discomfort with a child going without food.

But clearly, these supports are not adequate. This chapter addresses the subject of food deprivation in the United States and it's effects on children. Specifically, this chapter summarizes the latest research on the consequences of food deprivation on children's health, growth, and academic achievement, explores the multiple layers of effects that food deprivation can have on children within the context of their families, and describes recent research on Federal food security programs and child outcomes.

FOOD INSECURITY AND HUNGER

Today, Federal policymakers, antihunger advocates, and researchers use the terms "food insecurity" and "hunger" to describe the phenomenon of food deprivation in the United States.[5] Food insecurity is defined as "the limited or uncertain availability of nutritionally adequate and safe foods, or limited, or uncertain ability to acquire acceptable foods in socially acceptable ways," while hunger is more narrowly used to mean the "uneasy or painful sensation caused by a lack of food" or "the recurrent and involuntary lack of access to food."[6] The definition of food insecurity is based upon a consensus that hunger, or food restriction that elicits the sensation of hunger, is not the only socially meaningful characteristic of food deprivation that matters to society; the definition also encompasses the concepts of access, availability, and safety of food in addition to the social meaning of food acquisition methods.

Our current understanding of the phenomena of food insecurity and hunger draw from a rich research base of ethnographic research conducted with low-income North American women and families since the 1980s.[7] There are four flexible, though most commonly staged, components described by people experiencing household-based food insecurity. First, there is a sense of worry about the food situation as food resources diminish, a core characteristic of food insecurity that Radimer et al.[8] called "food anxiety" and Hamelin, et al.[9] labeled "preoccupation with access to enough food." This uncertainty often is about the immediate situation, but could also include longer-term worry about the future. Second, diminished resources result in constraints to purchase or acquire food that is not considered acceptable quality or types. This refers to meals that are monotonous and reflect a lack of intrameal and intermeal variety; and also to the safety freshness, and nutritional value of the food supply.[10] Eventually, food supplies could become small enough to result in a shortage of food in the household, the third component of food insecurity. Several studies have shown that food supplies are lower among food insecure households.[11] In addition, intake among some low-income families, and food stamp program recipients in particular, declines throughout the month as food resources become further unavailable.[12]

Finally, qualitative research has found a strong sense among food-insecure families of shame over a lack of control over their situation, as many resort to acquiring food in socially unacceptable ways, such as at shelters or by purchasing out-dated food.[13] Hamelin et al. labeled this core characteristic of food insecurity as "alienation: lack of control over the food situation," and "the need to hide it."[14] Acquiring food from food banks, soup kitchens, friends, or neighbors are strategies undertaken by households who no longer have other choices; further, there is a lack of choice in food type, quality, and quantity inherent in accepting food from most charitable sources. According to one study, this is "a state of frustration due to being deprived of access to food and subjected to unmodifiable conditions. Because the adults could not feed their household properly and did not anticipate any improvement in the near future, they felt they did not have a fit place in society."[15]

MAGNITUDE OF FOOD INSECURITY AND HUNGER IN THE UNITED STATES

Utilizing the conceptualizations of household food insecurity and hunger, a U.S. Household Food Security Survey Module (HFSSM) was developed in the early 1990's and has now been administered as part of the U.S. Census Bureau's Current Population Survey (CPS) annually since 1995.[16] The measure was developed with wide consensus among antihunger advocates, researchers, academics, and government officials and is broadly accepted, used, and disseminated by each of these sectors, including the Federal government. It includes 18 questions, asked of a household respondent—10 items about household food insecurity and adult hunger, and 8 items about child food insecurity and hunger. Households with children are asked all 18 items, while households without children are asked only the 10 items about household food insecurity and adult hunger. Households are thought to be "food insecure without hunger" if members are habitually concerned about their food situation or if the adult(s) in the household occasionally go without food (for example, skip meals).[17] A household will be categorized as "food insecure with hunger" if the adult(s) in the household go(es) without food or a child is cutting the size of their meals or "not eating enough."

In 2004, the prevalence of food insecurity in the United States was 11.9 percent of all households, and 3.9 percent of households experienced hunger at some point throughout the year.[18] Households with children are particularly at risk, and those with single parents even more so. Almost 17 percent of households with children experience food insecurity at some point throughout the year, and more than a third of female-headed households with children experience food insecurity.[19]

In 2001, Nord and Bickel published an in-depth analysis of children's food insecurity and hunger status using the CPS data from 1995 to 1999 and concluded that the prevalence of childhood hunger from 1998 to 1999 was 0.7 percent.[20] However, a reanalysis of the 1995 CPS data for a National Academy of Sciences report showed that, in 1995, 3.1 percent of households with children in that year responded positively to at least one of the items referring to child hunger, including: "cutting the size of children's meals," "children were not eating enough," "a child skipped a meal," or "a child did not eat for whole day."[21] In any case, the official figures are likely an underestimate; several vulnerable populations are not captured by the survey including the homeless or those households who do not have telephone service.

Food is just one of many material necessities that may be lacking in a poor family's life, and the trends in food insecurity closely track those of poverty in the United States. In this country, poverty is defined by a threshold income level defined by three times the USDA Thrifty Food Plan.[22] It is intended to be set at a level at which a family's income is inadequate to meet its basic material needs, such as housing, food, health care, child care, and clothing, although it is not tied to budgets that allow for those needs, except for food. While the percentages of Americans who are food insecure and poor are in close alignment, food-insecure households are not necessarily the same households that fall below the poverty line. Only 35.1 percent of households with incomes below the poverty line experienced food insecurity in 2003, and only approximately 50 percent of families affected by hunger have incomes below the poverty line.[23]

CONSEQUENCES OF FOOD INSECURITY AND HUNGER FOR CHILDREN IN UNITED STATES

Studies of poverty in the United States have also shown important consequences of children growing up without sufficient income resources. In a comprehensive review of the literature up until 1995, Crooks[24] concluded that poor children were more likely to have low birthweight, chronic illness, and lead poisoning, higher rates of stunting, and deficits in cognitive and academic functioning. In their summary of several longitudinal studies in *Consequences of Growing Up Poor*, Duncan and Brooks-Gunn[25] also conclude that poverty has a strong effect on children's cognition and academic achievement and later earning ability.

Fewer studies have been conducted in the United States to understand the consequences specifically associated with food deprivation. The distinction is important because, as stated previously, not all poor children are hungry or food insecure; and not all food insecure children have family incomes below the poverty line. Until recent developments in measuring food insecurity, hunger, and food insufficiency (defined as "an inadequate amount of food intake due to lack of resources" and used by some government surveys before the development of the HFSSM), indicators of malnutrition in poor children, such as anthropometric measures, were used as a proxy for food deprivation. These studies often found positive relationships between height or weight, and either cognition, achievement, or both.[26]

The main problem with these studies is that anthropometric indicators of nutrition status (such as height and weight) are not specific, nor sensitive enough for policy purposes. Food and income assistance programs are designed to aid families and children who do not have access to enough food due to resource limitations. Height, or stunting, for example, is affected by genetic factors as well as malnutrition and associations with poor outcomes do not necessarily mean that hungry children do worse, or that shorter children do worse. In addition, labeling only shorter children as "hungry" will miss many children who did not get enough food to eat, but whose height was not affected.

In more recent years, researchers have documented effects of hunger for U.S. children using questionnaire-based methods. Various indicators of hunger, food insecurity or food insufficiency have been associated with child physical and psychological health outcomes in both community and national surveys, controlling for confounding factors such as family income, parent's education, and health insurance status. Child physical health outcomes associated with food insecurity, hunger, or food insufficiency include higher prevalence of fair/poor health status, increased stomach aches and headaches, increased hospitalizations, and increased colds (among preschool children).[27] Psychological and social outcomes that have been found to be associated with a measure of food deprivation include increased internalizing and externalizing behaviors, increased anxiety, increased aggression and difficulty getting along with other children, hyperactivity, impaired psychosocial functioning and social skills.[28] In one study, researchers found food insufficiency was associated with depression and suicidal symptoms among teenagers.[29] This finding was significant because poorer children were *less* likely to be depressed, except if they were food insufficient.

Food insecurity, hunger, and food insufficiency have also been shown to be associated with a range of academic outcomes among school-aged children, including lower math scores, repeating a grade, tardiness, and absenteeism.[30] However, reading scores are not lower among food insecure or hungry children, and importantly, food insufficiency and hunger has not been associated in the United States with cognitive measures, such as portions of the IQ test.[31]

In 1994, Dietz published a case study describing a child who was both hungry and overweight, and hypothesized that food insecurity could cause weight gain.[32] The theory is that individuals who are food deprived may tend to overeat when food does become available, and/or that individuals who are food insecure are more likely to eat cheaper foods, which tend to be energy-dense and nutrient poor.[33] This association has been tested in both adults and children data. While studies of weight among food insecure women has shown a significant association, there is little evidence of an association among children; if anything, food insecure and particularly hungry children are more likely to be underweight.[34]

HOW FOOD DEPRIVATION AFFECTS CHILDREN

Food shortage at the household level can affect children biologically, by causing a reduction of food intake among children within that household and/or the diminished nutritional quality of children's diets, such as nutrient deficiencies like iron or vitamin A. These concepts are traditionally what we have meant by the terms "hunger," the sensation that occurs when one is unable to eat, or does not eat to satiety, and "malnutrition." Poverty, malnutrition, and harsh environmental conditions are often much more severe and life-threatening in developing countries than they are in developed countries such as the United States and studies of malnutrition and hunger in poorer countries have clearly documented devastating consequences of food deprivation for children—including poor health status, delays in motor skills, cognitive deficits, decreases in school performance, greater rates of infection and death.[35] Current theory postulates that malnutrition's effect on children occurs through motivational and emotional behaviors.[36] Severely malnourished children have been shown to be apathetic, withdrawn, and passive and have decreased motivation and heightened anxiety.[37]

It is important to understand, however, that household food insecurity can also affect children even if they are eating "enough" to assuage hunger and nutrient deficiencies. In addition to actual deprivation, as stated above, food insecurity also causes a strong *sense* of deprivation.[38] This feeling associated with food insecurity may be of equal importance to the actual sensation of hunger and/or nutritional quality in terms of consequences of food insecurity, particularly with regard to outcomes such as depression.

A exceptionally illuminating paper describes in-depth qualitative interviews with Mississippi children 11–16 years of age about food insecurity and hunger among people they know.[39] In addition to food behaviors associated with food insecurity (eating less, eating "cheap" foods, eating less desirable foods, or eating larger amounts/faster), content analysis revealed that the children clearly recognized the social and psychological dimensions of family food insecurity. These included worry/anxiety/sadness about the family food supply ("They make those sad faces"; "They will look crazy and try to borrow food"); shame/fear of being labeled as "poor" (". . . well, where we stay, they will [tease them]. . . push them in the head and talk about them. They will bring up something like that that they had to come to their house and eat their food"); and limited participation in social activities (due to lack of money).[40]

It is also likely that family food insufficiency affects children's outcomes through food deprivation of their *parent(s)*. Food insecurity is a "managed process" affecting whole families, not just children.[41] There is strong evidence that food allocation in food-insecure and hungry families in the United States is such that parents (most commonly mothers) deprive themselves of food before they allow their children to go hungry.[42] Both qualitative and quantitative research has described the prioritization of children's food intake over their parents within households in North America.[43] Further, food insecure parents can also feel powerless in relation to their food situation. Words used by food insecure respondents to describe their feelings include: loss of dignity, shame, embarrassment, guilt, powerlessness, fear, and frustration. As one respondent stated: "Hunger is more than physical pain, it hurts inside."[44]

Among women and mothers, food insecurity has been shown to be associated with poorer health status, overweight, and importantly, depression.[45] A lack of food and/or the constant anxiety associated with not having enough food may cause parental distress or irritability which, in turn, can affect children through parenting behaviors.[46] Thus, it is possible that parental food deprivation can have developmental consequences for children, again, even if the children are eating "enough." Several of the respondents in Hamelin et al.'s study reported disturbed parent–child dynamics associated with lack of food.[47] For example, one respondent stated: "When I don't eat, I become aggressive (or rude or angered) with my children."[48] Parents' stress and psychological impairment are among the strongest predictors of child developmental and psychological problems.[49]

POLICIES THAT WORK

Education reformers recognize that the cure for distressed school districts (such as those in inner cities) necessitates addressing the poverty in which children in those school districts live. As Anyon states, "Attempting to fix inner city schools without fixing the city in which they are embedded is like trying to clean the air on one side of a screen door."[50] Children are whole individuals and cannot be compartmentalized into education, housing, food, and other single issues. Solving one of these without addressing the others does not create whole, healthy, successful students.

The same could be said for childhood hunger—ensuring that all children are fed without fixing the family economic insecurity underlying the problem will allow us to come closer to our goal of having healthy children, but will not succeed completely. Providing food to children while parents go without will not necessarily improve child outcomes, nor will ensuring that families have food, but not other necessities. *Food security*, in contrast to *food sufficiency* (an inadequate amount of food), requires ready availability of food as well as "the assured ability to acquire acceptable foods in socially acceptable ways (e.g., without resorting to emergency food supplies, scavenging, stealing, and other coping strategies)." This latter condition, "assured ability," is only possible for families who have sufficient resources, that is, who are economically secure. Economic security, as used here, incorporates not only the ideas of a family having income above the poverty line, but also a family's ability to endure sudden economic changes such as loss of employment or food stamps, or large expenses for health care, housing, or child care.

A main distinction is whether society supports low-income families by providing charitable food assistance, or by providing an economic structure whereby families are able to make ends meet for themselves through their own labor. This means employment locally available that pays enough; and if the pay is not enough (a common occurrence with the erosion of the minimum wage rate), then government supports are available to make up the difference. In addition to food (including cooking facilities), successful families require enough resources for safe housing, health insurance, clothing, child care, transportation, adequate training/education, and time off to care for illness. Increasingly, however, working families, with incomes below or sometimes up to twice the poverty line, are unable to meet these necessities with only the income and benefits provided by their employer.[51]

Many people think of antihunger programs as those program that provide food, but any program that increases families' resources acts as a buffer to hunger and food insecurity. Likewise, government food programs serve as both economic and food security needs. Recently, nutrition, medical, and policy researchers have turned their attention to the outcomes associated with Federal policies aimed at reducing poverty and the material hardships associated with poverty such as food insecurity, hunger, and homelessness. Although there are limitations in study designs due to selection bias (families who are worse off self-select to participate in programs), many studies that control for selection bias find that the federal programs we have in place *work* in terms of reducing food insecurity and improving outcomes for children, but the programs are inadequately funded and offered to cover enough children and their families to provide an adequate nutritional and economic safety net.[52]

For example, the Food Stamp Program has been shown to reduce the depth of poverty, increase family food purchases (among single-parent families), and improve food security status.[53] However, changes in the program administration that accompanied the 1996 Welfare Reforms significantly reduced food stamp coverage for many low-income families, including making it harder for families to receive benefits and reducing the benefit levels. Recent studies from the Children's Sentinel Nutrition Assessment Program have found that these losses are associated with increased food insecurity, and that participation in the Food Stamp Program reduces the negative effect of food insecurity on children's general health status.[54]

Similarly, the Special Supplemental Nutrition Program for Women, Infants, and Children (WIC), which currently provides benefits to almost half of all infants in the United States and about a quarter of the children ages 1–4,[55] has shown to be effective in increasing mean birthweight, reducing the incidence of low birthweight, decreasing birth-related Medicaid costs, increasing nutrient intake among infants and young children, and improving children's health status.[56] It is not clear, however, if WIC affects a family's food insecurity status. Two studies addressing improvements in food security status in families accessing WIC found conflicting results.[57]

There have been other studies that underscore the importance of whole family economic policies, not just those that address food issues. Two studies have examined the trade-off that low-income families face in winter months when faced with heating bills. One found that during winter months, poor families reduce food expenditures by roughly the same amount as the increase in fuel expenditures, while rich families increase their food expenditures. This translated into a reduction in about 200 kilocalories among poor adults and children during winter months.[58] Another study found that children who visit emergency rooms were twice as likely to be hungry or at risk of hunger if their families were without heat or were threatened with a utility turn-off during the previous winter. Further, children presenting during the winter months were more likely to have weight-for-age scores below the fifth percentile.[59] A recent study to determine variations in hunger rates among states found that "to reduce hunger rates, policymakers should consider ways to mitigate income shocks associated with high mobility (i.e., frequent housing moves) and unemployment and reduce the share of income spent on rent by low-income families."[60] Indeed, one study of housing subsidies among food insecure families showed a significant improvement in weight-for-age among those receiving the subsidy.[61]

The United States is the only industrial nation that has not yet ratified and signed the Convention on the Rights of the Child, which was adopted in 1989 and entered into force by the General Assembly of the United Nations in 1990.[62] This document establishes "the right of the child to the enjoyment of the highest attainable standard of health" and "the right of every child to a standard of living adequate for the child's physical, mental, spiritual, moral and social development."[63] Rights are not natural in the sense that humans have inherent rights as individuals, but they are instead socially negotiated and necessitate enforcement by societal institutions. Basic rights specify the basic minimum we believe no one should fall below. It can be argued that economic security or subsistence rights are no less basic or genuine than the civil and political rights the U.S. Constitution currently recognizes.[64] This review of child food insecurity and hunger in the United States demonstrates that the closer we come to achieving those rights, the more we will benefit our children, who are our nation's future.

NOTES

1. J Grisham. Somewhere for everyone. *Newsweek* February 9, 1998.

2. UNICEF. *Child poverty in rich countries, 2005.* Florence, Italy 2005.

3. B Bradbury, Jantti M. *Child poverty across industrialized nations.* Innocenti Occasional Papers, Economic Policy Series, Florence, Italy, 1999.

4. C DeNavas-Walt, Proctor B D, Lee C H. *Income, poverty and health insurance coverage in the United States: 2004*: U.S. Department of Commerce; 2005.

5. M Nord, Andrews M, Carlson S. Household food security in the United States, 2001 (FANRR-29). Alexandria (VA): U.S. Department of Agriculture, Food and Rural Economics Division, Economic Research Service; 2002. www.ers.usda.gov/publications/fanrr42_researchbrief.pdf

6. Life Science Research Office Federation of American Societies for Experimental Biology. Core indicators of nutritional state for difficult to sample populations. *Journal of Nutrition* 1990(102):1559–1660.

7. J Fitchen. *Poverty in rural America: A case study.* Boulder, CO: Westview Press; 1981; J Fitchen. Hunger, malnutrition, and poverty in the contemporary United States: Some observations on their social and cultural context. *Food and Foodways.* 1998;2:309–333; A Hamelin, Habict J, Beaudry M. Food insecurity: Consequences for the household and broader social implications. *Journal of Nutrition* 1999;129:525S–528S; A Hamelin, Habict J, Beaudry M. Characterization of household food insecurity in Quebec: Food and feelings. *Social Science Medicine* 2002;54:119–132; K Radimer. *Understanding hunger and developing indicators to assess it.* Dissertation/Thesis. Ithaca, NY, Cornell University Editor; 1990; K L Radimer, Olson C M, Campbell C C. Development of indicators to assess hunger. *Journal of Nutrition* 1990;120 Suppl 11:1544–1548; K Radimer, Olson C, Greene J, Campbell C, Habicht J. Understanding hunger and developing indicators to assess it in women and children. *Journal of Nutrition Education.* 1992;24:36S–45S; S Quandt, Rao P. Hunger and food security among older adults in a rural community. *Human Organization* 1999;58(1):28–35; C L Connell, Lofton K L, Yadrick K, Rehner T A. Children's experiences of food insecurity can assist in understanding its effect on their well-being. *Journal of Nutrition.* Jul 2005;135(7):1683–1690.

8. K Radimer, Olson C, Greene J, Campbell C, Habicht J. Understanding hunger and developing indicators to assess it in women and children. *Journal of Nutrition Education.* 1992;24:36S–45S.

9. A Hamelin, Habict J, Beaudry M. Food insecurity: Consequences for the household and broader social implications. *Journal of Nutrition* 1999;129:525S-528S; A Hamelin, Habict J,

Beaudry M. Characterization of household food insecurity in Quebec: Food and feelings. *Social Science and Medicine* 2002;54:199–132.

10. A Hamelin, Habict J, Beaudry M. Characterization of household food insecurity in Quebec: Food and feelings. *Social Science and Medicine* 2002;54:199–132.

11. L L Kaiser, Melgar-Quiänonez H, Townsend M S, Nicholson Y, Fujii M L, Martin A C, Lamp C L. Food insecurity and food supplies in Latino households with young children. *Journal of Nutrition Education and Behavior* May–Jun 2003;35(3):148–153; A Kendall, Olson C, Frongillo E. Validation of the Radimer/Cornell measures of hunger and food insecurity. *Journal of Nutrition.* 1995;125:2793–2801; D Matheson, Varady J, Varady A, Killen J. Household food security and nutritional status of Hispanic children in the fifth grade. *American Journal of Clinical Nutrition* 2002;76:210–217.

12. F E Thompson, Taren D L, Andersen E, Casella G, Lambert J K, Campbell C C, Frongillo E A, Jr., Spicer D. Within month variability in use of soup kitchens in New York state. P4. *American Journal of Public Health* 1988;78(10):1298–1301; P Wilde, Ranney C. *A monthly cycle in food expenditure and intake by participants in the U.S. Food stamp program.* Ithaca: Cornell University; March 1997. WP 97-04; P Wilde, Ranney C. The monthly food stamp cycle: Shopping frequency and food intake decisions in an endogenous switching regression framework. *American Journal of Agriculture Economics* 2000;82(2):200–213; D L Taren, Clark W, Chernesky M, Quirk E. Weekly food servings and participation in social programs among low income families. *American Journal of Public Health* 1990;80(11):1376–1378; D Matheson, Varady J, Varady A, Killen J. Household food security and nutritional status of Hispanic children in the fifth grade. *American Journal of Clinical Nutrition* 2002;76:210–217.

13. A Hamelin, Habict J, Beaudry M. Characterization of household food insecurity in Quebec: Food and feelings. *Social Science and Medicine* 2002;54:199–132; A Hamelin, Habict J, Beaudry M. Food insecurity: Consequences for the household and broader social implications. *Journal of Nutrition* 1999;129:525S–528S.

14. A Hamelin, Habict J, Beaudry M. Characterization of household food insecurity in Quebec: Food and feelings. *Social Science and Medicine* 2002;54:199–132.

15. Ibid.

16. W Hamilton, Cook J, Thompson W, Buron L, Frongillo E, Olson C, Wehler C. *Household food security in the United States in 1995: Summary report of the food security measurement project.* Alexandria, VA 1997.

17. G Bickel, Nord M, Price C, Hamilton W, Cook J. *Guide to measuring household food security, revised 2000.* Alexandria, VA 2000; M Nord, Andrews M, Carlson S. Household food security in the United States, 2001 (FANRR-29). Alexandria (VA): U.S. Department of Agriculture, Food and Rural Economics Division, Economic Research Service; 2002.

18. M Nord, Andrews M, Carlson S. *Household food security in the United States, 2004.* Alexandria, VA 2005. Economic Research Report No. (ERR11).

19. Ibid.

20. M B G Nord, Andrews M P M. *Estimating the prevalence of children's hunger from the current population survey food security supplement.* In: Anonymous, editor. Food Assistance and Nutrition Research Report No. 11-2; 2001:31.

21. K Alaimo, Froelich A. *Alternative construction of a food insecurity and hunger measure from the 1995 current population survey food security supplement data.* Washington, DC 2004.

22. C DeNavis-Walt. Income, poverty and health insurance coverage in the United States: 2003. *U. S. Government Printing Office* 2004;Series P60–201.

23. M Nord, Andrews M, Carlson S. Household food security in the United States, 2003, D Rose. Economic determinants and dietary consequences of food insecurity in the United States. *Journal of Nutrition.* 1999;129(2):517.

24. D Crooks. American children at risk: Poverty and its consequences for children's health, growth, and school achievement. *Yearbook of Physical Anthropology.* 1995;38:57–86.

25. J Duncan, Brooks-Gunn J. *Consequences of growing up poor.* New York, NY: Russell Sage Foundation; 1997.

26. J Douglas, Ross J, Simpson H. The relation between height and measured educational ability in school children of the same social class, family size and stage of sexual development. *Human Biology* 1965;37:178–186; L Humphreys, Dvey T, Park R. Longitudinal correlation analysis of standing height and intelligence. *Child Development* 1985;31(6):1465–1478; R Karp, Martin R, Sewell T, Manni J, Heller A. Growth and academic achievement in inner-city kindergarten children. *Clinical Pediatrics* 1992;31(6):336–340; G Richards, Marshall R, Kreuser I. Effect of stature on school performance. *Journal of Pediatrics* 1985;6(5):81–82; E Pollitt, Mueller W, Leibel R. The relation of growth to cognition in a well-nourished preschool population. *Child Development* 1982;53:1157–1163; R W Thatcher, McAlaster R, Lester M L, Cantor D S. Comparisons among EEG, hair minerals and diet predictions of reading performance in children. *Annals of the New York Academy of Science* 1984;433:87-96; D Wilson, Hammer L, Duncan P, Dornbusch S, Ritter P, Hintz R, Gross R, Rosenfeld R. Growth and intellectual development. *Pediatrics.* 1986;78:646-650; L Edwards, Grossman M, Mushkin S. The relationship between children's health and intellectual development. In: Anonymous, editor. *Health: What is it worth? Measures of health benefits.* New York: Pergamon Press; 1980:270–313.

27. K Alaimo, Olson C, Frongillo E, Briefel R. Food insufficiency, family income and health in U.S. Preschool and school-age children. *American Journal of Public Health.* 2001;91:781–786; P H Casey, Szeto K L, Robbins J M, Stuff J E, Connell C, Gossett J M, Simpson P M. Child health-related quality of life and household food security. *Archives of Pediatrics & Adolescent Medicine.* Jan 2005;159(1):51–56, P Casey, Szeto K, Lensing S, Bogle M, Weber J. Children in food-sufficient, low-income families. *Archives Pediatric Adolescent Medicine* 2001;155:508-514; P Casey, Goolsby S, Berkowitz C, Frank D, Cook J, Cutts D, Black M M, Zaldivar N, Levenson S, Heeren T, Meyers A, The children's sentinel nutritional assessment program study group. Maternal depression, changing public assistance, food security, and child health status. *Pediatrics* Feb 2004;113(2):298-304; J Cook, Brown J. Children's rights to adequate nutritious foods in the two Americas. *Food Policy* 1996;21(1):11–16; J T Cook, Frank D A, Berkowitz C, Black M M, Casey P H, Cutts D B, Meyers A F, Zaldivar N, Skalicky A, Levenson S, Heeren T. Welfare reform and the health of young children: A sentinel survey in 6 US cities. *Archives of Pediatrics & Adolescent Medicine* Jul 2002;156(7):678–684, J T Cook, Frank D A, Berkowitz C, Black M M, Casey P H, Cutts D B, Meyers A F, Zaldivar N, Skalicky A, Levenson S, Heeren T, Nord M. Food insecurity is associated with adverse health outcomes among human infants and toddlers. *Journal of Nutrition* Jun 2004;134(6):1432–1438; J T Cook, Frank D A, Levenson S M, Neault N B, Heeren T C, Black M M, Berkowitz C, Casey P H, Meyers A F, Cutts D B, Chilton M. Child food insecurity increases risks posed by household food insecurity to young children's health. *Journal of Nutrition* Apr 2006;136(4):1073–1076.

28. P H Casey, Szeto K L, Robbins J M, Stuff J E, Connell C, Gossett J M, Simpson P. Child health-related quality of life and household food security. *Archives of Pediatrics and Adolescent Medicine* 2005;159(1):51–56; R Kleinman, Murphy M, Little M, Pagano M, Wehler C, Regal K, Jellinek M. Hunger in children in the United States: Potential behavioral and emotional

correlates. *Pediatrics* 1998;101(1) p.e3; L Weinreb, Wehler C, Perloff J, Scott R, Hosmer D, Sagor L, Gundersen C. Hunger: Its impact on children's health and mental health. *Pediatrics.* 2002;110(4) p. e41; J Murphy, Wehler C, Pagano M, Little M, Kleinman R, Jellinek M. Relationship between hunger and psychosoci functioning in low-income American children. *Journal of the American Academy of Child Adolescent Psychiatry.* 1998;37(2):163–170; K Alaimo, Olson C, Frongillo E. Food insufficiency and American school-aged children's cognitive, academic, and psycho-social development. *Pediatrics* 2001;108(1):44–53; K Alaimo, Olson C, Frongillo E. Family food insufficiency, but not low family income, is positively associated with dysthymia and suicide symptoms in adolescents. *Journal of Nutrition* 2002;132:719–725; D F Jyoti, Frongillo E, Jones S. Food insecurity affects social children's academic performance, weight gain, and social skills. *Journal of Nutrition* 2005;135:2831–2839; R Dunifon, Kowaleski-Jones L. The influences of participation in the National School Lunch Program and food insecurity on child well-being. *Social Service Review* 2003;77:72–92, K S Slack, Yoo J. Food hardship and child behavior problems among low-income children. *Social Service Review* 2005;79:511–536.

29. K Alaimo, Olson C, Frongillo E. Family food insufficiency, but not low family income, is positively associated with dysthymia and suicide symptoms in adolescents. *Journal of Nutrition* 2002;132:719–725.

30. D F Jyoti, Frongillo E, Jones S. Food insecurity affects social children's academic performance, weight gain, and social skills. *Journal of Nutrition* 2005;135:2831–839; E Frongillo, Jyoti D F, Jones S. Food Stamp Program participation is associated with better academic learning among school children. *Journal of Nutrition* 2006;136:1077–1080; J Winicki, Jemison K. Food insecurity and hunger in the kindergarten classroom: Its effect on learning and growth. *Contemporary Economic Policy* 2003;21(2):145–157; K Alaimo, Olson C, Frongillo E. Food insufficiency and American school-aged children's cognitive, academic, and psycho-social development. *Pediatrics* 2001;108(1):44–53; J Murphy, Wehler C, Pagano M, Little M, Kleinman R, Jellinek M. Relationship between hunger and psychosoci functioning in low-income American children. *Journal of the American academy of Child and Adolescent Psychiatry* 1998;37(2):163–170.

31. K Alaimo, Olson C, Frongillo E. Food insufficiency and American school-aged children's cognitive, academic, and psycho-social development. *Pediatrics* 2001;108(1):44–53; E Frongillo, Jyoti D F, Jones S. Food Stamp program participation is associated with better academic learning among school children. *Journal of Nutrition* 2006;136:1077–1080.

32. W H Dietz. Does hunger cause obesity? *Pediatrics* 1995;95(5):766–767.

33. C M Olson. Nutrition and health outcomes associated with food insecurity and hunger. *Journal of Nutrition* 1999;129(2):521–524; K Alaimo, Olson C, Frongillo E. Low family income and food insufficiency in relation to overweight in US children. *Archives of Pediatrics and Adolescent Medicine* 2001;155:1161–1167.

34. S J Jones, Jahns L, Laraia B A, Haughton B. Lower risk of overweight in school-aged food insecure girls who participate in food assistance: Results from the panel study of income dynamics child development supplement. *Archives of Pediatrics & Adolescent Medicine* Aug 2003;157(8):780–784; S J Jones, Frongillo E A. The modifying effects of Food Stamp Program participation on the relation between food insecurity and weight change in women. *Journal of Nutrition* Apr 2006;136(4):1091–1094, D F Jyoti, Frongillo E, Jones S. Food insecurity affects social children's academic performance, weight gain, and social skills. *Journal of Nutrition* 2005;135:2831–2839; D Rose, Bodor N. Household food insecurity and overweight status in young school children: Results from the early childhood longitudinal study. *Pediatrics.*

2006;117(2):464–473; P Wilde, Peterman J. Individual weight change is associated with household food security status. *Journal of Nutrition* 2006;136:1395–1400; L Kaiser, Townsend M. Food insecurity among US children: Implications for nutrition and health. *Topics in Clinical Nutrition* 2005;20(4):313–320; L Kaiser, Melgar-Quiänonez H, Townsend M S, Nicholson Y, Fujii M L, Martin A C, Lamp C L. Food insecurity and food supplies in Latino households with young children. *Journal of Nutrition Education and Behavior* 2003;35(3):148–153; M Townsend, Peerson J, Love B, Achterberg C, Murphy S. Food insecurity is positively related to overweight in women. *Journal of Nutrition* 2001;131:1738–1745.

35. D Barrett, Frank D. *The effects of undernutrition on children's behavior.* New York: Gordon and Breach Science Publishers; 1987; D Levitsky, Strupp B. Malnutrition and the brain: Changing concepts, changing concerns. *Journal of Nutrition* 1995;125:2212S–2220S; B Strupp, Levitsky D. Enduring cognitive effects of early malnutrition: A theoretical reappraisal. *Journal of Nutrition* 1995;125:2221S–2232S; E Pollitt, Mueller W, Leibel R. The relation of growth to cognition in a well-nourished preschool population. *Child Development* 1982;53:1157–1163; E Pollitt. Poverty and child development: Relevance of research in developing countries to the United States. *Child Development* 1994;65:283–295; E Pollitt, Golub M, Gorman K, Grantham-McGregor S, Levitsky D, Schurch B, Strupp B, Wachs T A. A reconceptualization of the effects of undernutrition on children's biological, psychosocial, and behavioral development. *Social Policy Report* 1996;10(5):1–22; D L Pelletier, Frongillo E A, Jr., Schroeder D G, Habicht J P. The effects of malnutrition on child mortality in developing countries. *Bulletin of the World Health Organization* 1995;73(4):443–448; D L Pelletier, Frongillo E A, Jr., Schroeder D G, Habicht J P. A methodology for estimating the contribution of malnutrition to child mortality in developing countries. *Journal of Nutrition* 1994;124(10 Suppl):2106S–2122S.

36. B Strupp, Levitsky D. Enduring cognitive effects of early malnutrition: A theoretical reappraisal. *Journal of Nutrition* 1995;125:2221S–2232S; D Levitsky, Strupp B. Malnutrition and the brain: Changing concepts, changing concerns. *Journal of Nutrition* 1995;125:2212S–2220S; E Pollitt, Golub M, Gorman K, Grantham-McGregor S, Levitsky D, Schurch B, Strupp B, Wachs T. A reconceptualization of the effects of undernutrition on children's biological, psychosocial, and behavioral development. *Social Policy Report* 1996;10(5):1–24.

37. B Strupp, Levitsky D. Enduring cognitive effects of early malnutrition: A theoretical reappraisal. *Journal of Nutrition* 1995;125:2221S–223S; E Pollitt, Golub M, Gorman K, Grantham-McGregor S, Levitsky D, Schurch B, Strupp B, Wachs T. A reconceptualization of the effects of undernutrition on children's biological, psychosocial, and behavioral development. *Social Policy Report* 1996;10(5): 1–24.

38. A Hamelin, Habict J, Beaudry. Characterization of household food insecurity in Quebec: Food and feelings. *Social Science and Medicine* 2002;54:199–132; K Radimer, Olson C, Greene J, Campbell C, Habicht J. Understanding hunger and developing indicators to assess it in women and children. *Journal of Nutrition Education* 1992;24:36S–45S.

39. C L Connell, Lofton K L, Yadrick K, Rehner T A. Children's experiences of food insecurity can assist in understanding its effect on their well-being. *Journal of Nutrition* 2005;135(7):1683–1690.

40. Ibid.

41. K Radimer, Olson C, Greene J, Campbell C, Habicht J. Understanding hunger and developing indicators to assess it in women and children. *Journal of Nutrition Education* 1992;24:36S–45S.

42. K Radimer, Olson C, Campbell C. Development of indicators to assess hunger. *Journal of Nutrition* 1990;120 Suppl 11:1544–1548. J Fitchen. *Poverty in rural America: A case study.* Boulder, CO: Westview Press, 1981; M Devault. *Feeding the family: The social organization of caring as gendered work.* Chicago, IL: University of Chicago Press; 1991.

43. J Fitchen. Hunger, malnutrition, and poverty in the contemporary United States: Some observations on their social and cultural context. *Food and Foodways* 1998;2:309–333; L McIntyre, Glanville T N, Raine K D, Dayle J B, Anderson D, Battaglia N. Do low-income lone mothers compromise their nutrition to feed their children? *Canadian Medical Association Journal* 2003;168(6):686–691; K Radimer, Olson C, Greene J, Campbell C, Habicht J. Understanding hunger and developing indicators to assess it in women and children. *Journal of Nutrition Education* 1992;24:36S–45S; V Tarasuk. Household food insecurity and hunger among families using food banks. *Canadian Journal of Public Health* 1999;90(2):109–113; V Tarasuk. Household food insecurity with hunger is associated with women's food intakes, health and household circumstances. *Journal of Nutrition* 2001;131:2670–2676; V Tarasuk. Low income, welfare and nutritional vulnerability. *Canadian Medical Association Journal* 2003;168(6):709–710.

44. A Hamelin, Habict J, Beaudry M. Characterization of household food insecurity in Quebec: Food and feelings. *Social Science and Medicine* 2002;54:199–132.

45. J Stuff, Casey P, Szeto K, Gossett J, Robbins J, Simpson P, Connell C, Bogle M. Household food insecurity is associated with adult health status. *Journal of Nutrition* 2004;134:2330–2335; C M Olson. Nutrition and health outcomes associated with food insecurity and hunger. *Journal of Nutrition* 1999;129(2):521–524; M Townsend, Peerson J, Love B, Achterberg C, Murphy S. Food insecurity is positively related to overweight in women. *Journal of Nutrition* 2001;131:1738; K Nelson, Cunningham W, Andersen R, Harrison G, Gelberg L. Is food insufficiency associated with health status and health care utilization among adults with diabetes? *Journal of General Internal Medicine.* 2001;16:404–411; K Siefert, Heflin C, Corcoran M, Williams D. Food insufficiency and the physical and mental health of low-income women. *Women & Health* 2001;32(1):159–177; K Siefert, Heflin C, Corcoran M, Williams D. Food insufficiency and physical and mental health in a longitudinal survey of welfare recipients. *Journal of Health and Social Behavior* 2004;45(2):171–185.

46. R Conger, Conger K, Elder G, Duncan G, Brooks-Gunn J. Family economic hardship and adolescent adjustment: Mediating and moderating processes. In: Anonymous, editor. *Consequences of growing up poor.* New York, NY: Russell Sage Foundation; 1997; KS Slack, Yoo J. Food hardship and child behavior problems among low-income children. *Social Service Review* 2005;79:511–536.

47. A Hamelin, Habict J, Beaudry M. Characterization of household food insecurity in Quebec: Food and feelings. *Social Science and Medicine* 2002;54:199–132.

48. Ibid, 126.

49. G Brody, Stoneman Z, Flor D, McCrary C, Hastings L, Conyers O. Financial resources, parent psychological functioning, parent co-giving, and early adolescent competence in rural two-parent African-American families. *Child Development* 1994;65:590–605; K Dodge, Pettit G, Bates J. Socialization mediators of the relation between socioeconomic status and child conduct problems. *Child Development* 1994;65:649–665; C Holohan, Moos R. Risk, resistance, and psychologica distress: A longitudinal analysis with adults and children. *Journal of Abnormal Psychology* 1987;96(1):3; V McLoyd, Jayaratne T, Ceballo R, Borquez J. Unemployment and work interruption among African-American single mothers: Effects on parenting and adolescent socioemotional functioning. *Child Development* 1994;65:562–589; V McLoyd.

The impact of economic hardship on Black families and their children: Psychological distress, parenting, and socioemotional development. *Child Development* 1990;61:311–346.

50. J Anyon. *Ghetto schooling: A political economy of urban educational reform.* New York, NY: Teachers College Press; 1997.

51. L Mishel, Bernstein J, Allegretto S. *The state of working America 2004/2005.* Ithaca, NY: Cornell University Press; 2005.

52. N Neault, Cook J. *The safety net in action: Protecting the health and nutrition of young American children*: C-SNAP (Children's Sentinel Nutrition Assessment Program); July 2004.

53. D Jolliffe, Tiehen L, Gundersen C, Winicki J. *Food stamp benefits and child poverty in the 1990s*: USDA; September 2003. Report No: FANRR-33; J Winicki, Jolliffe D, Gundersen C. How do food assistance programs improve the well-being of low-income families?; Food Assistance and Nutrition Research Report No. (FANRR26-9), October 2002:4; B O Daponte. Private versus public relief: Use of food pantries versus food stamps among poor households. *Journal of Nutrition Education.* 2000;32:72–83; G J Borjas. Food insecurity and public assistance. *Journal of Public Economics.* 2004;88:1421–1443; N S Kabbani, Kmeid M Y. The role of food assistance in helping food insecure households escape hunger. *Review of Agricultural Economics.* 2005;27(3):439–445.

54. J T Cook, Frank D A, Berkowitz C, Black M M, Casey P H, Cutts D B, Meyers A F, Zaldivar N, Skalicky A, Levenson S, Heeren T. Welfare reform and the health of young children: A sentinel survey in 6 US cities. *Archives of Pediatrics and Adolescent Medicine* 2002;156(7):678–684; P Casey, Goolsby S, Berkowitz C, Frank D, Cook J, Cutts D, Black M, Zaldivar N, Levenson S, Heeren T, Meyers A. Maternal depression, changing public assistance, food security, and child health status. *Pediatrics* 2004;113(2):298–304; J T Cook, Frank D A, Levenson S M, Neault N B, Heeren T C, Black M M, Berkowitz C, Casey P H, Meyers A F, Cutts D B, Chilton M. Child food insecurity increases risks posed by household food insecurity to young children's health. *Journal of Nutrition* 2006;136(4):1073–1076.

55. J Hirschman. *Review of WIC food packages. Paper presented at: Expert Committee for Review of Food Practices, 2004*; February 26, 2004; Institute of Medicine.

56. MK Fox, Hamilton W, Lin B. *Effects of Food Assistance and Nutrition Programs on Nutrition and Health: Volume 4, Executive Summary of the Literature Review.* Washington, D.C.: Economic Research Service, USDA; November 2004.

57. D Herman, Harrison G, Afifi A, Jenks E. The Effect of the WIC Program on Food Security Status of Pregnant, First Time Participants. *Family Economics and Nutrition Review* 2004;16(1):21–29; M M Black, Cutts D B, Frank D A, Geppert J, Skalicky A, Levenson S, Casey P H, Berkowitz C, Zaldivar N, Cook J T, Meyers A F, Herren T, the Children's Sentinel Nutritional Assessment Program Study Group. Special supplemental nutrition program for women, infants, and children participation and infants' growth and health: A multisite surveillance study. *Pediatrics* Jul 2004;114(1):169–176.

58. J Bhattacharya, DeLeire T, Haider S, Currie J. Heat or eat? Cold-weather shocks and nutrition in poor American families. *American Journal of Public Health* 2003;93(7):1149–1154.

59. D Frank, Roos N, Meyers A, Napoleone M, Peterson K, Cather A, Cupples L A. Seasonal variation in weight-for-age in a pediatric emergency room. *Public Health Reports* 1996;111:366–371.

60. J Taponga, Suter A, Nord M, Leachman M. Explaining variations in state hunger rates. *Family Economics and Nutrition Review.* 2004;16(2):12–22.

61. A Meyers, Cutts D, Frank D A, Levenson S, Skalicky A, Heeren T, Cook J, Berkowitz C, Black M, Casey P, Zaldivar N. Subsidized housing and children's nutritional status: Data from a

multisite surveillance study. *Archives of Pediatrics & Adolescent Medicine.* Jun 2005;159(6):551–556.

62. J Cook, Brown J. Children's rights to adequate nutritious foods in the two Americas. *Food Policy* 1996;21(1):11–16.

63. UNICEF. *The state of the world's children.* Oxford: Oxford University Press; 1991.

64. H Shue. *Basic Human Rights: Subsistence, Affluence, and U.S. Foreign Policy.* Princeton, NJ: Princeton University Press; 1980; J Nickel, Aiken W, LaFollette H. A human rights approach to world hunger. In: Anonymous, editor. *World Hunger and Morality.* Upper Saddle River, NJ: Prentice Hall; 1996.

CHAPTER 3

BREATHING POORLY: CHILDHOOD ASTHMA AND POVERTY

Cindy Dell Clark

Although one in five American children are poor, poverty has not been childproofed. Being poor reeks havoc on children's health in a variety of ways, starting with higher rates of infant mortality, lower birthweight, and followed by a myriad of problems sustained throughout childhood including missed school days and days spent in bed.[1] Asthma, the most common chronic illness among American children, disproportionately burdens poor children in America. In total 6.2 million children under 18 had asthma in 2003, of which 4 million experienced an asthma attack that year. Pediatric deaths from asthma nearly tripled in the United States from 1979 to 1996, reflecting a worsening of the illness in the United States as well as elsewhere.[2] Yet the total of 6.2 million children with asthma obscures marked differences above and below poverty levels.[3] Among welfare or TANF-receiving families in 2003, 11 percent of children had asthma, versus a 5 percent level among children in families not receiving aid.[4]

Asthma is more prevalent and especially more severe among urban, African American poor children than among poor children of other ethnicities. African American children are more likely to die of asthma than white or Latino children, and are more likely to have intensely severe cases of asthma.[5] (Among Latino children, Puerto Ricans have the highest prevalence of asthma, but not to the degree of African American youngsters.)[6] To date, no scientific or scholarly consensus exists on a model of why asthma severity is so problematic for African American children, whose rates of hospitalization and death from asthma are unduly high. Do high levels of poverty explain inner-city asthma? Is it related to culturally distinctive practices? Is it traceable to biological sources, such as genetics? What is clear is that inner-city living patterns (housing, external environment, interactions with medical care, and other factors) place poor, African American inner-city children at a pronounced risk for asthma, and especially severe asthma, relative to other groups.

This article will consider the factors that seem orchestrated to create this risk, as well as the consequences for children in life experience and personal well-being.

ASTHMA AND ITS TREATMENT

Asthma occurs when the airways are obstructed by inflammation, occurring in response to stimuli. The breathing passages in effect become narrowed, as the muscles around the airways tighten and mucus is secreted to further impede the flow of air. Breathing, a process normally taken for granted by most people most of the time (unless exposed to extreme irritants such as smoke from a fire), is challenged in asthma by tightened and inflamed airways. Wheezing is a common outer sign that the air required to oxygenate the blood is not passing freely. From the child's perspective, the breathlessness often carries anxious implications, for children (and no doubt adults) associate breathing with maintaining life.[7]

The stimuli that give rise to this response, known in medical parlance as "triggers," vary from child to child. Triggers are wide-ranging, including some entities highly pervasive in children's lives: colds and infections, exercise, mold, pollen from trees, grass and other plants, particular foods and additives, animals (dogs, cats, horses, birds, cockroaches, dust mites, mice, rats), smoke, air pollution, wind, rain, cold air, aspirin, beta-blockers, aerosol sprays, odors, dust, paint fumes, perfume, extended stress, laughing, crying, hyperventilation, and perhaps ironically, holding one's breath.[8] A child under medical treatment for asthma is assessed (with parental input) for which particular triggers are known to be problematic. Then parents are instructed to eliminate or minimize key triggers from the child's life: to keep the child indoors on days of extreme cold or high air pollution, to get rid of pets, to remove draperies and carpeting that could increase dust levels, to obtain a humidifier which will reduce air-borne triggers, to prevent the child from sleeping with transitional objects that may be dust-carrying (security blankets or teddy bears), to have parents quit smoking, and so on.

Treating severe asthma typically involves a complex regimen of prescribed medications and monitoring. One category of medicines, bronchodilators, acts to open the airways to make breathing easier, reversing airway obstruction. Another category of medicines (corticosteroids) prevents inflammation and must be taken preventively. A third group of medicines, such as chromolyn, interferes with the allergic process, and so are taken as prevention. Bronchodilators can be used during an attack to bring relief immediately, and are known as "rescue" or "quick relief" medicines. Corticosteroids and chromolyn work in a long-term fashion, precluding an attack, but only if taken regularly as prescribed for prevention.

Drugs are likely to be prescribed in combination for severe asthma, sometimes involving a fairly intricate timetable for giving children the varied prescribed medicines. Medicines for childhood asthma necessitate owning or using devices more complicated than the usual spoon or glass of water used to take ordinary pediatric medicines. That is, prescribed substances may be taken in liquid form (or pill form for older children), but may also be taken through an inhaler for which there is a particular, proper inhalation technique. For inhaled medications to be optimally delivered to children's lungs, a "spacer," a kind of extension tube that improves drug delivery, may be provided to attach to a child's inhaler. Prescribed drugs may also be taken through a nebulizer, a machine using tubing and a facemask to deliver medication, inhaled over a prolonged period as the child is tethered (by tubing) to the nebulizer.

Much as a thermometer is used to monitor a child's temperature, it is recommended that asthma be monitored using a peak flow meter, a device gauging the child's maximum breath as a means to catch early signs of deterioration. Research shows, however, that a peak flow meter is not actively possessed or used by many children, despite the recommendations of clinicians, just one example of the problematic level of adherence to asthma treatment prevailing across social groups.[9] Medication taking and medical appointments are also subject to nonadherence by young asthmatic patients. Adherence is an especially pronounced problem among inner-city children.

Asthma is known to recur within families, and research into the genetic transmission of asthma has been underway for several years.[10] Still, available evidence finds that the higher the degree of poverty within an ethnic group such as African Americans, the more concentrated are the differences in asthma severity, suggesting that social and environmental exposures may accompany or in some ways overshadow genetic factors in inner-city asthma.[11] Indeed, a complex array of conditions imposed on inner-city children can be linked to asthma incidence and severity, based on mounting evidence from a large and growing body of research.

FACTORS IMPLICATED IN INNER-CITY ASTHMA

The levels and severity of inner-city asthma have led to what amounts to a physical injustice: African American inner-city children suffer twice the incidence of asthma, are hospitalized and visit emergency rooms more, and are six times as likely to die from asthma as white children.[12] Moreover, the price tag to American society for treating poor children's asthma in emergency rooms and hospitals is high, with more money going to "crisis therapy" following an asthma attack than to prevention.[13] These disturbing facts, with obvious implications about children's suffering, have motivated considerable investigation of the factors entailed in urban asthma.

The trail of investigation has led to a multifactorial explanation for the problem of inner-city asthma in children, including: (1) asthma resultant from the physical environment outside the home, such as pollution; (2) asthma resultant from indoor environmental factors; (3) asthma related to indoor, sedentary lifestyles; (4) asthma traceable to a lack of proper medical care; (5) asthma traceable to a lack of family adherence to care provisions; (6) unbridged sociocultural differences between medical care providers, on one hand, and caretakers and patients, on the other hand; and (7) issues of mental health, including caregiver depression and psychological response to community violence. There is no single quick fix to the problem of inner-city asthma, but a need to understand and address a full gamut of interacting and entwisted factors.

Physical Environment Outside the Home

Respiratory problems (including childhood asthma) have become indicative markers of poor air quality. Children, research has shown, are more physically susceptible than adults to the impact of environmental pollution.[14] Even prenatally, exposure to airborne particles from diesel exhaust and other combustion sources (polycyclic aromatic hydrocarbons) is associated after birth with childhood respiratory impairment.[15] In cities the world over, outdoor air pollution correlates with emergency room visits for asthma, in line with increased symptoms and decreased lung function.[16] Ozone, nitrogen oxide, sulfur dioxide, and particulates in the air all lead to increased respiratory risk for children.[17]

When traffic is reduced in an urban area, this translates to less pollution and improved asthma. For instance, during the Olympic games, weekday traffic volumes in Atlanta fell 22 percent, resulting in a 28 percent drop in peak daily ozone levels and a large reduction in visits to treat acute asthma. Plant closures (such as during a strike at a Utah steel mill) have also been shown to decrease hospital admissions for asthma. Economically disadvantaged children more often live and go to school close to automotive traffic, which is known to increase asthma severity.[18] Outdoor exercise for children living in polluted inner-city places can, due to pollution, promote respiratory illness instead of the intended health.

In short, poor inner-city children are disadvantaged in the very air they breathe, a factor predisposing them to asthmatic symptoms. This problem of pollution as a factor in poor inner-city neighborhoods increases asthma risk in low-income African American children.

Indoor Environmental Factors

Inner-city children living in high-crime, densely populated settings spend ample time indoors, breathing indoor air. Poor African American children are prone to live in public and substandard housing in urban areas, settings in which indoor air quality is not ideal. A study of the residences of school-age youth living in Baltimore, for example, found that children's homes were deteriorating, with a quarter of the homes having leaking roofs. Plaster was broken, paint was peeling, and/or there were cracks in the walls or doors in the majority of dwellings. Cockroach and rodent infestation was common.[19] When samples were taken of particulate matter in children's sleeping rooms, mouse was an allergen found in large quantity and in more concentrated amounts than cat or dog allergens. Altogether, the elevated levels of indoor pollution and allergens (often found together with pollutants from tobacco smoke) are all significant risk factors for asthma exacerbation.

Nor were these concentrations of indoor air pollution restricted to Baltimore's low-income residences. Another study done in impoverished Boston neighborhoods surveyed residents and found that housing conditions were characterized by moisture and mold growth (a common allergen), by infestation by allergen-causing pests such as mice, cockroaches, and dust mites, by inadequate ventilation, and by other indoor hazards.[20]

Even school locations can be hazardous environments for children's health, as documented by a study conducted within the Los Angeles Unified School District. This study examined the relationship between educational outcomes and respiratory risks due to factors of school environment. Substantial differences were found in schools with the highest estimated respiratory hazard, whose students performed 20 percent lower in academic performance relative to students in other schools.[21]

One factor of children's indoor environments that correlates with low income and poverty is cigarette smoking, a known respiratory hazard for children inhaling secondary smoke. Tobacco marketers have saturated inner-city African American communities with cigarette billboards; to take the example of Baltimore, the intensity of cigarette billboards has been 3.8 times greater in African American neighborhoods than in white neighborhoods—and billboards have occupied positions next to homes, schools, churches, parks, playgrounds, health centers, and stadiums. Among national magazines, the most intense concentration of tobacco advertisements can be found in African American publications.[22] In line with such racially skewed promotion of cigarette use, smoking is common in the homes of poor African American children, including children with asthma. Exposure to smoking in turn leads to infantile and childhood wheezing, increased hospitalizations for lower respiratory tract infections, elevated sensitization to allergens, and hyperresponsive airways.[23] The combined exposure to outdoor pollutants and indoor tobacco smoke increases respiratory symptoms and asthma risk as early as 12–24 months of age.[24] In a major investigation of inner-city African American children with asthma, the proportion of children living with at least one smoker was 59 percent, with 48 percent of children having urine tests showing significant tobacco smoke exposure.[25] Cigarette smoke is an irritant to already inflamed lungs, contributing to children's asthma.

Sedentary Lifestyles

Increased attention and research has been devoted to the study of childhood obesity, which like asthma, is a pronounced problem for African American inner-city poor children. Low-income children, regardless of their respiratory health, have elevated chances of developing obesity.[26] A body of evidence now suggests that obesity and asthma occur in correlation, although it is unclear what the causative connection might be. Many experts have assumed that poor breathing, in asthma, makes it difficult to exercise, leading to obesity.[27] Yet obesity may at the same time leave children vulnerable to asthma; obese children wheeze more, have more unscheduled emergency room visits, and receive more medications for asthma.[28]

Children with asthma face a number of restrictions, but limitations on physical activity resulting from disabling asthma are particularly influential on children's lives. Children with uncontrolled asthma are limited in their sports performance, which becomes stigmatizing and marginalizing, especially for boys. It can seem as if, one boy in an interview study put it, one can "never catch up" with the others. Boys and girls alike face physical restrictions during recreation and school activities, stemming from asthma.[29]

Children living in high crime, poor neighborhoods are vulnerable to living a life restricted in its outdoor activities, made worse when poorly controlled asthma necessitates further reductions in activity. Reciprocal problems of inactivity, obesity, and asthma morbidity seem to conspire to promote childhood asthma in the inner city.

Lack of Proper Medical Care

The optimal and most economic way to care for childhood asthma places emphasis on prevention. Good preventive treatment would normally involve a long-term relationship with the same health-care provider, an advantage often missing from the treatment of poor, African American children.[30] Ironically, urban impoverished children with asthma access more expensive forms of care than do children with greater means. Low-income minority children are more apt to use emergency departments rather than primary care providers as sources of asthma care, thereby reducing their access to sustained continuous care by the same provider.[31] In one investigation, 75 percent of urban parents of asthmatic children identified the emergency department as their usual source of care.[32]

Overall, the asthma of inner-city children is often undertreated and not addressed preventively, despite frequent asthma symptoms. Even though 92 percent of inner-city children surveyed in a major study had health insurance (73% Medicaid, 11% health maintenance organizations, 9% private insurance), the majority had difficulty obtaining follow-up care.[33] Poor continuity of care with a particular provider is associated with less use of preventive anti-inflammatory asthma medications, and with a lack of a prescribed parental action plan to be followed during asthma exacerbations.

Studies indicate that poor African American asthmatic children make fewer visits to physicians than others. Yet they experience more hospitalizations.[34] While impoverished children may have some source of care, then, barriers and deficiencies in care are evident.

Families of these children may have difficulty obtaining the supplies needed to manage children's asthma; a study of 100 pharmacies in the Bronx, New York, found spacers for metered dose inhalers to be in stock in only 68 percent of pharmacies, with even lower availability for nebulizers (33%) and peak flow meters (17%).[35]

Guidelines established by National Heart, Lung and Blood Institute (NHLBI) for home management of asthma episodes are not followed or even known in many families of poor inner-city children. Only half the families of children hospitalized for asthma at one urban medical center had a written asthma action plan, only 30 percent had peak flow meters, and only 39 percent were providing children with anti-inflammatory agents as recommended by the NHLBI guidelines. These same families generally did not know the recommended steps to follow during an acute asthma exacerbation.[36]

Responsibility for proper treatment of a child with asthma lies with the clinician and the child's family caretaker, who ideally work together to keep symptoms at bay and to keep the child as well as possible. When there is no continuous relationship between caretaker and clinician, this is not likely to happen.[37]

As for the child's family caretaker, effective prevention calls for keeping medical appointments, having emergency plans, dispensing medications, and optimizing the home environment (e.g., eliminating tobacco smoke and allergens). In a report, a physician's assistant detailed how families at an inner-city clinic lacked preparedness to prevent further emergency department visits or hospitalizations for their child.[38]

> At the clinic . . . we see a population of parents who invariably come in after an ED visit or a hospitalization. Parents do not know exactly when to use one inhaler instead of another for their children, and rarely are patients maintained on inhaled corticosteroids [anti-inflammatories]. The new leukotriene inhibitor . . . Singulair, is not in the formulary; often peak flow meters, spacers, and nebulizers are unavailable. We have the luxury of a part-time nurse health educator, but seeing her the day of an acute visit is usually not feasible and patients rarely return for follow-up education.

Poverty brings with it deficits and crises of many sorts, and the management of children's asthma care is no exception. Preventive care requires particular resources of technical knowledge, services and supplies, all relatively lacking for caretakers of poor asthmatic children. Unprevented asthma in poor, urban children of color is more likely to reach the point of severe, dangerous crisis.

Adherence to Care Provisions

Following a regimen of asthma treatment is no easy task, even for economically advantaged families. The activities of treatment involve time and effort: making follow-up visits or calls to a physician, having the inventory of proper medicines and supplies on hand, competently giving a child his or her medicine according to the proper schedule, and enforcing the prescribed activity when the treatment is disliked or boring to the child (such as nebulizer treatment).[39] Adherence to treatment for asthmatic children within the total population (let alone among stressed, inner-city families) is typically reported as less than 50 percent.[40] Despite the availability of effective treatments, children do not always get the medical benefit of the optimal approaches: medicines left untaken cannot stave off asthma emergencies. As mentioned earlier, adherence is especially a problem for preventive, anti-inflammatory medicines that professional guidelines consider to be a standard part of the treatment regimen for children with severe asthma.

Among poor, urban children of color, the majority of children with moderate or severe asthma do not receive anti-inflammatory, preventive medicines.[41] This lack of preventive treatment is at least partly due to physicians' not prescribing anti-inflammatory medicines or making an inaccurate assessment of asthma severity.[42] The result of underuse of preventive treatment, unfortunately, is an increased risk of avoidable hospitalization for asthma.[43]

Even when preventive, anti-inflammatory drugs are prescribed appropriately, parental or caretaker follow-through in administering preventive treatment is apt to be incomplete. It is as if parents treat asthma as an acute disorder, using corrective medicines for the attack but avoiding preventive treatments, while physicians see asthma as a chronic disorder, in which preventive medicines should be taken to eliminate or minimize attacks. Many urban parents do not follow the asthma management plan prescribed by their health-care provider, but instead modify the plan based on their personal health beliefs. For example, parents might put aside the preventive medication and instead try nonmedical alternatives such as calming breathing or diet manipulations. Resistance to "pushing drugs" for children who are not, at the moment, having an obvious crisis is an attitude that impedes acceptance of preventive medicines.[44] Waiting to see if the early signs of asthma clear up on their own, rather than treating emergent asthma symptoms with anti-inflammatory medicine, is a predilection seen both inside and outside the inner city.[45] In one study of impoverished children with asthma, 29 percent of family caretakers whose child received a prescription for inhaled anti-inflammatory medicine were not convinced that the medicine would help their child. In the same study, 35 percent of family caretakers expressed fear about possible addiction to the medicine, and 42 percent admitted fear of side effects.[46] Much nonadherence is intentional rather than due to economic constraints, suggesting that issues of meaning and values (how treatments and illness are perceived and culturally represented) are significantly at stake in low adherence.[47]

Children play a role in adherence as well, since they are active participants and hold some responsibility in treatment,[48] such as when awaking with nocturnal asthma exacerbations and treating themselves[49] or when recognizing and seeking care for symptoms at school.[50] Coping with asthma is a shared matter between the child and the parent,[51] with children rating themselves to have more responsibility for self-care than parents estimate.[52] Accomplishing the needed technique for using inhalers, spacers, and nebulizers involves challenges to young users. Inhalers can be awkward for children (and some parents) to use properly. Keeping inhalers and nebulizers clean can be a problem, too. Since children may need parental help with these tasks, the time-consuming treatments may be skipped at times. Among younger children, nebulizer treatments may be confining and/or frightening due to the required facemask, resulting in adherence to nebulizer use that is as low as 33 percent in some studies.[53] A national research project conducted for the American Lung Association showed that many parents in the overall population underrate their child's symptoms, relative to the child's own assessment of breathing problems, coughing, wheezing, and shortness of breath. Children in this study reported more symptoms and more impeded activities due to symptoms than their parents did.[54] It is possible that parents, underestimating their child's breathing distress, may modify the treatment plan toward a more passive approach, perhaps at the very times when their child is experiencing difficulty. At the very least, studies show that parents believe that children are more actively adherent than they really are. Developing methods to help parents to exercise closer supervision and monitoring could be helpful.[55]

In the final analysis, successful treatment of childhood asthma is a three-pronged interactive effort between the parent, the child, and the medical practitioner.[56] Adherence depends to a large degree on the effective communication and interaction between these parties, a process made particularly difficult when there are social class and/or ethnic differences between the medical provider and the child's family care-taker (a topic to be discussed in the next section). Neither parents nor physicians are consistently good at communicating with children and understanding experiences with illness from the youngster's perspective. In a national survey across all social groups, 77 percent of parent–child pairs answered differently when asked how often asthma led children to cancel, postpone, interrupt, or stop an activity. The survey, reporting an array of factors for which parental and child reports did not match, concluded that the disparity between child and adult perceptions could be problematic: "Parents cannot always be with their child to observe symptoms—and children do not want to worry others about their symptoms."[57] Other studies have also shown that a lack of parental supervision can lead to poorer adherence than parents seem aware.[58]

Physician–child communication also raises concerns. Many physicians more readily communicate with parents than with children, due to parents' roles as primary agents of care.[59] Overall, more research on inner-city children's own roles in treatment would be worthwhile. Such child-centered research might lead to approaches that enhance adherence and well-being, in the face of numerous stresses and burdens for impoverished family caretakers.

Unbridged Sociocultural Differences

Investigations of adherence to asthma treatment often cite the doctor–patient relationship as a crucial way to advance, or on the other hand to scuttle, adherence. As one study concluded, "Continuity of care enhances the provider's ongoing knowledge about the child, family, and parental capabilities in problem solving and management of asthma and provides the family with security that the provider truly knows and respects them."[60] An ongoing relationship with a medical care provider creates the circumstances and mutual give and take needed for adherence. Conflict between a family and a physician is associated with poor adherence, even a child's increased risk of death from asthma.[61] As already explained, low-income inner-city children often depend for treatment on emergency rooms and hospital stays, which are not very suited for establishing continuous, familiar relationships of trust.

Another barrier to adherence-enhancing health-care relationships has to do with the elusive gaps between the cultural world of the inner-city family versus the cultural world of medical care providers. This is, in part, a matter of language: to avoid misunderstanding, health-care providers need to communicate in the language of the patient rather than in jargon that is meaningless to the patient.[62] It may be that poor African American families differ even from middle-class African American families in their manner of communication with their physician. Annette Lareau, in her book on family class distinctions, described a physician's visit by a middle-class African

American child that involved comfortable conversational exchange with the doctor by both the child and parent. Neither was intimidated or afraid to raise issues to be discussed with the physician. But an African American family living in a housing project, also studied by Lareau, conducted the visit and behaved very differently; the verbal rejoinders were more strained and indicated a lower level of trust extended by the mother. The mother in the latter family was quiet or even inaudible during the doctor's visit, and had a difficult time answering the doctor's questions. She did not know some of the terms used by the physician, and answered vaguely and timidly, as did her son. According to Lareau, these distinctions reflect sociocultural behavior patterns practiced at home and elsewhere, by which conversational exchange and verbal discourse is less emphasized in working-class and poor families than in middle-class families.[63] The fact that clinical conversation may be intimidating to some families raises an important challenge, since to form a treatment-building alliance works best when the patient and mother feel able to react openly about specific recommendations, in an atmosphere of mutual exchange.

It is essential, studies suggest, that medical personnel treating inner-city children seek to understand the culture and everyday dilemmas of low-income families with asthmatic children. Clinicians should adjust the interaction in the medical encounter to bring about a mutual, level playing field. Demonstrations and hands on approaches might go further than strictly verbal explanation, especially for children. In the end, the medical encounter at its best is a mutual interaction that organizes and interprets the child's asthma in a manner that participants find credible and sensible, with the result that the agreed upon course of handling the illness is *mutually* acceptable.[64]

Issues of Mental Health, Depression, and Violence

To say that life in the inner city is stressful for families is an understatement. With extensive hardships, and fewer means of coping with hardship, poor children are prone to find themselves in families marked by depression or other mental health challenges, all the while living amidst violent, high crime surroundings. A child's asthma is more likely to be fostered in such a family ecology. Stress, research has established, is a risk factor for asthma morbidity.[65]

In one study focusing on exposure to violence, caretakers of inner-city asthmatic children reported on the violent events in their neighborhoods during 6 months. Such events were strikingly evident. Fights including weapons occurred in 28 percent of locations, violent arguments between neighbors took place in 33 percent of places, gang-related violence in 15 percent of locations, and robberies or muggings in 38 percent of locales.[66] Fully 38 percent of those queried expressed fear that their child could be hurt by the reported violence nearby, with 34 percent of caretakers keeping their child indoors as a safeguard from violence. Smoking by caretakers and skipping of medications both occurred more often with such violent exposure, thereby connecting urban violence to increased health risk and increased nonadherence.

Conflict among a child's relations has also been shown in studies to indicate increased risk for asthma morbidity, including increased risk of mortality from asthma.

Notably, when a parental caretaker is in conflict with the child, or the child lacks secure attachment to the parent, this serves to differentiate urban children likely to have asthma from those who are healthy. Asthma morbidity and hospitalizations have been shown to worsen in line with life stress or compromised mental health of the caretaker.[67]

The hopelessness and lessened sense of control of impoverished lives takes a toll on the mental health of parents, as does dealing with anxious concerns, including asthma. One review showed that 44.5 percent of welfare recipients caring for asthmatic children reported depressive symptoms, a factor correlating with severity of their children's asthma.[69] Mothers with depressive symptoms are apt to have reduced adherence to medication regimens, such as difficulties with children's proper use of inhalers.[70] Issues of stress, anxiety, depression, and violence conspire to degrade the health of children with asthma in the inner city.

THE EXPERIENCE OF ASTHMA

Asthma is by no means an illness for which a single-minded, reductionist rendering of cause and effect is a workable model. A quick fix, simple solution is not likely to be effective against asthma in poor African American children, especially if it does not account for the multifaceted human factors involved. Even biomedical treatment innovations cannot necessarily improve the condition of inner-city childhood asthma, for noncooperation or nonadherence with biomedical treatment is an issue that can short-circuit biomedical drug delivery, even in families with insurance. The way in which biomedical care takes into account the mindset and everyday life context of young sufferers is crucial to achieving good outcomes.

The horrible factors contributing to inner-city asthma are in effect orchestrated to make children vulnerable to the respiratory ravages of asthma: the environment inside and outside their homes and schools, the family stresses accompanying poverty and violence, the cultural discomfort with health-care institutions and clinicians all contribute.

Above and beyond all these contributing factors, it is worthwhile to consider how asthma affects the child's sense of self and personal experience. Asthma is more than a diagnosis, more than a sick role fulfilled by the child, but a felt experience of the young patient—an aspect of the illness experience not always captured in analyses of asthma as a biological disease entity.

Illness is known to be grounded in the selfhood and daily worlds of sufferers, and asthma is a case in point. Studies exploring subjective experiences of asthma among inner-city children have found, often through child-engaging qualitative methods, that particular recurring themes characterize children's own experiences of asthma. For example, asthma is an illness experienced with unsettling anxiety and feelings of vulnerability. Breathlessness is associated by children, including urban children, as being a dire threat to existence.[71] Feelings of panic and fear commonly accompany the onset of a severe attack, feelings that do not always dissipate with repeated experience of attacks.[72] The sense of helplessness that accompanies worsening respiratory distress was videotaped in a study by Michael Rich and Richard Chalfen, who found that the videotape informed even the most experienced clinicians about the powerless and fearfulness of an urban child's asthma attack as she traveled to the hospital, driven by her mother.

> For four long minutes, one watches as JW's respiratory distress increases. She coughs, followed by high-pitched wheezing exhalations. Initially, as her breathing worsens, she remains calm, closing her eyes to focus on the problem. As JW tires, her eyes widen with fear. It becomes increasingly hard to breathe. There are deep audible wheezes throughout her breathing cycle. As they pull into the parking lot, JW purses her lips, blowing hard to maintain air pressure in her lungs. Finally, in the well-lit emergency room, we hear the reassuring hiss of JW's medication nebulizer. JW relaxes, inhaling the relieving medicine, wiping her brow.[73]

When this video was shown to clinicians, even the most experienced found the segment difficult to watch; the video captures, and then replicates in those who view it, the "helplessness, fear and uncertainty with which many young people with asthma live their *lives*."[74] Interview studies with children have similarly concluded that asthma conveys a sense of powerlessness and anxiety, along with a reliance on reactive responses ("I lay down," "drink water" or "go to the hospital") and identification of danger signs as asthma worsens ("ears will turn blue").[75] Children's experiences of asthma, in an urban environment, are punctuated by breathless crises and trips to the emergency room or hospital for treatment (but not necessarily marked by proactive prevention). This experience is emotionally laced with intermittent trauma and powerlessness.

Another trend of thought among youthful asthma sufferers is the way in which the risk of asthma is felt to pervade children's sense of place and experience. A study in which children were shown photographs of places found that children with asthma described unfamiliar places (such as a forest and a mountainside lake) as scary and isolating, a finding consistent with other research.[76] Children often mentioned asthma as a reason to be concerned about safety, which contrasted with healthy children, who felt that violence threatened safety. In other words, to asthmatic children the lack of safety associated with asthma was a more salient concern than violence. Summing up, the authors stated, "children with asthma find threats in environments that other people would describe as harmless."[77] Moreover, inner-city children with asthma have limitations on activity, which in many ways hems in their life experience: They are limited in how well they breathe, and this places restrictions on how they live. Asthma is a powerful interruption of daily life—in how much time a child can spend outside, in how much time a child can be fully active, and (stemming from the prior two problems) in how much time they can be with friends.[78] Overall, while the restricted breathing of an asthma attack may be short-lived once treated at the emergency room, the way in which asthma restricts an urban child's daily life is pervasive, and contributes to a sense of being unsafe and hindered.

A final dimension uncovered in research on children's felt experiences of asthma has to do with the pronounced gap between the biomedical messages conveyed by professional clinicians and the reality of day-to-day family living. Based on videos of children's own environments presented by children themselves, the number of asthma triggers to which children are exposed far exceed what is disclosed when a physician takes a medical history. Exposures to dust, mold, tobacco smoke, pets, and other indoor hazards are more common, in videotape, than in reports to medical professionals. One participant, for example, lived in the same residence as several cats belonging to her mother, but asserted that the cats were not allowed in her room. Nevertheless, the child's video revealed a kitten sleeping in her bed.[79]

Moreover, videotaped observations focusing on children's own lives also confirm that medicines are not necessarily taken using the proper technique, even in circumstances where explicit instruction was part of comprehensive clinic education.[80] Patients' own notions of illness, attitudes, and actions govern the outcomes of treatment. Adherence to asthma treatment is so partial that inner-city parents may be said to have an inclination to treat asthma as an acute crisis, rather than a chronic condition necessitating ongoing, preventive measures. This possibility would explain the reliance on emergency treatment and hospitals rather than being dedicated to preventive management in conjunction with a trusted care provider.

Whether or not patients live the life their doctors would prescribe to prevent childhood asthma, it is clear that no biomedical intervention can fully dictate or mold the family's role in treatment. Neither children nor parents can be regarded as the means to an end, that is, the means to the delivery of biomedical treatment.[81] On the contrary, each child and family ought to be regarded as the goal of treatment, not the means. The intrinsic value of children and families should be the central, humane thrust to any program of treatment, for ultimately, only a humane and holistic effort will be able to empower and improve the environments and lives of poor asthmatic children.

Implied in a humane and holistic approach is the need for society to work toward a clean, nontoxic urban environment rather than marginalizing the poor to places of greatest risk. Asthma has become the touchstone of vulnerable children living in marginalizing urban poverty, pollution, mental health problems, violence, vermin, and lack of medical literacy. Unless asthma is tackled broadly, there is a danger that unaddressed factors will ultimately outweigh half done interventions. Unless asthma is countered humanely, issues of meaning may be overlooked, to the detriment of adherence and family cohesion and coping. (Family rituals, for example, help children to cope with the stressors of asthma, and such vehicles of resilience need to be fostered.[81]) Eliminating asthma, closely tied to stubborn challenges of poverty, will require a committed and integrated approach, if poor African American children are to be released from asthma's disabling grip.

NOTES

1. J. Lawrence Aber, Neil G. Bennett, and Jiall Li "The Effects of Poverty on Child Health and Development," *Annual Review of Public Health* 18 (1997); Montserrat Graves, Christina Adams, and Jay Portnoy, "Adherence in Young Children with Asthma," *Current Opinion in Allergy and Clinical Immunology* 6 (2006), pp. 463–484.

2. Hope Cristol, "Childhood Asthma Rises in Europe, U.S.," *The Futurist* 36(5) (2002).

3. Lauren Smith et al., "Rethinking Race/Ethnicity, Income, and Childhood Asthma: Racial/Ethnic Disparities Concentrated among the Very Poor," *Public Health Reports* 120 (2005).

4. Child Trends, "Child Trends Data Bank," (2006).

5. Diane R. Gold and Rosalind Wright, "Population Disparities in Asthma," *Annual Review of Public Health* 26 (2005).

6. Jane Brotanek, Jill Halterman, Peggy Auinger, and Michael Weitzman "Inadequate Access to Care among Children with Asthma from Spanish-Speaking Families," *Journal of Health Care for the Poor and Underserved* 16(1) (2005).

7. Cindy Dell Clark, *In Sickness and in Play: Children Coping with Chronic Illness* (New Brunswick, NJ: Rutgers University Press, 2003).

8. Ibid.

9. B.G. Bender and S.E. Bender, "Patient-Identified Barriers to Asthma Treatment Adherence: Responses to Interviews Focus Groups and Questionnaires," *Immunology and Allergy Clinics of North America* 25(1) (2005).

10. Hakon Hakonarson and Eva Halapi, "Genetic Analyses in Asthma: Current Concepts and Future Directions," *American Journal of Pharmacogenomics* 2(3) (2002).

11. Smith et al., "Rethinking Race/Ethnicity, Income, and Childhood Asthma."

12. Leslie Kole, "Rectifying Color and Class Disparities in Health Care," *Journal of the American Academy of Physician Assistants* 13(6) (2000).

13. Bengt Jonsson, "Measuring the Economic Burden in Asthma," in *Asthma's Impact on Society: The Social and Economic Burden*, ed. Kevin Weiss, A. Sonia Buist, and Sean Sullivan (New York: Marcel Dekker, 2000).

14. Rachel Morello-Frosch, Manuel Pastor Jr., and James Sadd, "Integrating Environmental Justice and the Precautionary Principle in Research and Policy Making: The Case of Ambient Air Toxics Exposures and Health Risks among Schoolchildren in Los Angeles," *The Annals of the American Academy of Political and Social Science* 584 (2002).

15. Rachel Miller, Robin Garfinkel, Megan Horton, David Camann, Frederica Perera, Robin Wyatt, and Patrick L Kinney, "Polycyclic Aromatic Hydrocarbons, Environmental Tobacco Smoke, and Respiratory Symptoms in an Inner-City Birth Cohort," *Chest* 126 (2004).

16. Patrick Breysse, P. N. Breysee, T. J. Buckley, D. Williams, C. M. Beck, S. J. Jo, B. Merriman, K. A. Callahan, A. M. Butz, C. S. Rand, A. M. Moseley, J. Curtin-Brosnan, N. B. Durkin, and P. A. Eggleston, "Indoor Exposures to Air Pollutants and Allergens in the Homes of Asthmatic Children in Inner-City Baltimore," *Environmental Research* 98(2) (2005).

17. H. Patricia Hynes, Doug Brugge, Neal Osgood, John Snell, Jose Vallarino, and John Spencer, "'Where Does the Damp Come From?' Investigations into the Indoor Environment and Respiratory Health in Boston Public Housing," *Journal of Public Health Policy* 24(3/4) (2003).

18. Robert Byrd and Jesse Joad, "Urban Asthma," *Current Opinion in Pulmonary Medicine* 12 (2006).

19. Breysse et al., "Indoor Exposures to Air Pollutants and Allergens in the Homes of Asthmatic Children in Inner-City Baltimore."

20. Hynes et al., "'Where Does the Damp Come From?'"

21. Morello-Frosch Jr. and Sadd, "Integrating Environmental Justice and the Precautionary Principle in Research and Policy Making."

22. Barbara Lynch, Richard Bonnie, and Institute of Medicine, *Growing up Tobacco Free* (Washington DC: National Academy Press, 1994).

23. M.J. Federico and A.H. Liu, "Overcoming Childhood Asthma Disparities of the Inner-City Poor," *The Pediatric Clinics of North America* 50 (2003).

24. Miller et al., "Polycyclic Aromatic Hydrocarbons, Environmental Tobacco Smoke, and Respiratory Symptoms in an Inner-City Birth Cohort."

25. Evelyn Grant, Hande Alp, and Kevin Weiss, "The Challenge of Inner-City Asthma," *Current Opinion in Pulmonary Medicine* 5(1) (1999).

26. Richard Strauss and Judith Knight, "Influence of the Home Environment on the Development of Obesity in Children," *Pediatrics* 103(6) (1999).

27. Kathleen Sheerin, "The Link between Asthma and Obesity," *Allergy & Asthma Advocate* (Summer 2005).

28. Peter Belamarich, Elizabeth Luder, Meyer Kattan, Herman Mitchel, Shaheen Islam, Henry Lynn, and Ellen F. Crain, "Do Obese Inner-City Children with Asthma Have More Symptoms Than Nonobese Children with Asthma?" *Pediatrics* 106(6) (2000).

29. Jonathan Gabe, Michael Bury, and Rosemary Ramsay, "Living with Asthma: The Experiences of Young People at Home and at School," *Social Science and Medicine* 55 (2002).

30. Arlene Butz, Kristin A. Riekert, Peyton Eggleston, Marilyn Winkelstein, Richared E. Thompson, and Cynthia Rand, "Factors Associated with Preventive Asthma Care in Inner-City Children," *Clinical Pediatrics* 43(8) (2004).

31. Lauren Smith and Jonathon Finkelstein, "The Impact of Sociodemographic Factors on Asthma," in *Asthma's Impact on Society*, ed. Kevin Weiss, A. Sonia Buist, and Sean Sullivan (New York: Marcel Dekker, 2000).

32. Andrea Wallace, Ellen Johnson Silver, Mary P. McCourt, and Ruth E. K. Stein, "Impoverished Children with Asthma: A Pilot Study of Urban Healthcare Access," *Journal for Specialists in Pediatric Nursing* 9(2) (2004).

33. Federico and Liu, "Overcoming Childhood Asthma Disparities of the Inner-City Poor."

34. Smith and Finkelstein, *Asthma's Impact on Society*.

35. Federico and Liu, "Overcoming Childhood Asthma Disparities of the Inner-City Poor."

36. Karen Warman et al., "How Does Home Management of Asthma Exacerbations by Parents of Inner City Children Differ from NHLBI [National Heart, Lung and Blood Institute] Guideline Recommendations?" *Pediatrics* 103(2) (1999).

37. Frederick Leickly et al., "Self-Reported Adherence, Management Behavior, and Barriers to Care after an Emergency Department Visit by Inner City Children with Asthma," *Pediatrics* 101(5) (1998).

38. Kole, "Rectifying Color and Class Disparities in Health Care."

39. Clark, *In Sickness and in Play*.

40. Bruce Bender, Henry Milgrom, and Frederick Wamboldt, "Measurement of Treatment Nonadherence in Children with Asthma," in *Promoting Adherence to Medical Treatment in Chronic Childhood Illness*, ed. Dennis Drotar (Mahwah NJ: Lawrence Erlbaum, 2000).

41. Karen Warman, Ellen Johnson Silver, and Ruth Stein, "Asthma Symptoms, Morbidity, and Anti-Inflammatory Use in Inner-City Children," *Pediatrics* 108(2) (2001).

42. Jill Halterman, Lorrie Yoos, Jeffrey M. Kaczorowski, Kenneth McConnochie, Robert J. Holzhauer, Kelly M. Conn, Sherri Lauver, and Peter G. Szilagyi, "Providers Underestimate Symptom Severity among Urban Children with Asthma," *Archives of Pediatric & Adolescent Medicine* 156 (2002).

43. Doreen Matsui, "Children's Adherence to Medication Treatment," in *Promoting Adherence to Medical Treatment in Chronic Childhood Illness*, ed. Dennis Drotar (Mahwah NJ: Lawerence Erlbuam, 2000).

44. Mona Mansour, Bruce Lanphear, and Thomas DeWitt, "Barriers to Asthma Care in Urban Children: Parent Perspectives," *Pediatrics* 106, no. 3 (2000).

45. Graves, Adams, and Portnoy, "Adherence in Young Children with Asthma."

46. Wallace et al., "Impoverished Children with Asthma."

47. Roberto Rona, "Asthma and Poverty," *Thorax* 55 (2000).

48. Bruce Miller and Beatrice Wood, "Childhood Asthma in Interaction with Family, School, and Peer Systems: A Developmental Model for Primary Care," *Journal of Asthma* 28(6) (1991).

49. Clark, *In Sickness and in Play*.

50. Miller and Wood, "Childhood Asthma in Interaction with Family, School, and Peer Systems."

51. Gabe, Bury, and Ramsay, "Living with Asthma."

52. Shari Wade et al., "Psychosocial Characteristics of Inner-City Children with Asthma: A Description of the NCICAS Psychosocial Protocol," *Pediatrics Pulmonology* 24 (1997).

53. Graves, Adams, and Portnoy, "Adherence in Young Children with Asthma."

54. Schulman, Ronca and Bucuvalas, Inc. (SRBI), "Children and Asthma in America," (Asthma Action America, 2004).

55. Leickly et al., "Self-Reported Adherence, Management Behavior, and Barriers to Care after an Emergency Department Visit by Inner City Children with Asthma."

56. Elisa Sobo, "Prevention and Healing in the Household: The Importance of Sociocultural Context," in *Child Health Services Research: Applications, Innovations and Insights*, ed. Elisa Sobo and Paul Kurtin (San Francisco: Jossey-Bass, 2003).

57. Graves, Adams, and Portnoy, "Adherence in Young Children with Asthma."

58. Leickly et al., "Self-Reported Adherence, Management Behavior, and Barriers to Care after an Emergency Department Visit by Inner City Children with Asthma."

59. Graves, Adams, and Portnoy, "Adherence in Young Children with Asthma."

60. Kathleen Peterson-Sweeney, Ann McMullen, H. Lorrie Yoos, and Harriet Kitzman, "Parental Perceptions of Their Child's Asthma: Management and Medication Use," *Journal of Pediatric Health Care* 17(3) (2003).

61. Astrida Seja Kaugars, Mary Klinnert, and Bruce Bender, "Family Influences on Pediatric Asthma," *Journal of Pediatric Psychiatry* 29(7) (2004).

62. Thomas Creer, "Medication Compliance and Childhood Asthma," in *Developmental Aspects of Health Compliance Behavior*, ed. Norman Krasnegor, Leonard Epstein, Suzanne Bennett Johson, Norman A. Krasnegor, Sumner J. Yaffe. (Hillsdale NJ: Lawrence Erlbaum, 1993).

63. Annette Lareau, *Unequal Childhoods: Class Race, and Family Life* (Berkeley: University of California Press, 2003).

64. Viky Divertie, "Strategies to Promote Medication Adherence," *MCN the American Journal of Maternal Child Nursing* 27(1).

65. Byrd and Joad, "Urban Asthma."

66. Rosalind Wright, Rosalind Wright, Herman Mitchell, Cynthia M. Visness, Sheldon Cohen, James Stout, Richard Evans, Diane Gold, "Community Violence and Asthma Morbidity: The Inner-City Asthma Study," *American Journal of Public Health* 94(4) (2004).

67. Wade et al., "Psychosocial Characteristics of Inner-City Children with Asthma."; Constance Weil et al., "The Relationship between Psychosocial Factors and Asthma Morbidity in Inner-City Children with Asthma," 104(6) (1999).

68. Pamela Wood et al., "Relationships between Welfare Status, Health Insurance Status, and Health and Medical Care among Children with Asthma," *American Journal of Public Health* 92(9) (2002).

69. Susan Bartlett, K. Kolodner, A. M. Butz, P. Eggleston, F. J. Malveaux, and C. S. Rand, "Maternal Depressive Symptoms and Adherence to Therapy in Inner-City Children with Asthma," *Pediatrics* 113(2) (2004).

70. Clark, *In Sickness and in Play.*

71. Gabe, Bury, and Ramsay, "Living with Asthma."

72. Michael Rich and Richard Chalfen, "Showing and Telling Asthma: Children Teaching Physicians with Visual Narrative," *Visual Sociology* 14 (1999).

73. Rich and Chalfen, "Showing and Telling Asthma."

74. Kirsten Rudestam, Phil Brown, Christina Zarcadoolas, and Catherine Mansell, "Children's Asthma Experience and the Importance of Place," *Health: An interdisciplinary journal for the Social Study of Health, Illness and Medicine* 8(4) (2004).

75. Clark, *In Sickness and In Play.*

76. Rudestam et al., "Children's Asthma Experience and the Importance of Place."

77. Ibid.

78. Michael Rich, Steven Lamola, Colum Amory, and Lynda Schneider, "Asthma in Life Context: Video Intervention/Prevention Assessment," *Pediatrics* 105 (2000).

79. Rich et. al., "Asthma in Life Context."

80. Charles Oberg, Nicholas Bryant, and Marilyn Bach, *America's Children: Triumph or Tragedy* (American Public Health Association, 1994).

81. Samia Markson and Barbara Fiese, "Family Rituals as a Protective Factor for Children with Asthma," *Journal of Pediatric Psychology* 25(7) (2000).

CHAPTER 4

CHILDHOOD DISABILITY AND POVERTY: HOW FAMILIES NAVIGATE HEALTH CARE AND COVERAGE

Debra Skinner, William Lachicotte, and Linda Burton

Poverty, disability, and poor health are conjoined for a substantial number of families in the United States. Environmental and social conditions associated with poverty can cause or exacerbate disabilities and chronic health problems,[1] and medical costs associated with health problems or loss of employment due to illness or disability can plunge a family into poverty.[2] Prevalence studies bear out this association. Census 2000 data indicate that families with members with a disability are more likely to be in poverty (12.8%) compared to families who do not experience disability (7.7%).[3] Conversely, studies indicate that both child and adult rates of disability are higher among poor families. In 1996, the rate of disability for children aged 3–21 at or below the poverty line (11%) was nearly twice that of children above the poverty line (6%).[4] Studies of adult welfare recipients show high rates of mental health impairments and physical disabilities.[5] A nationwide 1999 Survey of Income and Program Participation (SIPP) found that 44 percent of welfare beneficiaries reported physical or mental impairments at three times the rate of the nonwelfare population.[6] Major depression, a significant barrier to work, may alone affect approximately 25 percent or more adult women welfare recipients.[7] Health-care access and coverage are of vital importance to all families, but especially to those who have members with chronic illness or physical or mental disabilities. For low-income families, Medicaid is the primary means of health-care coverage. Since its inception under Title XIX of the Social Security Act of 1965, the Medicaid program has grown with the expansion of the health-care sector of the economy. In 2002, Medicaid accounted for 17 percent of all health-care expenditures in the United States—1,236 billion dollars. Twenty-five million children (more than 1 in 4), and 26 million adults were covered under the program.[8] Medicaid, along with charity care, is the foundation of what has been called the "medical safety net" for low-income Americans. Yet Medicaid remains a net with large holes, especially for adults. Among low-income individuals in the United States, it is estimated that 21 percent of children, 36 percent of adults with dependent children, and fully 42 percent of adults without dependents remain uninsured.[9]

Other means-tested programs for low-income families, such as Supplemental Security Income (SSI), Temporary Assistance for Needy Families (TANF), food stamps, and housing assistance also provide crucial resources to families who care for individuals with disabilities. Families often "bundle" these resources to meet the needs of their members, but these programs are increasingly difficult to access, and come with stringent eligibility requirements.[10] Finding out about these services, providing all the requisite materials to access them and multitudinous records to maintain them, going through eligibility redeterminations, and correcting mistakes made by agencies take an enormous amount of caregivers' time and resourcefulness.

While research on families in poverty and on families of children with disabilities has been extensive, relatively few studies have examined the unique set of challenges brought about by the intersection of poverty and disability. We know little about how low-income families access necessary medical and therapeutic services, make ends meet, and negotiate the governmental programs that support, or sometimes hinder them, in these efforts. The ethnographic account presented here of 42 low-income families of young children with moderate to severe disabilities portrays caregivers' intense efforts to care for their children while navigating the complex worlds of disability and poverty programs, and suggests ways in which programs could be reformed to improve delivery of services.

THE STUDY

This study is based on 3 years of ethnographic research with 42 families (12 African American, 14 non-Hispanic white, and 16 Hispanic/Latino) who had at least one child 8 years of age or younger, with moderate to severe disabilities (e.g., moderate to severe delays in cognitive, communicative, behavioral, motor, and/or adaptive skills). It is a component of a larger, multimethod study of family life conducted in Boston, Chicago, and San Antonio during 1999–2003, a period in which the early effects of welfare reform were becoming manifest (a detailed description of the Welfare, Children and Families: A Three-City Study and a series of reports are available at www.jhu.edu/~welfare).

All 42 families had household incomes that were below 200 percent of the federal poverty line (in 2001, the federal poverty level for a family of three was $14,630 per year, or $1,219 per month). At the time of recruitment, 22 households received TANF, and five were former beneficiaries. The vast majority of primary caregivers were the child's biological mother (81%). About one-fourth of the caregivers were married and the remainder were never married, divorced, separated, or widowed. Only 10 primary caregivers were working at the time of recruitment, mostly at part-time and low-paying jobs with no benefits.

Fieldworkers interviewed the primary caregiver of each family approximately once a month for 12–18 months and then conducted follow-up interviews every 6 months until the end of the study to ascertain changes in families' lives. Interviews addressed a wide range of topics, including health and health access; families' experiences with TANF, SSI, Medicaid, and other public assistance programs; work experiences; family economics and support networks; and child care. Ethnographers also engaged in participant observation, following caregivers and children to welfare offices, health centers, grocery stores, and workplaces, and taking note of the interactions and contexts of those places. The resulting datasets of interview transcripts and fieldnotes were coded in QSR6, a computer software program that aids in qualitative data analysis. We also used matrices to record specific information related to health care and coverage for each family and compiled "family profiles," or case summaries of families' perspectives on and experiences with health care and social welfare programs.

FINDINGS

Health Status of Children, Caregivers, and Other Household Members

Because this was a study of the impact of childhood disability on low-income families, we purposely recruited families who had at least one child with a disability significant enough to affect daily functioning and family routines. Diagnoses of the focal children in the 42 families included cerebral palsy, Down syndrome, seizure disorder, severe ADHD, significant developmental delays, visual and hearing impairments, spina bifida, Pervasive Developmental Disorder, autism, chondrodysplasia punctata, various syndromes (e.g., Kartagener syndrome, Angelman syndrome, and Cri-du-chat syndrome), severe asthma, and other involved medical conditions (e.g., heart congenital heart problems; brain damage, lung disease) that resulted in developmental delay and disability. Over half the children had multiple disabilities. Because of their conditions, the children had extensive health-care needs. Most were receiving medical and therapeutic treatments. Some required periodic hospitalizations and operations, as well as specialized equipment for feeding, mobility, or communication. Others had significant mental health disorders that called for behavioral interventions and medications.

In addition to childhood disability, we found general poor health among caregivers. Only a few mothers stated that they thought their health was good.[11] Over the course of the project, a majority of the caregivers reported mental health problems (e.g., depression, anxiety), chronic physical health problems (e.g., arthritis, diabetes), and learning disabilities (e.g., dyslexia) that, while not disabling, caused them some difficulty in carrying out daily activities. In addition, 29 percent of the caretakers reported having a disability (e.g., sickle cell anemia, bipolar disorder, epilepsy, cerebral palsy) that limited their ability to perform major life activities, including work and child care. Ten of the households had additional children or adults with a disability. In all, 83 percent of the households had two or more members with conditions or disabilities that resulted in some functional limitations.

Caregivers' Activities

Mothers' activities revolved around caregiving; accessing medical, educational, and therapeutic services, and managing the bureaucracy of social service programs needed for financial assistance. Many mothers worked long hours to attend to their children's health-care needs and accessing a range of services. None of the mothers of children with disabilities under the age of 3 was employed outside the home. Center-based child care was not an option for most of these families since slots available for young children with moderate or severe disabilities are rare.[12] Even if caregivers could have found child care, they did not trust that others would provide the specialized care their children with disabilities required, and feared that they might be harmed. At the end of the ethnographic study in 2003, few caregivers had been able to get or keep full-time jobs. Even if the child with a disability was in child care or a school setting, caregivers still felt they were "on call" for medical and behavioral emergencies. Several mothers lost their jobs over the course of the study because of having to miss work to handle their children's needs.[13]

Mothers were not only the primary caregivers of their children with disabilities, but also acted as their therapists, service coordinators, and advocates. In addition to taking care of other children and adults in the household, mothers' daily and weekly schedules often involved multiple doctors' appointments; meeting with early interventionists; administering recommended therapies; preparing and feeding of special diets, procuring specialized equipment, seeking out needed services, and arranging transportation. They were also crisis managers when their children's conditions required emergency care or hospitalizations. Their responsibilities lessened only slightly when their children were old enough to attend center or school-based programs. Mothers were frequently called to school to deal with their children's medical or behavioral problems. Most mothers who attempted to work outside the home found they had to miss numerous days taking care of their children's special needs, with some losing their jobs because of this. Janice's case in this regard is not unusual. Janice lived in Chicago with her four children, including Elisa, a 4-year-old daughter with multiple severe disabilities. Janice's husband left her 2 months after Elisa was born and did not provide any financial support. Elisa required specialized care around the clock. Although Janice had some in-home nursing care for her daughter, nurses frequently called in sick and she had to take over their shifts. Janice said that even if she could find a child-care center that would accept her daughter, she did not trust that they could care for her properly. In spite of these issues, Janice's welfare caseworker could not understand why she was unable to find and keep a job.

Most caregivers also had to search out social services and public assistance programs to provide necessities for the child and family (e.g., SSI, TANF, food stamps, Medicaid, transportation, specialized equipment); and other family supports (e.g., counseling, parent education, advocacy and legal efforts). Locating and managing health and social services was time-consuming and required stamina, persistence, and skills. With the exception of early intervention services, most disability and poverty programs were not easily accessed, and often necessitated ponderous paperwork and numerous applications and appeals. The caregiver's ability to locate services, correctly do the paperwork involved, get around bureaucratic quagmires, and advocate for their child's services and rights made a difference in the health care their children received and the overall quality of life of the household.

Health Coverage and Access Issues

For caregivers of children with disabilities and chronic health problems, health-care coverage and access were paramount. By most caregivers' assessments, children with disabilities were receiving adequate or even high quality care, and they did not ordinarily lack insurance coverage. All but five of the children with disabilities were covered by Medicaid, four had Medicaid and private insurance; and one child was covered entirely by private insurance. Coverage for caregivers was not as uniform. Twenty-four of the 42 primary caregivers were covered solely by Medicaid, one had Medicaid and private insurance, six were covered solely by private insurance, and 11 were uninsured. Nearly half of the uninsured caregivers lived in San Antonio, where Medicaid coverage was relatively restrictive.[14]

For the most part, Medicaid was working well for the child with disabilities, providing a comprehensive benefit package and access to medical specialists for these children with special health-care needs. It also covered most of the children's medications, therapies, and equipment.[15] For Emily, these benefits provided crucial services for her daughter, Suzy, who had severe visual impairment and developmental delays. Medicaid covered Suzy's visits to numerous medical specialists. She also received diapers, along with the shampoos and lotions she needed for her sensitive skin. Emily's only problem with Medicaid was getting Suzy a special wheelchair and a helmet to protect her head. Caregivers noted that many of these services were not covered by private plans and they appreciated that Medicaid did not impose premiums or co-pays that would be hard for them to meet given their limited budgets. They also were grateful that Medicaid covered many medications and procedures that private plans (in this age of "managed care") do not.

Overall, caregivers positively evaluated Medicaid's coverage for their children with disabilities, but there were some problems. Health insurance—whether private or Medicaid, HMO or fee-for-service—was confusing. The first problem is one familiar to most Americans these days: how to choose a plan among the options available to you? Medicaid is now provided with a number of optional, "HMO-like" managed care plans. These options are intended to provide different kinds of services depending on the needs of families. However, as one particularly savvy mom remarked, it is hard to figure out the advantages and disadvantages of the plans, indeed, hard to determine what is covered and what is not even for those who are highly literate or experienced in strategic planning. Caregivers shared the popular distrust of HMOs and other managed care programs. Many, especially in Chicago, expressed a preference for "straight" Medicaid, the classic, fee-for-service option. The basis of this preference was not just its familiarity, but the consumers' belief that the "straight plan" preserved a broader choice of providers.

Another problem with Medicaid included problematic gaps in coverage. Many beneficiaries avoided treatment for services that were not covered. Preventive or restorative dental care for adults was rarely covered, or covered only under certain options. For example, many of the Chicago parents had bad teeth because, while children's cleanings were covered, Medicaid only covered extraction for adults. One mother reported that she had not had her teeth cleaned since she was a little girl because Medicaid did not cover this service. However, since Medicaid covered extractions, she had an abscessed tooth removed. Caregivers also noted that is difficult to find the specialized dental care that is required for children with disabilities.

Other challenges to health care included the slowness of allowance or denial of reimbursement. The latter posed particular problems for those who qualified for alternative coverage of certain services (such as durable medical equipment) only after Medicaid denied coverage. Another problem, more common in Chicago, concerned what appeared to be the monthly delivery of the card that certified Medicaid eligibility. Some of the caregivers spoke of having to delay medical treatment because their cards went awry, either in the mail or in issuance. These problems were mainly nuisances, but they sometimes delayed care in situations where time was critical. In other cases, the regulations of Medicaid and other programs combined to create highly problematic situations for some families. One such case involved Alicia, who lost Medicaid benefits for her son when she moved from one Boston neighborhood to another. She had changed her address with MassHealth, but her card had not arrived. Without the card, she had no proof of insurance, and so had to stop taking Jonathan, her son with behavioral disorders, to therapy sessions. As a consequence, the Department of Social Services charged Alicia with neglect. Alicia was outraged because she had to wait for the insurance to be restored to pay for the therapy. Though the neglect charge was eventually resolved, it took time and created additional stress.

Some families had a difficult time finding physicians who would accept Medicaid. In Chicago, especially, parents complained about limited appointment times for families on public assistance that meant long waits for appointments or having to take their children out of school because they could only be seen in the mornings. For example, Connie, whose 8-year-old son had cerebral palsy, did not like the fact that there were only limited appointment times for "public aid patients" at her health-care center in Chicago. She could only get appointments in the morning, as the more convenient evening hours were reserved for private pay patients. Dan had up to ten appointments in a month, so Connie could not keep mornings free for work.

Whether insured by Medicaid or private companies, coverage and access did not come easy. Caregivers had to devote a great deal of time and energy to locating appropriate health services and negotiating gaps or lapses in coverage. Families often did not receive adequate information about what services were available to them or how they should access and choose among services. Also, a lack of information in Spanish created difficulties for Latino families who were not proficient in English. There were also numerous challenges in obtaining equipment and medication that were ruled not to be medically necessary. For example, one mother encountered a problem getting Medicaid to cover a car seat that cost $500 for her son with multiple disabilities because he did not weigh the requisite 46 pounds. Another mother could not get approval for both a wheelchair and stroller, although her daughter needed both. Helena, mother of David, an eight-year-old with Down syndrome, a hearing impairment, and other health problems, detailed the efforts needed to obtain a portable nebulizer. Helena first called her Blue Cross HMO and was told that she could rent one but that it would take 2 months and she would first need her doctor to write a referral. Even with the referral, the HMO denied the request because they had replaced David's regular electric nebulizer when it had broken. Helena called every day and eventually the HMO approved it. Said Helena "This is what you do, you spend hours on the phone with people." These stories of making numerous phone calls, following up daily, and fighting for services were common.

Another major health-care challenge was finding appropriate care and coverage for mental health diagnostics and treatment for children with psychiatric disorders.[16] Parents reported feeling that doctors did not understand the nature or depth of their children's behavioral and mental conditions. For example, Tonya, the mother of Andy, her 3-year-old adopted son diagnosed with severe ADHD and a sensory perceptual disorder, suspected that Andy may have been misdiagnosed. She thought he really suffered from bipolar disorder, a condition exacerbated by the antidepressants prescribed for him. Another family in Texas could not get appropriate services for their son, Jerry, diagnosed with severe ADHD, oppositional-defiant disorder, and bipolar I disorder with psychotic features. Jerry was sometimes violent and had injured family members. His family located a psychiatrist, who prescribed medication, but his mother thought the treatment was only superficial, and that Jerry needed to be in a group home to get the help he needed. They were told that Medicaid would only cover the cost of residential care if they made Jerry a ward of the state, but once he became a ward of the state, they could not take him back.

Families with private insurance were not necessarily better off than those receiving Medicaid. They often got hit with steep copayments, especially on prescriptions, and these out-of-pocket costs created financial hardships. For the few families who had private insurance coverage through work, there was one rule: don't change jobs; don't change plans. Helena, introduced above, who herself suffered from a disabling rheumatic disorder, made clear the reasons for the rule. She and her child were covered under her husband's insurance, provided by his employer in Chicago. Her husband wanted to change to a better job, but the family's health needs were a part of calculating the benefits of any such move. Helena explained that her and her son's disabilities—the "preexisting conditions" that no insurer would want to underwrite—constituted one large roadblock. Only employers with a sufficiently large group policy could "write off" (defray in an actuarial sense) the problem cases, and, even so, the vendors or administrators of the plan might deny them. Since these kinds of employers are rare, job mobility was, in effect, not much of an option for families with members with disabilities. Helena had the sense of being trapped by this lack of "portability." These concerns of portability and insurability also affected families with more income and fewer needs than Helena's.

Navigating Health Care in Contexts of Poverty and Social Programs

Many factors coalescenced to affect families' abilities to obtain the health care and other services their children required. One was the health of the caregiver. Caregivers had to amass time and energy to locate and access health care and social services. This was a challenge for all caregivers, but especially for those with poor physical and mental health. Sometimes the effort and frustration involved in caring for their children, getting services, and making ends meet took their toll. Caregivers talked about being constantly worried, feeling overwhelmed and stressed, and being depressed. Their own health suffered, and was often exacerbated by forfeiting or postponing health care for themselves. Some mothers would not take prescription drugs, either because they could not afford them or because the side effects made them too sleepy to care for their children. Others refused operations or other medical treatments because they felt they could not take time away from their child care duties. One such case involved Marjorie, a mother living in Boston, who neglected seeking treatment not only for her enduring psychiatric disorder, but also for cervical cancer. She said that treatments left her too exhausted to watch her four children, three of whom had special needs. At one point, her doctor wanted to hospitalize her for pneumonia, but she had no one to care for her four children and could not obtain emergency child-care funds, so she recovered at home. In spite of multiple health problems, Marjorie spent a great deal of effort managing her children's services and took justifiable pride in her parenting, but some days she just did not have the energy to deal with everyday routines. Postponing health care proved to be a counter-productive strategy when the caregiver's health deteriorated to a point where it affected everyday activities, including child-care and accessing services.[17]

Another factor determining health-care access was the nexus of social and disability programs that caregivers found themselves in, and the myriad policies that regulated eligibility for Medicaid and monetary benefits such as TANF and SSI. Welfare reforms of 1996 uncoupled or "delinked" eligibility for TANF and Medicaid. Families who were not eligible for enrollment in TANF, or who left TANF, were not always aware that they could still qualify for Medicaid. Indeed, studies have shown a decline in families receiving Medicaid once off TANF rolls, although it is not clear the extent to which this is due to families no longer being eligible or to their not being aware of continuing eligibility.[18]

Caregivers in the study feared losing Medicaid for the child with disabilities if they returned to work. The type of jobs most of them could obtain were those that offered few, if any, benefits. If health insurance was offered, they could not afford the premiums. Choosing between work with no or limited benefits and keeping Medicaid was a major decision for some families. Yet for those welfare recipients who were not exempt from work participation requirements or time limits, staying on welfare was not an option. At the time of the study, Massachusetts's TANF program allowed exemptions from both time limits and work requirements if the caregiver had disabilities or was caring for a disabled household member. Texas exempted these individuals from work, but not from the 60-month lifetime limit for TANF.

In Illinois, persons with disabilities or their caregivers were not considered exempt from the 5-year TANF time limit, but they could be temporarily exempted from work participation because of medical or other barriers. In the majority of states (28), caregivers of a child or adult with a disability were not exempt from the time limit and, presumably, needed to enter the workforce once their TANF benefits ended.[19] This situation created real dilemmas for a number of families who shared the fear of losing Medicaid and not being able to obtain other health insurance for their children.

This was the case for Emily, a mother of a child with disabilities, who lived in Illinois and was therefore subject to TANF time limits. Emily experienced intense stress from the dilemmas she faced in trying to make ends meet and care for Suzy, her daughter who had multiple disabilities. Emily wanted to work, but did not want to stop her daughter's therapies during the day, nor were child-care slots available for children like Suzy. Emily was enrolled in a cooking school and planned to work as a chef when Suzy became old enough to go to a school-based child-care program, but she worried about being able to keep a job because of Suzy's extensive health-care needs. She also worried about losing Medicaid for Suzy once she got a job, and not being able to obtain private insurance because of Suzy's preexisting medical conditions. The threat of losing TANF and Medicaid and not being able to work due to her daughter's condition increased her stress, and she often felt overwhelmed and hopeless. Her physical and mental health deteriorated over the course of the study.

SUPPORTING FAMILIES OF CHILDREN WITH DISABILITIES

There are many supports that would assist low-income families of children with disabilities in their move to work and economic security. To work outside the home, they need child-care providers who can provide the specialized care their children require.[20] They need a flexible workplace, flexible work hours, and an employer that understands when time has to be taken away from work to manage the child's medical, educational, and therapeutic needs. Families also need affordable health-care coverage for their children and for themselves, and to be assured that coverage of their children with disabilities will not be put in jeopardy by their working.

This 3-year ethnographic examination of low-income families with children with disabilities highlights several important points that should be considered in any further reforms in TANF, SSI, and Medicaid. During the time of the study, we found that Medicaid worked for children with disabilities. For the most part, these children had access to a wide range of specialists who were dedicated to their health care and development. Although some families experienced scheduling difficulties and long waits, overall, most parents positively evaluated the services their children received through Medicaid programs.

However, Medicaid could be improved. Caregivers spoke of a need to have clearer explanations (and to have explanations in Spanish) of benefits and options. They preferred plans that could be tailored for their individual situations, like MassHealth.

They told of problems that stemmed from lack of coverage of dental care for adults, inadequate mental health services, and lack of coordinated care between mental health and substance abuse services. They discussed the need for better assessments of what specialized equipment is required for individuals with disabilities and the need for service providers to offer more flexible appointment times.

We also found uneven insurance coverage within families. Whereas a disability, especially one that meets the criteria for SSI benefits, virtually guarantees access to Medicaid for the individual with the disability, other members of the family, especially adults, may not be covered. They may not have access to other insurance plans through the workplace, or can afford them if they do.[21] In this study, all of the caregivers wanted to work and had plans for work when they could locate appropriate child care. Yet, they feared that they would lose Medicaid once their income increased and not be able to obtain insurance through the workplace, especially for the child with disabilities. For these families, transitional Medicaid that could be extended even longer than the current 1-year limit would be a major incentive and support to work. But what working poor and nonworking families need most is a universal health-care program that covers all family members, not just those with "eligible" disabilities. Health coverage is a crucial support to families in their quest to care for their children and attain economic security.[22]

Since universal health care may not occur in our lifetime, what can help families now is more collaboration between disability agencies and poverty programs. For the most part, professionals who work with individuals with disabilities are not familiar with poverty programs or the needs of poor families. Conversely, TANF caseworkers are largely unaware of the difference disability makes in families' abilities to meet program requirements or of disability programs that could assist these families.[23] What would help low-income families who have children with disabilities is for disability professionals to refer families to appropriate programs and services for those in poverty, and vice versa. For example, TANF caseworkers could receive training on childhood disability and its impact on caregivers' ability to work. They could maintain a list of agencies to which they could refer clients for additional resources and supports. Conversely, disability professionals such as early intervention caseworkers could receive training on how to assist families in applying for and appealing applications to TANF, Medicaid, SSI, and other means-tested programs. Such information and supports would better aid families in being able to access and provide health care for all their members.

NOTES

1. Gary Evans, "The Environment of Childhood Poverty," *American Psychologist*, 59 (2004):77–92; James Garbarino and Barbara Ganzel, "The Human Ecology of Risk," in *Handbook of Early Childhood Intervention*, 2nd ed., ed Jack P. Shonkoff and Samuel J. Meisels (Cambridge: Cambridge University Press, 2000).

2. Anna Lukemeyer, Marcia K. Meyers, and Timothy M. Smeeding, "Expensive Children in Poor Families: Out-of-Pocket Expenditures for the Care of Disabled and Chronically Ill Children in Welfare Families," *Journal of Marriage and the Family* 62 (2000):399–415; Katherine

Seelman and Sean Sweeney, "The Changing Universe of Disability," *American Rehabilitation* 21 (1995):2–13.

3. US Census Bureau, "Disability and American Families: 2000," (July 2005), http://www.census.gov/prod/2005pubs/censr-23.pdf (accessed June 16, 2006).

4. Glenn T. Fujiura and Kiyoshi Yamaki, "Trends in Demography of Childhood Poverty and Disability," *Exceptional Children* 66 (2000):187–199.

5. Amy Johnson and Alicia Meckstroth, "Ancillary Services to Support Welfare to Work," *Mathematica Policy Research Report to the Office of the Assistant Secretary for Planning and Evaluation, U.S. Department of Health and Human Services* (June 22, 1998), http://aspe.hhs.gov/hsp/isp/ancillary/front.htm. (accessed June 16, 2006); Eileen P. Sweeney, "Recent Studies Indicate that Many Parents Who are Current or Former Welfare Recipients Have Disabilities or Other Medical Conditions," *Center for Budget and Policy Priorities* (February 29, 2000), http://www.cbpp.org=29-00wel.pdf (accessed June 16, 2006).

6. General Accounting Office (GAO), "*Welfare Reform: More Coordinated Effort Could Help States and Localities Move TANF Recipients With Impairments Toward Employment* (GAO-02-37) (October, 2001), http://www.gao.gov/new.items/d0237.pdf (accessed June 16, 2006).

7. Mary Corcoran, Sandra K. Danziger, and Richard Tolman, "Long Term Employment of African-American and White Welfare Recipients and the Role of Persistent Health and Mental Health Problems," *Women & Health* 39 (2004):21–40; Mary C. Lennon, Juliana Blome, and Kevin English, "Depression among Women on Welfare; A Review of the Literature," *Journal of the American Medical Women's Association* 57 (2002):27–32.

8. Kaiser Commission on Medicaid and the Uninsured, "The Medicaid Program at a Glance," (May, 2006), http://www.kff.org/medicaid/upload/7235.pdf (accessed June 16, 2006). The Henry J. Kaiser Family Foundation, especially through the Kaiser Commission on Medicaid and the Uninsured, provides current information on Medicaid and the state of public health in the United States. It issues numerous reports, briefs, and factsheets, most of which are available through its Web site (http://www.kff.org).

9. Amy Davidoff, Anna S. Sommers, Jennifer Lesko, and Alshadye Yemane, "Medicaid and State-Funded Coverage for Adults: Estimates of Eligibility and Enrollment," *The Kaiser Commission on Medicaid and the Uninsured* (April, 2004), http://www.kff.org/medicaid/7078.cfm (accessed June 16, 2006). For an analysis of inequities, along class and ethnic lines, in the health care safety net, and for people's accounts of living without health insurance, see Gay Becker, "Deadly Inequality in the Health Care Safety Net: Uninsured Ethnic Minorities' Struggle to Live with Life-Threatening Illnesses," *Medical Anthropology Quarterly* 18 (2004):58–275.

10. Committee on Children with Disabilities, "The Continued Importance of Supplemental Security Income (SSI) for Children and Adolescents with Disabilities," *Pediatrics* 107 (2001):790–793; Mark Nadel, Steve Wamhoff, and Michael Wiseman, "Disability, Welfare Reform, and Supplemental Security Income," *Social Security Bulletin* 65 (2003/2004):14–30; Debra Skinner, William Lachicotte, and Linda Burton, "The Difference Disability Makes: Managing Childhood Disability, Poverty, and Work," in *Doing Without: Women and Work after Welfare Reform*, ed. Jane Henrici (Tucson: University of Arizona Press, in press).

11. This pattern is comparable to that found in the larger Three-City Study sample reported in Ronald J. Angel, Laura Lein, and Jane M. Henrici, *Poor Families in American's Health Care Crisis* (New York, Cambridge University Press, 2006) and also in Andrew London, John Martimez, and Denise Polit, "The health of poor urban women; Findings from the project on

devolution and urban change," *MDRC report* (May, 2001), http://www.mdrc.org/publications/77/execsum.html (accessed June 16, 2006).

12. Appropriate and quality child care is a problem for families, regardless of income or disability status, but is particularly acute for low-income families of children with disabilities. A review of studies on the availability of child care for families of children with special needs indicates that whereas many centers may serve children with mild to moderate delays, there are very few child-care slots for children with significant disabilities (Mark Wolery and Ariane Holcombe-Ligon, "The Extent and Nature of Preschool Mainstreaming: A Survey of General Early Educators, *Journal of Special Education* 27 (1993):222–234. Challenges of finding child care for children with special needs is also documented in Cheryl Ohlson, "Welfare Reform: Implications for Young Children with Disabilities, Their Families, and Service Providers," *Journal of Early Intervention* 21 (1998):191–206; and Elisa A. Rosman and Jane Knitzer, "Welfare Reform: The Special Case of Young Children with Disabilities and their Families," *Infants and Young Children* 13 (2001):25–35. For barriers to child care for children with disabilities, see Cathryn Booth-LaForce and Jean F. Kelly, "Childcare Patterns and Issues for Families of Preschool Children with Disabilities," *Infants and Young Children* 17 (2004):5–16; Jack P. Shonkoff and Deborah Phillips, eds., *"From Neurons to Neighborhoods: The Science of Early Childhood Development"* (Washington, DC: National Academy of Science, 2000).

13. For other studies of the intersection of caregiving, childhood disability, and work, see Valerie Leiter, Marty W. Krauss, Betsy Anderson, and Nora Wells, "The Consequences of Caring: Effects of Mothering a Child with Special Needs," *Journal of Family Issues* 25 (2004):379–403.

14. For factors affecting health insurance coverage for families in The Three-City Study, see Angel, Lein, and Henrici.

15. Ronald J. Angel, Laura Lein, Jane Henrici, and Emily Leventhal, "Health Insurance Coverage for Children and Their Caregivers in Low-Income Neighborhoods," *Welfare, Children & Families: A Three-City Study Report* (July, 2001), www.jhu.edu/~welfare/18581_WelfareBriefSummer01.pdf (accessed June 16, 2006.)

16. See David Mechanic, ed., *Managed Behavioral Health Care: Current Realities and Future Potential* (San Francisco: Jossey-Bass, 1998); Howard Waitzkin, Robert L. Williams, John A. Bock, Joanne McCloskey, Cathleen Wiliging, and William Wagner, "Safety-Net Institutions Buffer the Impact of Medicaid Managed Care: A Multi-Method Assessment in a Rural State," *American Journal of Public Health* 92 (2002):598–610.

17. See also Jane Henrici, this volume.

18. Angel, Lein, and Henrici; Karl Kronebusch, "Children's Medicaid Enrollment: The Impacts of Mandates, Welfare Reform, and Policy Delinking," *Journal of Health Politics, Policy and Law* 26 (2001):1223–1260.

19. *Center on Budget Priorities' State Policy Documentation Project* (2000), www.spdp.org, updated June 2000, (accessed December 20, 2001.)

20. See also Susan L. Parish, Jennifer M. Cloud, Jungwon Huh, and Ashley N. Henning, "Child Care, Disability, and Family Structure: Use and Quality in a Population-Based Sample of Low-Income Preschool Children," *Children and Youth Services Review* 27(2005):905–919.

21. According to the Kaiser Commission on Medicaid and the Uninsured, four out of five (81%) of uninsured individuals are in working families. See "The Uninsured and Their Access to Health Care," (November 2005) http://www.kff.org/uninsured/upload/The-Uninsured-and-Their-Access-to-Health-Care-Fact-Sheet-6.pdf (accessed June 16, 2006).

22. See also Henrici this volume and Angel, Lein and Henrici.

23. Jennifer Pokempner and Dorothy Roberts. "Poverty, Welfare Reform, and the Meaning of Disability, *Ohio State Law Journal* 62 (2001); David Whittenburg, "A Health-Conscious Safety Net? Health Problems and Program Use among Low-Income Adults with Disabilities," *The Urban Institute* (September 2004), http://www.urban.org/UploadedPDF/311065_B-62.pdf (accessed June 16, 2006).

CHAPTER 5

CHILDREN, RURAL POVERTY, AND DISABILITY: CASE STUDIES FROM THE HEARTLAND

Cynthia Needles Fletcher and Mary Winter

THE RURAL CONTEXT

About 1 in 5 Americans (17%) live in rural areas. A careful study of rural areas reveals a great deal of demographic and economic diversity. The proportion of the total population and the absolute numbers of children that are rural continue to shrink, although urban expansion, high immigration and birth rates, and the migration of retirees all have boosted the population in some rural areas. In addition to changes in population size, rural areas also are becoming more diverse racially, ethnically, and economically. In general, lower levels of human capital, higher underemployment rates, and lower wages distinguish rural economies compared to urban centers.[1] Poverty is more prevalent and more persistent in rural America. Nearly 14 percent of rural Americans live below the poverty line and 95 percent of persistent-poverty counties, designated so if 20 percent or more of their populations were living in poverty over the last 30 years, are rural.[2]

Consistent with national trends, Iowa's economic base and much of its population are moving from strictly rural areas to urban areas in the state. The rural population in Iowa continues to shrink, although a few communities have experienced an influx of immigrants attracted by jobs in food processing plants. Iowa ranks near the bottom among all states in terms of population growth and near the top, second only to North Dakota, in the proportion of its population age 85 and older. Nearly half of Iowa's counties, primarily rural, experienced population loss during the 1990s. The state lags the nation in per capita and median household income levels. Iowa has a lower incidence of rural poverty (9.2 %) and, in contrast to national averages, there is no rural-urban difference in the poverty rate. No Iowa counties are counted among the persistently poor.[3] These structural shifts create challenges in how best to serve Iowa's most vulnerable rural citizens: poor children and poor elderly.

Rural areas, as a whole, are more disadvantaged than urban ones across numerous health indicators. Access to health-care facilities is more limited; rates of health insurance coverage are similar in rural and urban areas, but private insurance is less common in rural areas; and spells without insurance coverage are longer. Many studies illustrate that the structure, access to, and use of social supports and institutions differ between rural and urban communities. Many rural areas have seen health-care facilities shuttered. Lack of transportation is a key barrier to accessing services in rural communities. These findings, culled from national data sets mask local differences, however.[4] For example, state-specific data reveal that rural-urban differences in access and utilization are not present to the same degree in all states.[5] Observations from community case studies in the seven Iowa communities that were the sites for this study provide county-specific data that are consistent with the state-specific findings. In each county, the health-care system met the most basic needs of low-income families to varying degrees. No community seemed to address all the difficulties inherent in trying to meet the needs of a geographically dispersed, low-income population, however. In particular, rural residents routinely traveled to metropolitan areas to obtain highly specialized health-care treatment.[6] A growing body of literature demonstrates that long-term economic trends, coupled with low population densities and limited community resources, affect health-care service delivery and, in turn, the well-being of rural children and their families. Few studies, however, have used a qualitative approach to understand what it means to be poor, to cope with a child's health problems, and to navigate a rural health-care system.

DATA AND METHODS

Data for this study are from a series of in-depth interviews with 35 families (five families in each of seven Iowa communities) who were receiving payments under Iowa's cash assistance program, called the Family Investment Program or FIP, in mid-1997. The focus on recipient families was one phase of a comprehensive study of welfare reform in Iowa.[7] The seven communities represented a continuum ranging from an extremely rural community with a population of 1,800 to a metropolitan community of 109,000. Families were selected randomly from the list of welfare recipients in each of the seven counties in which the targeted communities were located. Two Iowa State University Extension staff members who served the community conducted each interview, taking detailed notes and tape recording the interview.

The interview protocols were a combination of structured and semistructured questions. Six in-depth interviews were conducted approximately every 6 months between late 1997 and early 2001. Parents—primarily mothers—discussed many dimensions of family life, including the health status of each family member. The respondent was the same through all interviews; however, other people (usually her partner) often were present during the interviews. Tapes were transcribed and coded following standard qualitative research protocols. Baseline demographic and program participation characteristics were entered into a database for quantitative analysis. Qualitative data analysis was completed the old-fashioned way: by reading and rereading the transcripts, searching for common themes throughout the interviews. The three families featured in this chapter all live in rural communities. The names, places, and some of the circumstances that might identify a particular family have been changed, but the stories told present a detailed picture of the tremendous challenges faced by rural poor families with children who have significant physical and behavioral health problems.

CHILDREN'S HEALTH IN RURAL AREAS

Our examination of the data identifies several themes. First, a striking number of the families have a child with significant chronic health problems. We draw upon the data to develop thick descriptions of the health conditions of the children. Second, we describe the challenges of accessing health care and support services for disabled children in rural areas and the roles that mothers play as advocates for their children in obtaining services. Third, we describe some of the effects that having a child with health problems have on the family.

The Children in the Study

At the time of the first interviews, 74 children lived in the 35 households. They ranged in age from $3\frac{1}{2}$ weeks to 17 years. Thirteen of the children, *more than one-sixth of the kids*, were disabled or had other serious health problems, according to a report from a parent. The health problems of the children included autism, developmental delays, seizures, skeletal problems that led to several surgeries, mental retardation, and Attention Deficit Hyperactivity Disorder (ADHD). In three of the 35 families, children either had been removed from the home or were removed over the course of the interviews, and placed in foster care. Two older boys in one family were in trouble with the law for vandalism. The situations of three children and their families illustrate the themes that have emerged from the data.

Bailey's Health

Bailey, the 8-month old daughter of Mary and Tom, lives in a very small community in northern Iowa with her parents and her half-sister, Sally; during the course of the interviews, a baby brother is born. Bailey suffers from seizures and is on heavy medication. She requires special liquid formula at $20 per can because of concerns about food allergies. At the first interview, Mary reported that Bailey recently was ill and lost about 2 pounds—dropping from 19 to 17 pounds. The family travels to Des Moines, the nearest metro area—135 miles one way—for appointments with a specialist every 2 or 3 months. At the second interview, Mary describes Bailey's very serious health problems: ".... she's been in the hospital every 2 weeks [in the past 6 months]. She has uncontrollable epileptic seizure disorder. She has febrile seizures and epileptic seizures. The hospital stay we just got done with is a little different. They finally got the seizures under control, then we transferred to [specialized university hospitals in] Iowa City. Her temperature at [the children's hospital in Des Moines] got to 107.2 degrees. We sat up in Iowa City—they're good doctors—they ran every test they could to find out what's going on with her. . . . All her tests came back negative. They did find an infection in her bowels that was causing it [high temperatures] really bad."

At the third interview, Mary reflects on the challenges of raising Bailey: ". . . her longest seizure has been $3\frac{1}{2}$ hours and that's the one that put her on life support. It's like a constant battle. Actually we're doing really good right now. She's been sick this week and had seizures. In the last 6 months it was every 2 weeks on the dot, we were in the Des Moines hospital. We were Life Flighted [or] rushed by ambulance. Sometimes we'd actually already be in Des Moines because we had just been to the doctor that day. When she gets sick she gets sick fast . . . that's another reason why we don't leave the house very often. She's very prone to any illnesses or viral infections that go around. She catches them."

At the fifth interview, Bailey—almost 3—is still facing many health problems. Her mother reports: "We've been up in Des Moines and Iowa City every week for the last . . . I don't know how many weeks. We've been to every specialist there is. . . . She has always been on the 95th percentile for her height and weight—always. Right now she is 55 percent for her height and she is 27 percent for her weight. She is losing weight . . . big time. They don't seem to be concerned about it but, I'm sorry, the kid's wrists are the size of a newborn's. She aches like she has arthritis. January 3 we go to Iowa City to see a bone specialist. We've seen an allergist. We've seen a behavior specialist. We've seen a dietitian. They said we're doing every thing we should be doing—giving her the extra butter, extra peanut butter, extra fat. . . . She eats all the time, and she's still losing weight."

Devon's Autism

At the first interview, Devon, age 6, lives with his parents, Cindy and Bob, and 4-year-old brother, David, in a small town in west central Iowa. At the age of 3, Devon was diagnosed as autistic by specialists in Minneapolis. The diagnosis was the beginning of a long and often frustrating journey for Devon's parents. "They [the doctors in Minneapolis] were talking way over our heads. We didn't understand a thing. We had no clue what they were talking about." The interviews provide a glimpse of both the physical and behavioral health problems of this young boy.

A chronic digestive problem has resulted in a swollen esophagus that the local doctor was unable to treat. In the second interview, Cindy describes the problem and treatment: ". . . . vomiting but he [Devon] won't vomit, he swallows it back. . . . We doctored with Dr. Swanson and he said 'I can't do no more'. The only scope in Iowa is Iowa City. . . . Every three months we have to go back [to Iowa City]." At this same interview, Cindy notes behavioral changes in Devon: "The attitude he's had through the sickness is not good. . . . It's not violent, but he's back into the biting stage. His autism is more demanding."

At the last interview, Devon—now age 9—has made great progress in school. Cindy observes, "Devon's physical [condition] is tremendously better.... Mrs. Beem [his teacher] says he's come a long way with friends and being social." However, in the same interview Cindy describes a recurrence of Devon's digestive problems and ponders the cause: "... you don't know what it is—if it's physical, mental or.... So we're going down to see the upper GI doctor on the same date with an ear specialist, plus his autism doctor."

Jake's Learning Disability

Jake, age 17, lives with his father, Bill, his step-mother, Patsy, and 13-year-old sister, Brandy, in a small town in western Iowa. At the first interview, his stepmother says Jake is retarded. He would like to be a policeman or fireman, but the family is aware that he will not be able to meet those goals. In addition to being labeled as learning disabled, Jake has a history of depression and violence. During the course of the interviews, he is taking Prozac. When he has forgotten to take his medicine, he has dark moods, and has hit his mother and his sister. Patsy tells the interviewer "It's up and down. If he forgets to take his Prozac it gets bad." And Jake replies, "Sometimes I take it late; sometimes I forget."

Jake's physical health is also at issue. He is obese and has high cholesterol. Patsy reports that Jake "weighs 300 pounds. That's a little too overweight.... We had him to the doctor.... They said to watch his cholesterol because it was high at the time, but he won't listen. We went to church one Sunday and came back and he had cooked himself three pounds of hamburger and didn't leave none for anybody else. He's a meat eater—constantly into meat every half hour. He just eats constantly. He don't know when to quit."

Jake is listed as being in "eighth grade special education" during the first two interviews, and in "ninth grade special education" at interview three. At interview four, he is 18 and has graduated from high school. While still in high school, Jake begins to participate in the local work activity center. When asked how he received that opportunity, Patsy replies, "His teacher at school does that for the kids—for all of the kids that have slow learning disabilities. She puts all her class in there that needs it." He continues to work through this program after he leaves school, going to several different communities each week. When asked what he does, Patsy responds, "At [business] he puts boxes together. At [another business] he's a custodian. At [a third business] he packs boxes of cheese ... and he loves it." At the last interview, he is 20, living at home and looking for work.

Access to Health Care and the Advocacy Role of Mothers

Families in rural areas must travel long distances to access specialized medical care for their children. Although Bailey might be better served elsewhere, her mother describes a decision to stick with services in Des Moines rather than continuing treatment at the University Hospitals in Iowa City, more than 200 miles from her home: "Des Moines has to be the break off point because it's half way between for her medical emergency. It's [Iowa City] too far for Life Flight to come. Otherwise it's an 8-hour trip for an ambulance to come down and get us and take us back—it's too far. We're still going to deal with our doctors in Des Moines."

Devon's mother also has had to make difficult choices about dealing with her son's autism, particularly in the quest for an "autism doctor." Cindy describes one series of interactions with the various systems: "I called . . . [Devon's] autistic doctor in Iowa City. He's no longer in practice. So now I have to sign on with a doctor in Des Moines. This afternoon I have to go through paperwork to resubmit him with a doctor. DHS [the Iowa Department of Human Services] says to me, 'we might not be able to pay for this because [Devon] was signed on with a doctor and that doctor hasn't told us he was out of practice.' So we might have to pay for another doctor's evaluation. . . . The reevaluation runs anywhere from $2000 to $4000. . . . This is our third diagnosis because we've been to Minneapolis because they [presumably DHS] wanted to try out this new doctor in Minneapolis. She's wonderful. But her Minnesota title won't fit Iowa. So then two years later we go to Iowa City. I loved [the physician in Iowa City], he helped me in a lot of different ways, but he didn't tell us he was quitting. *So here we go.* This is all happening this month."

Devon's disability has thrown his mother into the labyrinth of support systems for children with conditions like autism: the school system, the Area Education Agency (AEA), the Department of Human Services (DHS), and the medical system, none of which are located in their community. The DHS office is located in the county seat, 10 miles away, and the respite care facilities are in a neighboring county 40 miles to the northwest, the opposite direction from Des Moines and Iowa City. On the day of one of the interviews, Cindy describes her attempt to find an orthodontist who will take an autistic patient with Title XIX (Medicaid): "I've called nine today and no one will take him." She finally finds one, about 50 miles away.

Poor rural families are very reliant on private transportation to meet regular health-care appointments. Personal vehicles owned by poor families are often not reliable. Mary describes her transportation problems: "It's [her van] really reliable—except when the alternator belt falls off. We got stuck that one Saturday night . . . the coldest wind chill factor of the year. . . . We were stranded. . . . We got cold. It took them an hour to get us." Long distances complicate the ability of rural families to maintain relationships with their doctors. Cindy reflects that she "couldn't really keep much contact with Minneapolis doctors because they're so far away. We called for help and it took them three or four days . . . to get the message." In addition to trips for medical care, Cindy comments on the travel costs of attending educational workshops: "Just to learn about autism . . . those big meetings I go to in Des Moines—just to go there it's $50. That's a lot of money."

A recurring theme throughout the interviews is the critical role that poor mothers can play in diagnosing and monitoring their child's health and then advocating for services within the health-care system. Mary describes her frustrations and her proactive role: "They keep saying, 'well, we can't find anything wrong.' We know there is something wrong, and I'm going to make them find it. I don't mean to sound harsh, but if something happens to her, I will sue. I'm not going to lose my kid over their mistake or me sitting back. She [Bailey] kept having these little seizures. I kept telling them, 'something is wrong—something is wrong.'.... She has delayed development of the brain. Her brain is smaller than normal—which means there's extra fluid there to fill up the space.... After I got this absorbed, I called up there [to the neurologist] and said 'what's the name of this'? They said, 'it doesn't have a name.' Microcephalic is smaller than normal brain. Hydrocephalic is extra water on the brain.... I asked [specialists at] Iowa City and they said *I was right.*"

Devon's mother has a high school education, but has self-diagnosed learning disabilities. She admits that sometimes the paperwork involved in getting assistance is overwhelming, but that "You have to stay on top of it. There's no way I could have a full-time job. I don't know how parents do it [employment] full time and deal with it ... with Devon's age I need all this extra assistance. So I have to stay on it full time." Although Cindy feels that her own learning disability sometimes makes it difficult for her to be a successful advocate for her son, she has found an ally in an educational program aide. "If I have any problems, I call Janice. I can deal with it. I've been dealing with it pretty good I think. I can do a certain amount, but then when it gets too hairy, or I get too frustrated, then that's when I call Janice."

Two instances, both reported to DHS, illustrate Cindy's experiences dealing with an autistic child and "the system." When Devon went to kindergarten, Cindy packed his lunch with foods he liked after he refused to eat school lunches. School officials viewed Cindy's lunches as "junk food." They "called DHS" and required her to work with a dietitian. In another instance, Cindy dealt with Devon's habit of biting his little brother by biting him herself: "I bit him. Now he knows what it feels like.... He doesn't know his own strength. He could bite an actual chunk out of David and not know it.... They'll [DHS] probably get me for abuse on that.... You're damned if you do and damned if you don't." One senses that Cindy's intentions are good, but her lack of knowledge and skills in parenting an autistic child have resulted in these run-ins with the system.

In the second interview, Devon is completing first grade. It is clear that his mother views his progress from a different perspective than the school: "Did you know that he missed 33 days [of school] this year? They [school officials] didn't think that was very good. *But look at what the child has been through.*" Cindy comments on the local school system: "I keep telling the teachers, 'hang in there, he's done good.' They've never dealt with autism. They're learning—we're all learning together." In a later interview, she complains that Devon's aide "... has no training. The therapist in Des Moines ... sent letters to the school that they wanted to go through some sort of autism training. The school hasn't followed through." At one point Devon's aide asks if his family will finance her (the aide) for training. Cindy sighs, "I didn't blow up at her...."

Although not the only reason, frustration with the school system is, in part, responsible for the family's move from their small older home they owned outright in a very small (less than 1,000 residents) community to 31 acres near a larger community. The family is pleased with their move. The school system is more responsive to Devon's needs, and being able to have animals at home has been a big help to him.

In contrast to the activism of Mary and Cindy by their own admission, Patsy and Bill are fairly passive in terms of finding support for Jake. They are content to let the school system take the lead, in part, perhaps, because school systems, even those in small communities, have more experience with children who are mentally delayed than with those with other disabilities. His stepmother says that Jake has always been labeled as retarded or learning disabled. When asked what the family has done to help with that condition, she replies, "We haven't done a whole lot. It's mainly the people that worked with us—the school system, etc." The interviewer follows up: "What does the school do for you?" Patsy: "Meetings." Interviewer: "Are they group–parent meetings?" Patsy: "Yes." Interviewer: "What do they tell you at these meetings?" Patsy: "They have a few good things to say about him, then there are things that they don't—that needs a little more work done with him. They do their part and we just sit in on the meetings and listen and learn what needs to be done."

Family Impact

The challenges and stresses that a chronically ill child places on any family are acute, but the lack of resources within poor families, coupled with the lack of services in rural communities exacerbate problems for the rural poor. Mary, who has not been employed since Bailey was born, describes the economic strain that Bailey's health-care needs have placed on the family. She aptly describes the dilemma of getting ahead and the need for medical care: "I imagine I could go to work and work 40 hours, lose touch with my kids and my family, but in the long run I can't afford to lose her [Bailey's] medical. That's the only reason I'm not working. I'm going nuts sometimes at home, but it's the only time I'm not working—but we'll lose her medical. We can't afford a $5,000 Life Flight bill. We're so much in debt right now it's not even funny anyway."

Financial stresses compound problems in Devon's family as well. During the course of the six interviews, his father holds several different jobs. He is unemployed at the last interview, and receiving Supplemental Security Income (SSI) disability payments. Like Mary, Cindy has not been employed outside the home since Devon's birth. She describes how Devon's needs limit her ability to seek employment: "Everybody calls at the last minute to make appointments. I have to jump. I'm not complaining, but in a way—financially—we could use some extra income. We deal with it."

Interviewers asked families to reflect back on family life at the beginning of the study and compare condition 3 years later. Mary replies: "Probably a 9 (on a 10-point scale). Life was pretty smooth. I think that was when Bailey was just born. Life was smooth—easy going. We both worked." And asked to evaluate life now: "Life in general kind of sucks. Put all the stress and change and everything together— probably a 2 or 3. Bailey's seizures, this disorder—it's put a lot of stress and strain on everything. It's had us totally where we had to rearrange our lives around this. . . . We always end up in Des Moines at the hospital—Life Flighted, ambulance and all that.

We lived with suitcases packed; we had no choice.... Last year it's gotten easier ... but it's still the stress of all the appointments, juggling Sally being in school, two kids at home, keeping the house clean, doing the doctor's appointments—especially when most doctor appointments are in Des Moines or Iowa City. It's just kind of nuts sometimes."

In contrast, Cindy says that their lives are getting better, in part because of their move to an acreage and in part because of her spouse's eligibility for SSI disability. Having horses and pigs and chickens on an "Old MacDonald Farm" has been a good thing for the boys, especially Devon. "It takes Devon $2\frac{1}{2}$ hours to come in from the bus. He talks to every animal. He loves his horses. He just loves his horses." Although they still must travel long distances for special medical services, those provided by the school system and the Area Education Agency are superior to the ones they left. And, at 9, Devon is easier to handle than he was at age 6. Throughout the interviews, Bob had moved between part-time employment without benefits and being jobless. His eligibility for SSI has stabilized the family's income and has given him access to Medicaid coverage. This change has also removed an uncertainty about loss of Medicaid eligibility for the children; however, Cindy remains uninsured.

Patsy also reports that life is better at the last interview. The four of them have just moved to a different house in a smaller community, a house purchased with Bill's $14,000 lump sum disability settlement from Social Security as a down payment. The family has lived in the house for three weeks when interviewed, and are still basking in the large amount of space in the new dwelling and that they are now owners. In response to a question about why they like this house so much, Patsy replies, "It's ours. That's what I like most about it. It belongs to us. We don't have to worry about landlords. . . . In about five years we'll have it all paid off. It will be ours and we don't have to worry about nobody else. It's home. That's what I love about it." The house needs a lot of work, however, and the family has not begun to deal with the repairs needed. "I don't know what we're going to do. The porch leaks, we've had a few other leaks since we got here. One thing or another.... "

After working in the employment training program, Jake is now unemployed. He is looking for a job at a local store. His dad says, "He's got an application he's going to put in at the store . . . maybe in March when it's warm...." When asked about challenges they are still facing, Patsy responds, "About the same old thing: their [Bill's and Jake's] tempers. . . . It's not as bad now that they are on the pills as it was before. It's not as often because this used to go on just about every day before Dr. Peterson put them on Prozac. Now it's more calm. It don't happen as often as before ... [Jake] likes to tease when he isn't in one of his moods. . . . When he gets in one of his moods, he gets mean with me."

DISCUSSION

Case study findings illuminate the life experiences of poor rural families raising children with serious disabilities. Digging deep into a series of interviews with three families, patterns emerged; however our results cannot be generalized nor do they provide the basis for broad policy recommendations. Our findings do raise questions for future research. First, thick descriptions obtained through open-ended interviews paint a vivid picture that the needs of children with serious physical and behavioral health problems can play havoc with daily routines—imposing stress, conflict, uncertainty, and financial strains on families that are struggling to keep afloat. Understanding the combined effects of disability and poverty during childhood and exploring spatial effects on children's long-term outcomes will require different longitudinal data than are currently available.

Second, it is not obvious that Bailey, Devon, or Jake would obtain better or different health care if they were insured through private rather than public health insurance systems. One obvious difference between poor and nonpoor families with ill children is the availability of financial resources. The extent to which money matters—for example, providing options of respite care, creating access to goods and services not covered by insurance, making reliable transportation available, and reducing the financial pressures that full-time caregiving by a parent may place on the family—is not well understood.

Finally, one of the most intriguing findings from our study points to the important role that mothers can play as advocates for their children within the various social systems that they and their children interact, including neighborhoods, schools, and the health-care network. It is clear that this is not an easy role. Without persistence, the systems and the professionals therein are prone to dismiss these mothers. Gaining a better understanding of how the human and social capital within a child's family influences not only access to treatment, but the quality of health-care needs further consideration.

These findings and conclusions support Katherine Newman's view that "the intrinsic value of qualitative research is in its capacity to dig deeper than any survey can go, to excavate the human terrain that lurks behind the numbers. Used properly, qualitative research can pry open that black box and tell us what lies inside."[8] New knowledge will begin to unfold when investigators imbed qualitative studies inside quantitative studies that are either cross-sectional or longitudinal panel designs. The fusion of the two approaches provides greater confidence in the representative nature of qualitative samples, and the capacity to move back and forth between statistical analyses and patterns in life histories renders either approach the richer for its partner.[9] It is likely that this dual approach to the study of rural children's health will yield the body of knowledge on which truly effective interventions and policies can be built.

ACKNOWLEDGMENT

The research involved the collaborative work of more than 50 Iowa State University faculty and extension field staff members who carried out the fieldwork for this study. The project was supported by Iowa State University Extension and the Center for Family Policy, College of Family and Consumer Sciences. The authors are most grateful to the 35 families who generously shared their time and told their stories with candor and sincerity.

NOTES

1. Debra A. Strong, Patricia Del Grosso, Andrew Burwick, Vinita Jethwani, and Michael Ponza, *Rural Research Needs and Data Sources for Selected Human Services Topics: Vol. 1: Research Needs.* (Princeton, NJ: Mathematica Policy Research, Inc, 2005), 21–29.

2. Economic Research Service, U.S. Department of Agriculture. *Rural Income, Poverty, and Welfare: Rural Poverty.* Washington, DC, 2006.

3. Ibid; Economic Research Service, U.S. Department of Agriculture. *State Fact Sheets: Iowa.* Washington, DC, 2006; Economic Research Service, U.S. Department of Agriculture. *State Fact Sheets: United States.* Washington, DC, 2006; Cynthia Needles Fletcher, Jan L. Flora, Barbara J.Gaddis, Mary Winter, and Jacquelyn S. Litt, "Small Towns and Welfare Reform: Iowa Case Studies of Families and Communities," in *Rural Dimensions of Welfare Reform,* ed. Bruce.A. Weber, Greg.J. Duncan, and Leslie.A. Whitener, 201–229. (Kalamazoo, MI: Upjohn Institute for Employment Research, 2002); Wan He, Manisha Sengupta, Victoria A.Velkoff, and Kimberly A. DeBarros, *65+ in the United States: 2005* (Current Population Reports No. P23-209). Washington, DC: Special Studies, U.S. Census Bureau, 2005.

4. Claudia L. Schur and Sheila J. Franco, "Access to Health Care," in *Rural Health in the United States,* ed. Thomas C. Ricketts, III, 7–24. (New York: Oxford University Press, 1999); Strong et al., *Rural Research Needs and Data Sources for Selected Human Services Topics.*

5. Barbara A.Ormond, Stephen Zuckerman, and Aparna Lhila, *Rural/Urban Differences in Health Care Are Not Uniform Across States.* Washington, DC: The Urban Institute. Assessing the New Federalism Discussion Paper Series B, B-11, 2000, 4–5.

6. Fletcher et al., *Rural Dimensions of Welfare Reform*; Ormond, Zuckerman, and Lhila, *Rural/Urban Differences in Health Care Are Not Uniform Across States.*

7. Fletcher et al., *Rural Dimensions of Welfare Reform.*

8. Katherine S. Newman, "The Right (Soft) Stuff: Qualitative Methods and the Study of Welfare Reform," in *Studies of Welfare Populations: Data Collection and Research Issues,* ed. Michele Ver Ploeg, Robert A. Moffitt, and Constance F. Citro, 355–383. (Washington, DC: Committee on National Statistics, Division of Behavioral and Social Sciences and Education, National Academy Press, 2002), 357.

9. Ibid., 382.

CHAPTER 6

FACTORS AFFECTING UTILIZATION OF MENTAL HEALTH SERVICES BY LOW-INCOME LATINO CHILDREN: A MODEL OF PARENTAL HELP-SEEKING BEHAVIOR

Ricardo B. Eiraldi and Laurie B. Mazzuca

Despite a significant increase in the number of children who receive clinical services for mental health and academic problems, there is still a considerable level of unmet need among ethnic minority populations. Latino children continue to lag well behind their nonminority counterparts in the rate of diagnosis and treatment for behavioral, emotional, and academic disorders. A number of models have been proposed to assess the causes of service disparities. Several of the models focus on factors that affect parental help-seeking behavior. This chapter describes factors that are hypothesized to affect the help-seeking behavior of Latino parents who have children with behavioral, emotional, and/or academic disorders. Factors are integrated within the framework of a modified theoretical pathway model encompassing problem recognition, decision to seek help and service utilization. The authors hope that this model will spur research on the causes of service disparities among Latino children.

It is estimated that up to 20 percent of children in this country are in need of mental health services.[1,2] Research on the utilization of mental health services by children has yielded mixed results. Some reports indicate that service utilization has increased among children during the past 10 years, especially for pharmacological treatments.[3,4] However, in a recent analysis of three large population samples, only 2 percent to 3 percent of children ages 3–5 and 6 percent to 9 percent of children and adolescents ages 6–17 actually used mental health services during a 12-month period.[5] Nearly 80 percent of children and adolescents who were identified as needing mental health services in the 6- to 17-year-old age bracket, had not received care.[6] Studies also indicate that low-income and ethnic minority children continue to lag behind their middle-class, nonminority counterparts in the rate of service utilization.[7,8] There is clear evidence that unmet need for mental health services among Latino children is extraordinarily high, even as compared to African American children.[9,10]

Given that Latino children comprise the largest and fastest growing minority group in this country, the gap in service utilization for this population is a very significant public health problem. Unfortunately, to date there have been very few studies investigating factors contributing to service disparities among Latino children. For the most part, the research in this area lacks a strong theoretical foundation, and studies typically investigate only a few factors at a time. As William Vega and Steven Lopez point out, "fine grain research" is needed in order to elucidate the many potential factors that may be contributing to disparities in service utilization for mental disorders in various Latino communities.[11]

The low rate of service utilization among Latino children is probably the result of a myriad of systemic, individual and cultural factors, such as lack of health insurance, economic hardship, illegal residency status, lack of services, and lack of knowledge about the mental health system and about the warning signs of mental disorders. Also, it may be that low acculturation levels contribute to a lack of trust in doctors, and stigma and negative attitudes toward specific treatments such as treatment with medication.[12, 13] The purpose of this chapter is to present a theoretical model of help-seeking behavior that can be used to investigate factors that promote or hinder parental help-seeking behavior on behalf of Latino children with behavioral, emotional, or learning disorders.

LATINOS IN THE UNITED STATES

Latinos are individuals of "Cuban, Mexican, Puerto Rican, South or Central American, or other Spanish culture or origin, regardless of race" (Note 14 Office of Management and Budget, 1997). Although many Latinos share the same language, the same religion, and an emphasis on the importance of hard work and family, they have roots in countries with different histories and cultural influences. Latinos in the United States present vast differences in race, socioeconomic status (SES), education level, and legal residency status.[14] Intra-group differences among Latinos are so great, that questions have been raised as to the appropriateness of referring to all Latinos as if they are members of a homogeneous group. In fact, Martha Giménez suggests that Latinos should be identified by their subgroup (e.g., Puerto Rican, Mexican-American, etc.) to acknowledge the fact that they may share minority status in the United States , but can have different racial/ethnic backgrounds and nations of origin.[15] Latinos are the largest ethnic minority group in the United States with a population of more than 41 million. Without including the 3.9 million residents of Puerto Rico, Latinos in the United States now constitute 14 percent of the population.[16, 17] By the year 2030, it is estimated that Latinos will total over 73 million and constitute over 20 percent of the U.S. population.[18] The largest Latino subgroups in the United States are Mexican (67%), Central and South American (14%), Puerto Rican (9%), Cuban (4%), and Latinos of Other Hispanic (7%) origin.[19] Individuals of Mexican origin have the largest number of undocumented immigrants and the lowest level of health insurance coverage.[20] Those of Puerto Rican origin have the lowest income of all Latino subgroups, but they have better access to health insurance due to their U.S. citizenship status.[21]

SERVICE DISPARITIES AMONG LATINO CHILDREN

Several recent population-based studies have reported that Latino children are significantly less likely to be diagnosed and treated for a psychiatric disorder than non-Latino children. Based on the combined sample of three large household surveys of over 48,000 children, Latino children were much less likely to receive services (4.7%) than their non-Latino white (7.23%) and African American (5.9%) counterparts.[22] Latino children with significant impairment were more than two and half times more likely to have unmet needs than non-Latino white children.[23] Kristen McCabe and colleagues reported that Latino youth were the group most consistently underrepresented in five public sectors of care in San Diego, CA.[24] In a study conducted by Philip Leaf and colleagues comparing service use by children in the United States with those in Puerto Rico, only 20 percent of children meeting criteria for a psychiatric diagnosis in Puerto Rico had received services during the previous 12 months compared to 38 percent in Atlanta, GA, 44 percent in New Haven, CT., and 41 percent in New York.[25]

Disparity in service use is also apparent in inpatient settings. In a study designed to determine the incidence of mental illness hospitalizations among elementary-school age children, Anand Chabra and colleagues found that non-Latino white and African American children were five times more likely than Latino children to be hospitalized for any mental health disorder.[26] Compared to non-Latino white children, Latino children were between eight and eleven times less likely to be hospitalized for anxiety disorders, impulse control disorders, and bipolar disorder.[27]

THE INFLUENCE OF ETHNICITY AND POVERTY ON SERVICE UTILIZATION

Poverty exerts its influence on service utilization among Latinos through its effect on access to health insurance, the ability to afford additional costs associated with services (e.g., deductibles, transportation), and on the health status of Latinos. U.S. Census data show that Latinos are more likely to be unemployed and earn less money for year-round, full-time work than non-Latino whites.[28] In 2002, the average per capita income of Latinos was $13,487, compared to $15,441 for African Americans, and $26,128 for non-Latino whites.[29]

Latino children are more likely to live in poverty than non-Latino white children, and only slightly less likely to be poor than African American children.[30] Flores, Bauchner, Feinstein, and Nguyen[31] found that Native American, Latino, and African American children are the least healthy children in the United States, are more likely to live below the poverty level, and have fewer doctor visits than non-Latino white children. In other words, poor Latino children may actually have an increased risk for the development of health problems, yet, may be less likely to be able to afford healthcare services.

Research suggests that the Latino population in the United States is younger and less educated than is the non-Latino white population,[32, 33] and therefore, many working Latinos occupy low-wage or part-time jobs (i.e., agriculture, forestry, housekeeping, construction, labor, etc.) that may not provide employer-based health insurance. In fact, a study of working Latinos in California found that even those Latinos who held full-time, full-year employment were significantly less likely to have employer-based health insurance than non-Latino whites and African Americans.[34] Moreover, research shows that working Latinos who are low-wage earners often cite inability to pay premiums, copays, and deductibles as the primary reason for lacking health insurance, even when offered by employers.[35] Poverty can impede access to health insurance and ultimately service utilization on many levels and this "trickle down effect" of poverty may be especially salient for undocumented, immigrant Latinos. Not only are they likely to occupy "underground" low-wage jobs that do not offer employer-based health insurance (or legal work visas), but they often cannot pay for private insurance; are typically not eligible for public or government-based insurance programs because they lack legal residency status; and often are afraid of interacting with health-care providers for fear of deportation.[36-39]

In summary, there is now strong evidence that Latino children living in the United States as well as those living in Puerto Rico are much less likely to receive mental health services than non-Latino white children or African American children. Latino children and families have a high risk of living in poverty, being in poor health, and experiencing both the financial and cultural barriers to care that are associated with poverty. Unfortunately, whereas significant progress has been made quantifying the extent of ethnic disparities in service use, no comparable progress has been made in investigating the causes of the disparities. A useful approach for identifying predictors of service utilization is to examine the help-seeking behavior of those who need services.[40] What follows is a brief discussion regarding the evolution of help-seeking behavior models. The section ends with a proposed pathway model to study help-seeking behavior among Latino parents.

HELP-SEEKING BEHAVIOR MODELS

An important assumption of early and subsequent models of service utilization was that when faced with a general health or mental health concern, individuals must first accept the idea that they have a problem. Subsequently, they have to weigh the pros and cons of different ways of dealing with the problem and decide whether they are willing to seek help. In the final stage, individuals select and then apply the type of service they think they need. Specifically, the help-seeking stages are *problem recognition*, *decision to seek help*, *service selection*, and *service utilization*.[41, 42]

Ronald Andersen developed the most influential model for the study of access to medical care and help-seeking behavior, known as the Behavioral Model of Health Service Use.[43, 44] Andersen observed that use of health services is a function of the perceived need for services, predisposition to use services, factors that enable or impede their use, and need for care.[45, 46] Andersen's model advanced the field by providing a better understanding of the help-seeking process (i.e., how people get services), and by identifying predictors of service use.

Harold Goldsmith et al. presented a reformulation and expansion of earlier models of help-seeking.[47] Goldsmith and colleagues emphasized the cognitive decision-making process of individuals considering services.[48] In their view, the process leading to the decision to seek services involves a cost-benefit analysis (i.e., whether the benefits of seeking help outweigh the costs). They presented a three-stage help-seeking pathway (i.e., problem recognition, decision to seek help, and decision to select specific services) and identified factors that may influence each stage.

Debra Srebnik and colleagues proposed a further expansion of the mental health help-seeking model by acknowledging the influence of social networks on the help-seeking process and by adapting the model for children and adolescents.[49] According to a social network theory, the interactions individuals have with members of their social network form the principal mechanism through which they recognize health problems, contact health facilities, and comply with medical advice.[50] In the Srebnik et al. model, the influence of social networks on help-seeking behavior can be seen as a barrier or a facilitator of service utilization.[51] Social networks are hypothesized to facilitate treatment when members of the network influence the parent to seek professional help, and constitute a barrier when they influence the parent not to seek services.

Ana Mari Cauce and colleagues proposed a further revision of the model to facilitate understanding of cultural and contextual factors affecting ethnic minority adolescents' pathways into services for mental health disorders.[52] Cauce and colleagues argued that culture and context impact help-seeking behavior through the influence of the community. Adolescents in need of mental health services are more or less likely to seek help depending on prevalent cultural and other contextual influences present in the community.[53] In their view, the effects of culture and context pervade the whole help-seeking process, and therefore, do not have specific foci in the pathway.[54] This model posits that minority and nonminority populations use different help-seeking pathways largely because of cultural and other contextual factors and, consequently, should be studied separately. Related to the effects of culture on service use, Hortensia Amaro and colleagues cited five sociocultural factors that are important to the understanding of both health status and health-care utilization among the Latino population.[55] Those factors are poverty, cultural beliefs, immigration and cultural adaptation, structural barriers to healthy development and health-care access, and the heterogeneity of the Latino population. These factors influence how, when, where, and if Latinos utilize health-care services.[56]

Finally, Eiraldi and colleagues recently proposed a further revision of the help-seeking behavior model in order to address the unique aspects of parental help-seeking behavior on behalf of children with ADHD.[57] This latest revision incorporated features of the help-seeking behavior models reviewed above. The stages in the

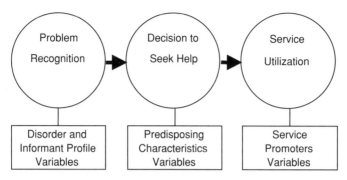

Figure 6.1
Stages of Help-Seeking Behavior. Adapted from Eiraldi et al., 2006; Goldsmith et al., 1988

help-seeking process (problem recognition; decision to seek help; service utilization patterns) are hypothesized to be influenced by characteristics of the disorder and the informant (e.g., parent), the predisposition to use services, factors that enable or impede the pursuit of services over time (see Figure 6.1).

It is hypothesized that most families who have children with emotional, behavioral, and/or learning disorders generally navigate the pathway in a voluntary and unidirectional fashion, first recognizing the problem, second deciding to seek help, and third, using services. However, as Pescosolido and colleagues have pointed out, sometimes individuals are made aware of the problem by others and at times they are forced or coerced into the mental health system.[58] For example, parents are sometimes made aware that their child has a problem by teachers or other professionals. Parents are sometimes influenced by school personnel into accepting services for their children (e.g., medication),[59] or in the case of children in the juvenile justice system, some may be pressured into continuing with treatment after the child is no longer in the system.[60]

The help-seeking process in most cases begins once the parent realizes or accepts the idea that the child might have a problem. *Disorder and Informant Profile* (see Figure 6.1) refers to a child's susceptibility to a given disorder or level of severity of symptoms and characteristics of adults involved in problem recognition. Some of the variables hypothesized to affect problem recognition are symptom severity, impairment level, parental psychopathology, parent–child relationship difficulties, and differential thresholds for distinguishing normal from abnormal behavior. Following problem recognition, parents need to decide whether to pursue further consultation or treatment. *Predisposing characteristics* are certain demographic characteristics such as age or gender, and relatively stable psychological and cultural factors that influence a person's readiness to seek help.[61] Psychological factors are aspects of an individual's personality that may increase or decrease readiness to seek help for a mental health condition. The term also pertains to beliefs about an individual's ability to perform certain expected roles related to help seeking[62] and his or her knowledge of the mental health system. Some of the variables thought to affect the decision to seek help are child's age and gender, stigma, apprehension about legal status, acculturation level, beliefs and expectations about mental health services, and knowledge about mental health disorders and how and where to obtain services.

Due to space limitations, we limit the discussion of factors affecting the different help-seeking behavior stages to only those hypothesized to influence service utilization. Careful consideration has been given to choosing variables that pertain to behavioral, emotional, and/or learning disorders and, to a lesser extent, that are likely to differentiate Latino children from children of other ethnic groups. A detailed discussion of issues related to these variables is beyond the scope of this chapter.

SERVICE UTILIZATION

Once parents have made the decision to seek services, they need to investigate what services the child should receive and which ones are available to them. Parents are more likely to make an appointment and begin using services if they are affected by factors that facilitate use of services and if they do not face any significant barriers. According to Srebnik et al.,[63] any social, economic, or environmental pressures that can occur at the family, community, or at the larger society level can be barriers or facilitators for using services. At a theoretical level, factors influencing access to services could affect parents at three separate points: (a) making an appointment, (b) using services for the first time, and (c) using services over time. What follows is a discussion of factors that are hypothesized to affect initial contact with service providers, followed by factors affecting initial use and use of services over time (see Figure 6.2).

Initial Contact

Most Latinos place great importance on having a strong identification with and attachment to their nuclear and extended families. Latinos tend to be very loyal to and supportive of their families. This relationship is known as *familism* or *familismo*.[64] When Latino children and adolescents experience emotional and behavioral difficulties, parents are much more likely to talk to members of their social network first; this in most cases would be the parents' extended family. If Latino parents do not make a decision regarding what to do with their child after consulting with their extended family, they might talk to other members of their social network such as teachers, friends, or other individuals from the community. Social network members could influence parents to make initial contact with service providers (e.g., making an appointment; asking for information about services) depending on the type of opinions they express about mental health service, or, whether or not they themselves are willing to provide direct assistance to the parents. Providing direct assistance such as babysitting, emotional support, etc., might diminish need for professional services, at least in the short term.

Service Utilization

Service Promoters

Making an Appointment

Community and Social Networks
—Familism
—Attitudes of network members toward mental health services

Initial Access to Services

Economic Factors
—Financial and social resources
—Health insurance
—Medicaid eligibility
—Transportation

Societal Factors
—Racial bias
—Racial discrimination
—Anti-immigrant attitudes

Use of Services Over Time

Service Characteristics
—Culturally sensitive staff
—Bilingual clinicians
—Availability of interpreters
—Patient-friendly administrative procedures
—English language proficiency (ELP)

Quality of Care
—Quality of services
—Fragmentation of care
—Coordination of care

Socio-cultural Norms and Values
—Simpatía and respeto

Figure 6.2
Service Utilization Factors for Latino Children with Behavioral, Emotional, or Learning Disorders. Adapted from Eiraldi et al., 2006; Goldsmith et al., 1988

Initial Access to Services

The low-income and low-insurability status of many Latinos represent a set of variables that potentially limit parents' ability to secure mental health services for their children. In the year 2004, 22.2 percent of Latinos lived in poverty compared to 8.4 percent of non-Latino white individuals.[65] As a group, Latinos have the lowest insurability rates of any ethnic group in this country. In the year 2000, 37 percent of Latino children did not have health insurance for all or part of the year. This is compared to 20 percent for non-Latino white and 23 percent of African American children.[66] Rates of insurability are much lower among Latino immigrants. In the year 1997, 49 percent of foreign-born Latinos were uninsured compared to 24 percent of U.S.-born Latinos.[67] In a recent study it was noted that Medicaid eligibility has a profound impact on the racial disparity associated with psychopharmacological treatment for mental disorders among youths.[68] Not having or not being eligible for Medicaid is a very strong predictor of unmet need among children.[69] Other major factors that may inhibit access to services are distance from specialized treatment sites, the availability of affordable transportation, complicated intake processes, long waiting lists, and limited operating hours.[70]

There are several societal factors that negatively affect the quality of services available to ethnic minorities in this country, and by extension, parental help-seeking behavior, and rates of service utilization. Those factors include racial bias, discrimination, and anti-immigrant attitudes.[71–73] In a large population study assessing quality of health services nationwide, it was found that 19.4 percent of Latinos in the sample reported having been treated with disrespect or looked down upon by medical staff, compared with only 9.4 percent of non-Latino white respondents.[74] Data from the 2000 National Survey of Early Childhood Health showed that many health-care providers hold stereotypical views of Latinos' child rearing practices and that Latino parents often feel that their health-care provider never or only sometimes takes time to understand their child's specific needs.[75] In a study that explored the effects of a ballot initiative designed to eliminate access to state-funded health services for undocumented immigrants in California, it was found that the rate of service utilization by Latino youth dropped by 26 percent after Proposition 187 received a majority of the "yes" votes.[76] This is a remarkable finding given the fact that this proposition never became law. Results of these studies indicate that such societal factors are likely to be barriers to help seeking for Latino parents.

Use of Services over Time

It is well established that Latinos use mental health services in low numbers. However, it is less well known that after the first visit to a mental health specialist, Latinos are unlikely to come back. The rate of attrition for mental health services among Latinos has been found in some studies to reach as high as 70 percent.[77]

There are many factors that may promote or diminish service utilization over time. Those factors could be divided into service characteristics, quality of care, and sociocultural norms and values. For example, a number of service characteristics such as the availability of culturally sensitive staff, bilingual clinicians or interpreters, doctors and staff of similar racial/ethnic background, and patient-friendly administrative procedures may increase the likelihood that the family will continue to use services.[78–80] Low English language proficiency (ELP) has been shown to be among the most significant access barriers to treatment for Latino children with health and mental health disorders.[81] Given that at least 31 percent of Latinos who speak Spanish in this country either do not speak English well or do not speak it at all,[82] low ELP is a major barrier for Latino parents.

Studies have reported that racial and ethnic minority populations in this country believe that they receive mental health services of substandard quality compared to those received by nonminority populations.[83] Several studies using objective measures support these perceptions.[84, 85] In a statewide, longitudinal study assessing the quality of publicly funded outpatient specialty mental health services in which the majority of participants were of ethnic minority background, Zima et al. found that clinics typically scored well below quality standards for most of the areas assessed, including service linkage with schools and PCPs, parental involvement, use of evidence-based psychosocial treatment, and patient protection.[86] Mental health care for children with disruptive disorders living in the inner city has been found to be highly fragmented and uncoordinated.[87] Based on these studies, it is reasonable to expect that low quality of services may be a significant factor in the high attrition rate in Latino child populations.

Sociocultural norms and values are also likely to play an important role in influencing families to stay in treatment. Two sociocultural constructs that have received empirical support in Latino populations are *Simpatía and Respeto*.[88] *Simpatía* means being kind, polite, and pleasant even in stressful situations. Avoiding hostile confrontations is also an important component. Latinos expect that the clinician is going to be polite, pleasant, and expressive. A reserved and nonexpressive clinician would normally not be well received by Latino patients or their families. Lack of *simpatía* could lead to decreased patient satisfaction, inaccurate reporting of history and symptomatology, nonadherence to therapy, poor follow-up and early drop out.[89] *Respeto* means "respect" and it is bestowed on professionals because of their position of knowledge and authority. Latinos also expect respect from the clinician, especially when the provider is younger than the parent. Unfortunately, this cultural value may lead patients and families to behave in an overly passive manner, for instance, not asking questions when instructions are unclear or questioning the clinician's diagnoses; all variables that would lead to high attrition rates.

SERVICE UTILIZATION PATTERNS

Table 6.1 presents some of the major systems available to Latino families. The list is divided into five categories: *Informal Support Network*; *School-Based*; *Primary Care*; *Mental Health Services*; and *Juvenile Justice System*.

There is some evidence indicating that in their quest for finding a solution to their child's difficulties, Latino families often consult and seek assistance from members of their nuclear and extended family first before reaching out to service providers.[90] It is not clear for what problems or in which circumstances would families need to continue their search for other sources of help beyond their social network. There are a number of other sources of support often used by Latino families, including community and religious organizations, folk healers, *botánicas* (herbal remedies) and

Table 6.1
Service Utilization Patterns

Service Categories Informal Support Network	School-Based	Primary Care	Mental Health Services	Juvenile Justice System
–Family and lay advisors	–Mental health clinic	–Referral services	–Pharmacological treatment	–Rehabilitation services
–Community/ religious organizations	–Individualized education plan (IEP)	–Pharmacological treatment	–Child and family therapy	–Counseling
–Promotores de salud	–Special accommodations (Section 504)	–Parent education	–Parent education	–Pharmacological treatment
–Botánicas	–After school program			

promotores de salud or health promoters.[91,92] However, it is likely that the use of these informal sectors of care vary according to country of origin and acculturation level.

Treatment and intervention for most Latino children with behavioral, emotional, and school problems are provided in schools or in primary care. Studies have consistently found that pharmacological treatment for behavioral and emotional disorders is often prescribed in primary care by practitioners without mental health training.[93] Latino children would be better served by specialized mental health providers. Unfortunately, access to a mental health practitioner is highly dependent on having health insurance with mental health coverage, a benefit that most Latino families do not have.[94]

The juvenile justice system is playing an increasingly important role in the mental health care of juveniles in the system.[95] Many Latino youth receive mental health services in this sector of care.[96] However, based on cultural norms and values (e.g., fear of stigma; lack of familiarity with mental health system), and socioeconomic and legal variables (e.g., lack of health insurance, residency status), schools appear to be the ideal setting for serving Latino children who exhibit behavioral, emotional, and/or learning disorders. The special role of schools in addressing children's mental health concerns is discussed in the next section.

SCHOOL-BASED MENTAL HEALTH SERVICES

Research suggests that low-income minority children and adolescents are more likely to seek mental health services from school-based health centers (SBHCs) or community-based providers, rather than through traditional hospital-based clinics or specialized mental health-care providers.[97–99] For example, Trina Anglin and colleagues reported that up to 63 percent of students with access to SBHCs utilized their services, with female Latina students having the highest rates of use; emotional problems represented the largest diagnostic category among this population.[100]

In an effort to reduce service disparities among low-income families, many health-care professionals now advocate for funding and resources to be directed toward the development of school-based mental health services in order to promote health-care utilization in underserved communities.[101–103] This impending shift toward expanded school mental health (ESMH) programs may have the greatest potential impact among the populations that experience significant barriers to health-care access, such as low-income, urban, Latino children.[104]

SBHCs have been used to address a wide range of behavioral, academic, and social issues.[105] There is a growing body of literature demonstrating that SBHCs can produce positive treatment outcomes for numerous behavioral health problems among Latinos,[106] and can help reduce underutilization among low-income populations.[107] Susan Foster and colleagues conducted a national survey of mental health services in a sample of over 2,125 public schools and 1,595 school districts, and reported that one fifth of students received some type of school-supported mental health services. In addition, approximately 80 percent of schools in the sample provided some type of mental health service.[108] However, the prevalence of expanded school mental health programs serving Latino youth and families has not yet been well-documented.

FUTURE DIRECTIONS

The help-seeking behavior pathway model may be useful in generating studies to investigate factors that hinder or facilitate the use of services by low-income Latino families. Although research demonstrates that poverty can potentially hinder service use among low-income Latino families through its influence on financial variables that affect help-seeking (e.g., access to health insurance, ability to afford costly services, etc.), more research is needed to investigate how SES moderates the relationship between culture and health-care utilization among low-income Latino families. For example, what is the role of poverty in the development of Latinos' beliefs about health, illness, and mental health treatment? Some research suggests that immigrant Latinos may hold cultural health beliefs that differ from those that dominate the traditional American biomedical model of health and illness,[109] yet, it is unclear to what extent lack of education, marginalization, and poverty contribute to the development and maintenance of these beliefs. Research also suggests that more educated Latina mothers are better able to understand complex treatment plans for children with ADHD, and therefore may be more likely to use and adhere to treatment than Latina mothers with less education.[110,111] Thus, other factors associated with poverty (i.e., poor educational opportunities, low literacy rates, marginalization) may help shape the cultural beliefs that ultimately contribute to help-seeking behavior among low-income Latinos.

Much research has been conducted on the role of acculturation on health outcome for Latinos. However, no studies have been conducted on the role of acculturation in parental help-seeking behavior. It would be important to know whether thresholds for differentiating normal from abnormal child behavior vary as a function of acculturation among Latino parents. It would also be important to know if acculturation moderates the effects of factors that predict problem recognition. Do stigma and attitudes toward mental health services predict the decision to seek help and does the prediction vary as a function of different acculturation levels? Does increased knowledge about mental health and the mental health system lead parents to become more active in seeking help for their children? With regard to service utilization, under what conditions do familism or social networks facilitate or hinder use of professional services? Would improving certain service conditions such as availability of interpreters and culturally sensitive staff lead to a decline in patient drop out rates?

Research using this model may facilitate decision-making regarding health policy, and health-care administration and practice. For example, decision makers in health policy might be interested in determining whether the gap in service use is smaller in high-risk communities that offer school-based behavioral health services to Latinos and other minorities, as compared to communities that do not. This type of research might lead to policies that support the creation of SBHCs in all underserved communities. Health policy decision makers may want to identify ethnic-specific strategies for disseminating information about mental health disorders to promote the development of health beliefs that are more consistent with what is known about the causes and treatments for mental health disorders, while promoting respect for the individual's cultural values and traditional beliefs. Decision makers in health-care administration might want to determine the acceptability and feasibility of offering mental health services in nontraditional settings such as in churches and other community settings. Would services provided in these settings lead to an increase in adherence to treatment and a decrease in attrition? Direct service providers might test the acceptability and adherence to effective treatments for common mental health disorders as originally developed, versus modified versions of those same treatments that incorporate culturally sensitive content.

In summary, Latino children continue to lag well behind their nonminority counterparts in the rate of diagnosis and treatment for behavioral, emotional, and academic disorders. This chapter describes factors that are hypothesized to affect the help-seeking behavior of Latino parents who have children with behavioral, emotional, and/or academic disorders. Factors are integrated within the framework of a modified theoretical pathway model,[112] encompassing problem recognition, decision to seek help, and service utilization. The authors hope that this model will spur research on the causes of service disparities among Latino children.

NOTES

1. Hector Bird Glorisa, Canino, Maritza Rubio-Stipec, M. S. Gould, Julio Ribera, M. Sesman, M. Woodbury, S. Huertas-Goldman, A. Pagan, A. Sanchez-Lacay, and M. Moscoso,

"Estimates of the prevalence of childhood mal-adjustment in a community survey in Puerto Rico: The use of combined measures," *Archives of General Psychiatry*, 45 (1988): 1120–1126.

2. E. Jane Costello, A. Angold, B. J. Burns, D. K. Stangl, D. L. Tweed, A. Erkanli, and C. M. Worthman, "The Great Smoky Mountains Study of Youth: Goals, design, methods, and the prevalence of DSM-III-R disorders," *Archives of General Psychiatry*, 53 (1996): 1129–1136.

3. Mark Olfson, Marc J. Gameroff, Steven C. Marcus, and Peter S. Jensen, "National trends in the treatment of attention deficit hyperactivity disorder," *American Journal of Psychiatry*, 160 (2003): 1071–1077.

4. Julie M. Zito, Daniel J. Safer, Susan dosReis, James F. Gardner, Laurence Magder, Karen Soeken, Myde Boles, Frances Lynch, Mark A. Riddle, "Psychotropic practice patterns for youth: A 10-year perspective," *Archives of Pediatric Adolescent Medicine*, 157 (2003): 17–25.

5. Sheryl H. Kataoka, Lily Zhang, and Kenneth B. Wells, "Unmet need for mental health care among U.S. children: Variation by ethnicity and insurance status," *American Journal of Psychiatry*, 159 (2002): 1548–1555.

6. See note 5 above.

7. Centers for Disease Control and Prevention, "Mental Health in the United States: Prevalence of Diagnosis and Medication Treatment for Attention-Deficit/Hyperactivity Disorder-United States, 2003," *MMWR*, 54 (2005): 842–847.

8. See note 5 above.

9. See note 7 above

10. Philip J. Leaf, Margarita Alegría, Patricia Cohen, Sherryl H. Goodman, Sarah McCue Horwitz, Christina W. Hoven, William E. Narrow, Michael Vaden-Kiernan, Darrel A. Regier, "Mental health service use in the community and schools: Results from the four-community MECA study," *Journal of the American Academy of Child and Adolescent Psychiatry*, 35 (1996) 889–897.

11. William A. Vega and Steven R. López, "Priorities issues in Latino mental health services research," *Mental Health Services Research*, 3 (2001): 194.

12. Ricardo B. Eiraldi, Laurie B. Mazzuca, Angela T. Clarke, and Thomas J. Power, "Service utilization among ethnic minority children with ADHD: A model of help-seeking behavior," *Administration and Policy in Mental Health and Mental Health Services Research*, 33 (2006): 607–622.

13. Albert M. Woodward, Alexander D. Dwinell, and Bernard S. Arons , "Barriers to mental health care for Hispanic Americans: A literature review and discussion," *The Journal of Mental Health Administration*, 19 (1992): 224–236.

14. Jorge G. García and Sylvia Marotta, "Characterization of the Latino population," in *Psychological Interventions and Research with Latino Populations*, ed. J.G. García and M.C. Zea, 1–14 (Boston, MA: Allyn and Bacon, 1997).

15. Martha Giménez, "Latino/Hispanic—who needs a name? The case against a standardized terminology," *The International Journal of Health Services*, 19 (1987): 557–571.

16. U.S. Bureau of the Census, "2004 American Community Survey Summary Tables," 2004, available at http://factfinder.census.gov.

17. U.S. Bureau of the Census, Annual Estimates of the Population of the United States and States, and for Puerto Rico: April 1, 2000 to July 1, 2005, (NC-EST2005-01). Population Division: U.S. Census Bureau (Washington, DC, 2005).

18. National Council of La Raza, *Critical disparities in Latino mental health: Transforming research into action* (NCLR: Washington, DC, 2005).

19. Roberto R. Ramirez, and G. Patricia de la Cruz, *The Hispanic population in the United Status: March 2002*, U.S. Census Bureau (Washington, DC: 2003).

20. Claudia L. Schur and Jacob Feldman, *Running in place: How job characteristics, immigrant status, and family structure keep Hispanics uninsured*, The Commonwealth Fund (New York: NY, 2001).

21. See notes 18 and 19 above.

22. See note 5 above.

23. See note 5 above.

24. Kristen McCabe, May Yeh, Richard L. Hough, John Landsverk, Michael S. Hurlburt, Shirley Wells Culver, and Beth Reynolds, "Racial/ethnic representation across five public sectors of care for youth," *Journal of Emotional and Behavioral Disorders*, 7 (1999): 72–82.

25. Philip J. Leaf, Margarita Alegría, Patricia Cohen, Sherryl H. Goodman, Sarah McCue Horwitz, Christina W. Hoven, William E. Narrow, Michael Vaden-Kiernan, and Darrel A. Regier, "Mental health service use in the community and schools: Results from the four-community MECA study," *Journal of the American Academy of Child and Adolescent Psychiatry*, 35 (1996) 889–897.

26. Anand Chabra, Gilberto Chávez, and Emily Harrison, "Mental illness in elementary-school-aged children," *Western Journal of Medicine*, 170 (1999): 28–34.

27. See note 26 above.

28. See note 16 above.

29. See note 16 above.

30. See note 16 above.

31. Glenn Flores, Howard Bauchner, Alvan R Feinstein, and Uyen-Sa Nyugen, "The impact of ethnicity, family income, and parental education on children's health and use of health services," *American Journal of Public Health*, 89 (1999): 1066–1071.

32. See note 16 above.

33. Howard Greenwald, Suzanne O'Keefe, and Mark DiCamillo, "Why employed Latinos lack health insurance: a study in California," *Hispanic Journal of Behavioral Sciences*, 27 (2005): 517–532.

34. E. Richard Brown, "Trends in health insurance in California, 1989–1993," *Health Affairs*, 15 (1996): 118–130.

35. See note 33 above.

36. Gilberto Granados, Jyoti Puwula, Nancy Berman, and Patrick T. Dowling, "Health care for Latino children: Impact of child and parental birthplace on insurance status and access to health services," *American Journal of Public Health*, 91 (2001): 1806–1807.

37. Cervando Martinez, "Mexican Americans," in *Clinical Guidelines in Cross-Cultural Mental Health*, ed. Lillian Comas-Diaz and Ezra Griffith, (New York: Wiley, 1988).

38. Eugenio M. Rothe, "Considering cultural diversity in the management of ADHD in Hispanic patients," *Journal of the National Medical Association* (Supplement), 97 (2005): 17S-23S.

39. See note 33 above.

40. David Mechanic, "The epidemiology of illness behavior and its relationship to physical and psychological distress," in *Monographs in psychosocial epidemiology. Symptoms, illness behavior and help-seeking*, ed. David Mechanic, (New York: Prodist., 1982).

41. See note 12 above.

42. Joseph Veroff, Richard A. Kulka, and Elizabeth Donovan, *Mental Health in America: Patterns of help-seeking from 1957–1976* (New York: Basic Books, 1981).

43. Ronald M. Andersen, "Revisiting the behavioral model and access to medical care: Does it matter?" *Journal of Health and Social Behavior*, 36 (1995): 1–10.

44. Ronald M. Andersen and John F. Newman, "Societal and individual determinants of medical care utilization in the United States," *Milbank Memorial Fund Quarterly Journal*, 51 (1973): 95–124.

45. See note 43 above.

46. See note 44 above.

47. Harold Goldsmith, David Jackson, and Richard Hough, "Process model of seeking mental health services: Proposed framework for organizing the research literature on help-seeking," in *Needs assessment: It's future*, ed. Harold Goldsmith, E. Lin, R. Bell, and David. Jackson, 49–64 (DHSS Publication No. ADM 88-1550) (Washington, DC: U.S. Government Printing Office, 1988).

48. See note 47 above.

49. Debra Srebnik, Ana Mari Cauce, and Nazli Baydar, "Help-seeking pathways for children and adolescents," *Journal of Emotional and Behavioral Disorders*, 4 (1996): 210–220.

50. Bernice A. Pescosolido, "Illness, careers and network ties: A conceptual model of utilization and compliance," *Advances in Medical Sociology*, 2 (1991): 161–184; Bernice A. Pescosolido, "Beyond rational choice: The social dynamics of how people seek help," *American Journal of Sociology*, 97 (1992): 1096–1138.

51. See note 49 above.

52. Ana M. Cauce, Melanie Domenech-Rodríguez, Matthew Paradise, Bryan N. Cochran, Jennifer M. Shea, Debra Srebnik, and Nazli Baydar, "Cultural and contextual influences in mental health help-seeking: A focus on ethnic minority youth." *Journal of Consulting and Clinical Psychology*, 70 (2002): 44–55.

53. See note 52 above.

54. See note 52 above.

55. Hortensia Amaro, Miriam Messinger, and Richard Cervantes, "The health of Latino youth: Challenges for disease prevention," in *Health issues for minority adolescents*, ed. Marjorie Kagawa-Singer and Phyllis A. Katz, 80–115 (Lincoln, NE: University of Nebraska Press, 1996).

56. See note 55 above.

57. See note 12 above.

58. Bernice A. Pescosolido, Carol A. Boyer, and Keri M. Lubell, "The social dynamics of responding to mental health problems," in *Handbook of the Sociology of Mental Health*, ed. Carol S. Aneshensel and Jo.C. Phelan, 441–460 (New York: Kluwer Academic/Plenum Publishers, 1999).

59. See note 50 above.

60. Karen M. Abram, Linda A. Teplin, Gary M. McClelland, and Mina K. Dulcan, "Co-morbid psychiatric disorders in youth in juvenile detention," *Archives of General Psychiatry*, 60 (2003): 1097–1108.

61. See note 49 above.

62. See note 47 above.

63. See note 49 above.

64. Ana Mari Cauce and Melanie Domenech-Rodríguez, "Latino Families: Myths and Realities," in *Latino Children and Families in the United States*, ed. Josefina M. Contreras, Kathryn A. Kerns, and Angela M. Neal-Barnett, 3–26 (Wesport, CT: Praeger Publishers, 2002).

65. U.S. Bureau of the Census, *Income, poverty, and health insurance coverage in the U.S.: 2004*, U.S. Department of Commerce; Economics and Statistics Division. U.S. Census Bureau (Washington, DC, 2005).

66. The Commonwealth Fund, *Health care quality survey*, (New York: 2001).

67. See note 20 above.

68. Julie Magno Zito, Daniel J. Safer, Ilene H. Zuckerman, James F. Gardner, and Karen Soeken, "Effects of Medicaid eligibility category on racial disparities in the use of psychotropic medications among youths," *Psychiatric Services*, 56 (2005): 157–163.

69. See note 68 above.

70. Glenn Flores, Milagros Abreu, Mary Anne Olivar, and Beth Kastner, "Access barriers to health care for Latino children," *Archives of Pediatrics & Adolescent Medicine*, 152 (1998): 1119–1125; National Hispanic/Latino Health Initiative: *Public Health Reports*, 108 (1993): 534–558.

71. U. S. Department of Health and Human Services. *Mental Health: Culture, Race and Ethnicity – Supplement to Mental Health: A Report of the Surgeon General*, U.S. Department of Health and Human Services, Public Health Service, Office of the Surgeon General (Rockville, MD, 2001).

72. Glenn Flores, Lynn Olson, and Sandra C. Tomany-Korman, "Racial and ethnic disparities in early childhood health and health care," *Pediatrics*, 115 (2005): e183-e193, URL: www.pediatrics.org/cgi/doi/10.1542/peds.2004-1474.

73. Judy Kendall and Diane Hatton, "Racism as a source of health disparity in families with children with attention deficit hyperactivity disorder," *Advances in Nursing Science*, 25 (2002): 22–39.

74. Janice Blanchard and Nicole Laurie, "R-e-s-p-e-c-t: Patient reports of disrespect in the health care setting and its impact on care," *Journal of Family Practice*, 53 (2004): 721–730.

75. See note 72 above.

76. Joshua Fenton, Ralph Catalano, and William Hargreaves, "Effect of Proposition 187 on mental health service use in California: A case study," *Health Affairs*, 15 (1996): 182–190.

77. See note 18 above.

78. See note 70 above.

79. Leo S. Morales, William E. Cunningham, Julie A. Brown, Honghu Llu, and Ron D. Hays, "Are Latinos less satisfied with communication by health care providers?" *Journal of Internal Medicine*, 14 (1999): 409–417.

80. See note 11 above.

81. See note 70 above.

82. U.S. Bureau of the Census, "Annual Estimates of the Population by Age and Sex of Hispanic or Latino Origin for the United States: April 1, 2000 to July 1, 2004," (NC-EST2004-04-HISP), 2004, http://www.census.gov/popest/national/asrh/NC-EST2004/NC-EST2004-04-HISP.xls

83. Marsha Lillie-Blanton, Mollyann Brodie, Diane Rowland, Drew Altman, and Mary McIntosh, "Race, ethnicity, and the health care system: Public perceptions and experiences," *Medical Care Research and Review*, 57 (2000): 218–235.

84. See note 71 above.

85. Bonnie T. Zima, Michael S. Hurlburt, Penny Knapp, Heather Ladd, Tang Lingqi, Duan Naihua, Peggy Wallace, Abram Rosenblatt, John Landsverk, and Kenneth B. Wells, "Quality of publicly-funded outpatient specialty mental health care for common childhood psychiatric disorders in California," *Journal of the American Academy of Child and Adolescent Psychiatry*, 44 (2005): 130–144.

86. See note 85 above.

87. James P. Guevara, Chris Feudtner, Daniel Romer, Thomas Power, Snejana Nihtianova, Janet Ohene-Frempong, and Donald F. Schwarz, "Fragmented care for inner-city minority children with attention-deficit/hyperactivity disorder," *Pediatrics*, 116 (2005): e512-e517; URL: http://www.pediatrics.org/cgi/content/full/116/4/e512

88. Ricardo B. Eiraldi, and Laurie B. Mazzuca, "Treatment of ADHD in Latino populations," *Behavioral Health Management*, 24 (2004): 34–36.

89. Glenn Flores, "Culture and the patient-physician relationship: Achieving cultural competency in health care," *The Journal of Pediatrics*, 136 (2000): 14–23.

90. Bernice A. Pescosolido, Eric R. Wright, Margarita Alegria, and Mildred Vera, "Social networks and patterns of use among the poor with mental health problems in Puerto Rico," *Medical Care*, 36 (1998): 1057–1072.

91. Alejandro Murguía, Rolf A. Peterson, and Maria C. Zea. "Use and implications of ethnomedical health care approaches among Central American immigrant," *Health and Social Work*, 28 (2003): 43–50.

92. Carlos Molina, Ruth E. Zambrana, and Marilyn Aguirre-Molina, "The influence of culture, class, and environment on health care," in *Latino Health in the U.S.: A growing challenge*, ed. Carlos W. Molina and Marilyn Aguirre-Molina, 23–43 (Washington, DC: American Public Health Association, 1994).

93. Kimberly Hoagwood, Kelly J. Kelleher, Michael Feil, and Diane M. Comer, "Treatment services for children with ADHD: A national perspective," *Journal of the American Academy of Child and Adolescent Psychiatry*, 39 (2000): 198–206.

94. Ruth E. Zambrana and Olivia C. Carter-Pokras, "Improving health insurance coverage for Latino children: A review of barriers, challenges and state strategies," *Journal of the National Medical Association*, 96 (2004): 508–523.

95. Michelle Wierson, Rex Forehand, and Cynthia Frame, "Epidemiology and treatment of mental health problems in juvenile delinquents," *Advances in Behaviour Research & Therapy*, 14 (1992): 93–120.

96. Ann F. Garland, Richard L. Hough, Kristen M. McCabe, May Yeh, Patricia A. Wood, and Gregory A. Aarons, "Prevalence of psychiatric disorders in youths across five sectors of care," *Journal of the American Academy of Child & Adolescent Psychiatry*, 40 (2001): 409–418.

97. Lori A. Barker and Howard S. Adelman, "Mental health and help-seeking among ethnic minority adolescents," *Journal of Adolescence*, 17 (1994): 251–263.

98. Susan R. McGurk, Jose Cárdenas, and Howard S. Adelman, "Utilization of a school-based clinic for identification and treatment of adolescent sexual abuse," *Journal of Adolescent Health*, 14 (1993): 196–201.

99. Linda Juszczak, Paul Melinkovich, and David Kaplan, "Use of health and mental health services by adolescents across multiple delivery sites," *Journal of Adolescent Health*, 32 (2003): 108–118.

100. Trina M. Anglin, Kelly Naylor, and David Kaplan, "Comprehensive school-based health care: high school students' use of medical, mental health, and substance abuse services," *Pediatrics*, 97 (1996): 318–330.

101. Sergio A. Aguilar-Gaxiola, Lynnette Zelezny, Christine Edmondson, Christine Alejo-Garcia, and William Vega, "Mental health care for Latinos: Translating research into action; reducing disparities in mental health care for Mexican Americans," *Psychiatric Services*, 53 (2002): 1563–1568.

102. Committee on School Health, "School-Based Mental Health Services," *Pediatrics*, 113 (2004): 1839–1845.

103. Mark D. Weist and Steven W. Evans, "Expanded school mental health: Challenges and opportunities in an emerging field," *Journal of Youth and Adolescence*, 34 (2005): 3–6; Mark D. Weist, Mark A. Sander, Christine Walrath, Benjaman Link, Laura Nabors, Steve Adelsheim, Elizabeth Moore, Jenni Jennings, and Kristine Carrillo, "Developing Principles for Best Practice in Expanded School Mental Health," *Journal of Youth and Adolescence*, 34 (2005): 7–13.

104. Christine M. Walrath, Eric J. Bruns, Karyn L. Anderson, Marcia Glass-Siegal, and Mark D. Weist, "Understanding expanded school mental health services in Baltimore City," *Behavior Modification*, 28 (2004): 472–490.

105. Gary D. Gottfredson and Denise C. Gottfredson, "What schools do to prevent problem behavior and promote safe environments," *Journal of Education and Psychological Consultation*, 12 (2001): 313–344; Jon Shepard and John S. Carlson, "An empirical evaluation of school-based prevention programs that involve parents," *Psychology in the Schools*, 40 (2003): 641–656.

106. Bradley D. Stein, Lisa H. Jaycox, Sheryl H. Kataoka, Marleen Wong, Wenli Tu, Marc N. Elliott, and Arlene Fink, "A Mental Health Intervention for Schoolchildren Exposed to Violence A Randomized Controlled Trial," *Journal of the American Medical Association*, 290 (2003): 603–611.

107. See note 104 above.

108. Susan Foster, Mary Rollefson, Teresa Doksum, Denise Noonan, Gail Robinson, and Judith Teich, School Mental Health Services in the United States, 2002–2003, DHHS Pub. No (SMA) 05-4068, Center for Mental Health Services, Substance Abuse and Mental Health Services Administration (Rockville, MD: 2005).

109. Emily Arcia and Maria C. Fernandez, "Cuban mothers' schemas of ADHD: Development, characteristics, and help seeking behavior," *Journal of Child and Family Studies*, 7 (1998): 333–352.

110. L. Eugene Arnold, Michael Elliot, Larry Sachs, "Effects of ethnicity on treatment attendance, stimulant response/dose, and 14-month outcome in ADHD," *Journal of Consulting and Clinical Psychology*, 71 (2003): 713–727.

111. See note 38 above.

112. See note 12 above.

CHAPTER 7

PERCEPTIONS OF HELP-SEEKING AND MENTAL HEALTH SERVICE USE AMONG PARENTS OF HEAD START CHILDREN

*Michael S. Spencer, Laura P. Kohn-Wood,
Rachael D. Jankowski, Stacey Lyn Grant,
and Jennifer Elizabeth McCall*

The 2001 Surgeon General's report on race, culture, and mental health states that ethnic minorities suffer from mental health disorders at approximately the same rate as nonminorities, but they do not seek or utilize services at the same rate.[1] Specifically, African American children tend to under-utilize outpatient mental health services compared to white Americans.[2] While African American children appear to be underserved by mental health service systems, they are over-represented in other service systems, including foster care and juvenile justice, and public institutions such as residential treatment centers and community mental health services.[3–6] Thus, research is necessary to understand why African Americans do not utilize services at the same rate as white Americans and what barriers might be perceived to children receiving early and effective interventions.

A number of factors have been suggested to explain the lower rates of mental health service utilization among African American children; most notably, barriers related to access and availability have been commonly cited in the literature.[7] However, less often discussed are attitudinal barriers toward mental health and service use that may be equally critical to determining timely service use. Cultural factors, such as race and low-income status, have been hypothesized to influence the attitudes and perceptions of parents toward mental health and service use, but these factors have not been examined thoroughly.[8] The purpose of this study is to examine low-income African American parents' perceptions of mental health services for preschool children in order to gain an understanding of how these perceptions might influence help seeking. The study uses in-depth qualitative interviews with parents of children enrolled in urban Head Start programs in the Detroit area.

BACKGROUND

Despite recent evidence that children's use of mental health services has almost doubled since 1986, ethnic minority children receive far fewer mental health services than white children.[9] According to a report funded by the Annie E. Casey Foundation, fewer black (19%) and Hispanic (14%) children receive services in comparison to whites (65%). The majority of children receiving services are adolescents aged 13–17 (51%), in comparison to children aged 6–12 (40%) and preschoolers (9%).[10] Research on the under-utilization of mental health services for African Americans has consistently pointed out that African Americans are less likely to have received care provided by mental health specialists, and less likely to have received services in outpatient and school settings.[11–14] The reasons for under-utilization have focused on various factors associated with help-seeking behavior, including instrumental and environmental factors such as socioeconomic status, lack of health insurance, and the inaccessibility and unavailability of services. Lack of heath insurance in particular is an accessibility barrier for African Americans, as nearly a quarter of African Americans are uninsured.[15] Also, research has shown that mental health services are not readily available in rural areas where higher proportions of African Americans live, particularly in the South.[16] In addition, in urban areas where services may be more readily available, service providers may not accept Medicaid or serve only high-need individuals who display severe, problems, thus rendering services unavailable to urban African Americans who are represented disproportionately in poor communities.[17]

However, these barriers may not be the only factors associated with help-seeking behavior. Research has shown that even when African Americans have health insurance, their levels of service use are still lower when compared to whites.[18] Specifically, attitudinal barriers associated with perceptions of mental health problems and service use may influence help seeking behaviors. Owens and colleagues found that of parents who reported barriers to mental health services, 20.7 percent reported structural constraints (e.g., too expensive, inconvenient, no transportation, unaware of where to go), 23.3 percent noted their perceptions of the mental health problem (e.g., problem not serious, decided to handle problems on own), and 25.9% cited negative attitudes toward services or the receipt of services as barriers (e.g., past negative experience, thought treatment would not help, stigma, did not know who to trust, child did not want to go).[19] Richardson uses social cognitive theory to understand how positive outcome expectations encourage the decision to engage in mental health service use. She reports that African American parents held disproportionately negative ideas and attitudes about the mental health profession and were twice as concerned about disapproval from family members, others knowing, and embarrassment about seeking services.[20] Research by Diala and colleagues found that African Americans had more negative views about the mental health field after receiving services when compared to whites.[21] In a study on attitudes of low-income Head Start parents toward seeking help with parenting, families were found to be less likely to believe in or seek out help than families with higher incomes.[22] Head Start families reported family, books and videos, telephone help-lines, and friends as the most frequent sources of help. However, using data from the Epidemiological Catchment Area (ECA) study, Snowden found that African Americans were less likely than whites to report turning for assistance to a friend, family member, or religious figure.[23] Snowden also found that African Americans tend not to use informal help as a substitute for formal help, but in conjunction with formal help.[24]

In addition, varying expressions and explanations for illness may influence service use and treatment seeking. A study of treatment preferences for depression found that urban African American adults were more likely to prefer to "wait it out" rather than seek professional help for depression, perhaps perceiving symptoms as likely to spontaneously remit.[25] In relation to service use, Snowden found that folk symptoms and idioms are associated with voluntary help seeking among African Americans.[26] Studies investigating cultural perceptions of illness and etiology associated with children's mental health are needed. If culturally based explanations are prevalent, this may explain why there is a delay in the use of early preventive services and greater use of public services and institutions when symptoms are more severe. In part, the purpose of this study is to investigate whether cultural perceptions may play a role in determining help seeking patterns. Understanding how low-income, African American parents perceive mental health service use is important for early childhood mental health research because it informs researchers and professionals of possible intervention strategies that might effectively reach the most children within this segment of the population.

METHODS

Sample and Procedures

Respondents in this study were parents of preschool children enrolled at Head Start centers in Detroit, Michigan. Head Start is a federally funded program designed to augment the academic, social, health and mental health development of children from poor families with quality preschool programs that provide instruction and services to benefit several aspects of child development at ages 3 and 4. The sample consisted of 29 primary caregivers (27 mothers and 2 fathers), all of whom were African American and low-income. Based on available demographic information on parents at participating centers, there were equal numbers of male and female children, 88 percent of families met the federal government poverty income standards, about 40 percent had not completed high school, and the highest level of educational attainment was a high school diploma for about 50 percent of the parents. About 80 percent of the parents were single parents and over half of all mothers were teen parents. In addition to parents, a smaller sample of 10 Head Start teachers were also interviewed, however, only parent data are utilized in the present study.

Participation in the study was voluntary, whereby parents responded to flyers posted in Head Start centers. Study staff also recruited parents through referrals from classroom teachers. Trained graduate and undergraduate research assistants participating in a yearlong community-based research and service learning internship conducted the interviews with parents (45–60 minutes per session). Parents were interviewed at their child's Head Start center in a private space (typically a conference room, unused classroom, or office) where confidentiality was assured. All of the interviews were audio taped with the permission of the parent. Parents were debriefed at the end of each interview and given contact information about the project and other community resources that provided more information about the interview topics.

Measures

The interview protocol was designed as an open-ended, semi-structured interview with the intent of initiating discussion related to several broad areas of parents' perceptions of child development, behavior problems, gender differences in behavior, risk and protective factors, and service utilization. We ended the interview with positive mood induction questions where parents could comment on their positive feelings about 3–5-year-old children.

At the beginning of the interview, parents were asked to think about a preschool-age child they knew that was not necessarily their own child. Parents could reference their own child, but were not asked to do so. We hoped that by not asking parents to reference their own child that it would elicit more honest and candid responses to the interview. Interviewers were trained to be nonjudgmental in their response to the answers that parents provided and were instructed to prompt parents for additional information or to provide clarifying statements that were nondirective and reflective of the meaning that parents derived from the questions.

Data Analysis

The audio taped interviews were transcribed verbatim into a text document format by undergraduate and graduate student research assistants and 25 percent were checked randomly for accuracy. Each interview was labeled specifically for the particular day and time of the interview and the type of interview (parents or teachers) was noted. Once the data was transcribed, it was formatted and loaded into ATLAS/ti, a qualitative software program that is used to organize data and aid in data analysis. The investigators conducted a two-stage coding procedure. The first stage of coding involved the development of a set of broad themes that reflected the research questions of interest. A total of 30 themes were developed (such as *environmental influence*, *origin of problems*, *service use*, and *potential solutions*) and definitions were developed for each theme to clarify the intended meaning and produce inclusion/exclusion criteria for the coders. The study investigators began by coding the data as a group and discussed the use of the codes extensively. Definitions for the themes were revised further to tighten the inclusion/exclusion criteria. Once consistency and understanding of the codes were established, two research assistants coded the remaining interviews independently. Codes were confirmed or revised under the supervision of the principal investigators (first and second authors) and queries were run using the ATLAS/ti software. The queries used the codes to pull units of data relating to the broad themes.

Three pairs of individuals on the research team were formed to analyze the units using both open and axial coding of the data to capture embedded concepts and meanings.[27] The pairs then met to compare their findings under the supervision of the investigators. Further, findings were discussed in ongoing meetings with Head Start program personnel, in an attempt to check the validity of the distilled data. The concepts that emerged from these analyses were confirmed or revised based on these meetings and repeated for all of the queries. The final step was to use these concepts and their text examples to organize evidence for the research questions. The results of these analyses are reported below.

RESULTS

Qualitative axial coding and analysis yielded several themes. Parents identified various resources for children's emotional and behavioral problems, including informal help seeking, self-reliance, formal services, and community resources. Specifically, parents had a stronger preference for informal help seeking and self-reliance. While parents endorsed formal service use as a possible resource, they expressed concerns that reflect the structural and sociocultural realities of low-income, African American communities.

Informal Help-Seeking and Self-Reliance

In response to where parents might seek help for a child displaying behavioral and emotional problems, parents overwhelmingly identified informal resources over formal mental health services. Informal resources include talking to friends or family members. Parents also spoke of getting advice from other parents who might be dealing with the same situation they are experiencing. Head Start teachers were another important resource cited by parents. It should be noted that many Head Start teachers are former Head Start parents and therefore could be possible role models in the community. Parents often expressed the need for "advice" for helping their child. For example, one parent reported,

> If my child had, was violent, or depressed, or displaying bad verbal behavior, I would turn to a neighbor, another family member, uncle, aunts, grandparents, you could also go to a teacher, there's so many, a coworker. I really would go to them.

Positive role models also could include other members of the community, particularly when children's home environments are less than ideal.

> Positive role models. A lot of times a child can come from bad home where emotional abuse happened. But if they have a community or teacher or positive role models. A lot of times that positive role model can grab that child and can teach them, you know, when

all the other brothers and sisters end up in jail. And this one child became an educated and successful adult, because of their positive role models.

The pastors and ministers also were cited often as important sources of advice. Spiritual guidance, expressed as going to church, was other ways in which religion and spirituality were important informal resources.

> With my family, because we go to church, so a lot of times if we're having problems, we can go to our pastor. You can ask him for advice, you know.

In addition to informal resources within the community, self-reliance in the form of "parent knows best" was a recurrent theme. This parent's response emphasizes the need to take care of one's own problems and not seeking advice or assistance outside the home.

> The only person I could see them asking would be their parents, like the current parents. I could never see myself asking a stranger for some advice on how to raise my son; you know that's like all instinct.

Also, parents talked about instilling certain "values" into the lives of their children as a way of dealing with emotional and behavioral problems. Some parents described what they themselves could do to mediate emotional and behavioral problems. These often were expressed through their perceptions of positive values and positive parenting practices. Not only did these values include moral values, but also parents emphasized the need for children to overcome their current situation, including poverty and high-risk neighborhood conditions, and to always strive to improve one's life.

> Well, yeah, um, I would think, regardless of where you live, good or bad community, you know, as long as you are there for your child, instill morals, go to church, positive things. Letting them know there's more to life than just here, where we live. You know, we're just here now, but when you get older you can become whatever you want. And if you choose to do better, fine. If you choose to stay, fine. But never become worse, always strive for better.

Formal Service Use

While parents typically endorsed informal resources and self-reliance for seeking help for children's emotional and behavioral problems, there was some discussion of the need to seek professional help. Several parents noted that they would only seek professional services as a secondary source of help or when a child displayed severe and consistent emotional or behavioral problems, and after other resources were attempted first.

> Number one thing would make this gentleman get better, is the parent have to get more involved. The parent not just getting involved in what he does, but get involved with him.

Sit him down, talk with him, um, let him understand something, if not, seek some professional help, um, because of what the child have seen over the years . . . Um, professional help, you know, and really home training, home training would take the course.

One parent described the need for professional help to assess why a child may be displaying difficult behaviors. This parent viewed professional services positively as a way to diagnose the problem without putting the blame on parents or the child.

I think if a child is showing violence or kinda withdrawn or is um, different things that they can do that sometimes its not just that parent that's doing something wrong, maybe something within the child. So I think if you're having these problems (with) your child, don't just naturally assume this is a bad child. You know, sometimes you need that professional advice to find out what it is.

Furthermore, when parents discussed the need for professional intervention it seems they were interested in seeking advice rather than obtaining medication or other formal interventions. In fact, no parent mentioned medication or psychotherapy specifically as sources of professional assistance they would seek out. In general, parents descriptions of formal services were vague and without detail. For example, specific services were not noted, nor were specific places where services might be obtained.

When parents were asked why they would not choose professional help first, they referenced many barriers, including lack of information about the availability of mental health services and an overall lack of formal resources in their neighborhoods. However, even when professional service may be available to them, many parents expressed feelings of distrust, skepticism, and fear of misunderstanding on the part of mental health professionals. Parents even questioned the competence of mental health professionals in truly being able to serve their children without stigmatizing them. For example, one parent stated:

They don't know that much about mental health. They think that um, a child, they put children in boxes of good and bad and they don't understand that some children don't, they lack skills and need assistance. They don't understand.

Also, parents expressed concern that they would be blamed for their child's behavioral or emotional problems and that the impact of community and structural barriers faced by these families would not be recognized. Again, self-reliance was the preferred alternative, which would assure that parents would not be blamed and children would not be "taken away" from parents. For example, one parent stated,

So just somebody who can actually give that kind of focus of help or psychological help. But then again, today's society is so afraid to do so because society is quick to take their kids. So it's a catch-22 thing. Like get help for my kid, then they're gonna blame me as the fault for it and then take my kids and I don't want that. So I do what is the best I know how. So society also has to let up on how much authority you can take from me.

Community Responsibility

In addition to informal and formal services, parents expressed a need for a community response to addressing the needs of children with emotional and behavioral problems. This response included structural changes in the social environment as well as enhanced community values such as cohesiveness, neighborly/village communication and involvement, safety, stability, and caring. For example, one parent stated,

> Ok, well . . . it goes back to getting involved, and looking at what's going on in the community, trying to put a halt to the situation, having development groups, having community involvement, having watch, neighborhood watch, having community awareness, police protection, just basically whole village involvement and to clean up the neighborhood, to clean up the community. And when we say clean up, let's go door to door, let's talk to families, let's see what's on families' minds, let's see what families are doing, what are their next steps. Are you shooting for the future or do you just want to stay in the past? And now, and now, are we going to get this neighborhood together? Are we going to live adequately or are we just going to live in dumps or are we going to live in good communities? Are we going to clean our areas up, not filthy? Get into the yards, let's clean things, now are we going to do this or are we going to stay right here? And that's definitely a big concern.

The theme of the "village" taking care of and looking after children was often repeated. The idea of the village extends the notion of informal help seeking, beyond family and friends to loose networks of parents and adults. However, in order for these systems to be effective, there needs to be greater sense of community and communication among its members. One parent summarized this idea in the following way:

> Yes, yes I do think it goes back to when I was talking about the village. If you would have or lived in a community of people that's just able to help one another um, we as generations coming up we need to be involved, we need to be involved, we need to help others, and helping others is not going to borrow nothing, but just helping means looking out, looking amongst what their children are doing. If the children are playing rough then go stop the children. If their doing something that you know that it's not right, stop them. Tell the parents, talk more. Nowadays, parents just run by each other. All they do is say hi and bye. The community is failing because there is no communication in the community, no communication.

DISCUSSION

A major goal of this study was to understand low-income, African American parents' perceptions of help seeking and use of children's mental health services. Several themes emerged from the data. First, a few parents endorsed the use of professional services, except for children and families experiencing severe problems. However, these endorsements lacked specificity and focused on advice and assessment rather than treatment modalities such as medication or psychotherapy. This finding is consistent with the literature that speaks to the under-utilization of services or the delayed use of services when problems become too difficult to deal with on one's own. Parents also discussed the lack of available services and noted several barriers to service use, including not knowing where to go or whether or not services would be provided in a respectful and understanding manner. Stigmatization is a major fear of parents who don't want to be blamed for their children's behavior problems and don't want their children labeled as "bad" children. Parents' fears of labels also may stem from not wanting their children to be placed in special education or self-contained classes, which they view as a trajectory of future failure.[28] Furthermore, parents who may use socially undesirable discipline techniques like corporal punishment to deal with their children's behavior problems may fear that their children might be taken away from them. Thus, the environmental conditions that lead to stress among families, which may lead to less than desirable parenting, and subsequent emotional and behavioral problems in children create a "catch-22" for parents who may know that they need help, but fear the consequences of seeking formal services rather than embracing the possibility that services might actually help their children or even help them to become better parents. In other words, parents fear that formal services will focus on the individual behaviors and troubles of parents and children rather than acknowledge and address structural issues, including poverty, which may be at the root of the problem.

Informal sources of support, on the other hand, were referenced by parents in greater detail and included the use of spiritual leaders, friends, relatives, coworkers, and other parents for help and advice. Trust, level of comfort, and accessibility of these resources are likely to inform the decision to seek help first from within the community before seeking out professional services. Teachers also were trusted sources and were viewed as positive role models for parents in their Head Start community. While these informal resources can prove to be an invaluable first line of defense for dealing with children's behavior problems, there are limitations to this approach. First, these individuals likely are not trained in children's mental health, and the advice offered may or may not be good. In fact, it may be detrimental. For example, friends or family members may suggest punitive or authoritarian approaches to parenting, which are not responsive to children's emotional needs.[29, 30] The use of ineffective approaches provided by informal resources also may delay the onset of service use that may be beneficial to children.

However, rather than discourage the use of these natural helpers in the environment, a more useful approach may be to provide information and training to these community resources who are most likely to be approached for advice, such as Head Start teachers and ministers. One possible approach to the use of natural helpers that has demonstrated effectiveness is the community health worker model, which enlists indigenous members of a given population to channel information, social support, tangible aid, and referrals to external resources to individuals and groups within the community. The success of community health worker interventions are evident in the Centers for Disease Control and Prevention's (1994) two-volume directory of lay health advisor projects and programs in the United States.[31] These studies have been found to be particularly successful in racial and ethnic minority communities (i.e., barbers and church members nominated by their pastors to encourage screening for hypertension among African Americans; migrant farm worker women served as *promotoras* to address the maternal and child health needs of families traveling in the Midwest and East Coast Migrant Streams). To date, this model has been used largely in the health arena, but could hold considerable promise in promoting effective parenting and positive mental health.

Parents also expressed concern about environmental conditions (e.g., drugs, violence, illegal dumping, and abandoned houses) and believe that children could be helped by communities taking greater responsibility for "cleaning up" the neighborhood. The concept of communal responsibility is congruent with popular notions of child well-being that evoke nostalgic feelings of the way things used to be when neighbors looked after one another and everyone knew whose child belonged to whom. Embedded in this concept is the notion of community empowerment and capacity building, where communities have the power and the ability to control their own destiny and future. Solutions for individual problems arise from collective action from within, and not necessarily from external political or economic forces or interventions. While this approach may be desirable and even advocated by community psychologists and social workers, poor communities of color should not bear the full burden of rectifying inequalities that are perpetuated by society at large. We can applaud and encourage the hope, and utilize the many strengths within poor communities of color, but at the same time, we must continue to work toward socially just policies and antipoverty approaches that will create structural changes to enhance a community's ability to help themselves. At the same time, we must also work toward eradicating the stereotypes of the poor and populations of color that maintain disparities in service use in formal settings.

While this study illustrates the importance of understanding parents' perceptions of help seeking and service use among poor, minority populations, the limitations of this study should be noted. First, the sample drawn for this study was not random and thus selection bias may have influenced the responses. It is possible that the sample consists of parents who were most willing to be interviewed and least likely to have children with mental health issues. Additionally, the sample is relatively small by the standards of quantitative research, but adequate for a qualitative study. Second, our data reflects parental perceptions and not actual behavior. In order to reduce bias and socially desirable responses, we did not ask parents directly about their own child or their past experiences with service use. Rather we assumed that parents would feel free to speak more candidly if they were asked questions about a hypothetical child they may know. Finally, our results may be biased by the use of university students as interviewers. Although these students also worked in the classrooms with teachers and children as part of a community service learning project for the entire academic year and parents had a number of opportunities to see and interact with the students, parents still may not have been comfortable interacting with students in the context of an interview or may not have wanted to appear lacking in competence around children's behaviors or parenting. Parents may have feared that information would be relayed back to teachers, despite assurances of confidentiality, or that their responses would be tied to their own child's classroom behavior. Student interviewers were generally not from the Head Start communities we drew our sample from and their status as outsiders may have been a barrier to participation in the study or may have influenced parents' responses. Race and class differences between interviewers and parents may have also contributed to bias in responses.

Overall, the results of this study suggest that understanding parents' perceptions of help seeking and services has implications for the design of interventions for low-income, African American families. Barriers to service use associated with socio-cultural conceptualizations could be reduced through careful consideration of these perceptions in early prevention models of practice and intervention development. Increased access to preventive practices could have implications for reducing more serious problems that limits opportunities in adolescence and adulthood. For low-income, African American parents, we must start by changing perceptions through increased culturally appropriate and acceptable services that begin in early childhood.

ACKNOWLEDGMENTS

The authors would like to acknowledge the support of our Head Start partners, Valerie Vanelas, Joya Rush-Keli, CaroleAnn Beaman, Toni Hartke, James Carr, and the families of the Detroit Head Start program who allowed us to work with them. This study was funded by the W.K. Kellogg Foundation's Global Program for Youth (GPY) awarded to the University of Michigan, School of Social Work, Paula Allen-Meares (P.I.).

NOTES

1. U.S. Department of Health and Human Services (USDHHS). *Mental health: Culture, race, and ethnicity-A supplement to mental health: A report of the Surgeon General-Executive Summary.* Rockville, MD: Substance Abuse and Mental Health Services Administration, Center for Mental Health Services, Office of the Surgeon General, 2001.

2. P.J. Cunningham and M.P. Freiman. "Determinants of ambulatory mental health service use for school-age children and adolescence." *Mental Health Services Research* 31 (1996): 409–427.

3. K.V. Bui and D.T. Takeuchi. "Ethnic minority adolescents and the use of community mental health services." *American Journal of Community Psychology* 20 (1992): 403–417.

4. N. Halfon, G. Berkowitz, and L. Klee. "Mental health service utilization by children in foster care in California." *Pediatrics* 89 (1992): 1239–1244.

5. K.M. McCabe, R. Clark, and D. Barnett. "Family protective factors among urban African American youth." *Journal of Clinical Child Psychology* 28 (1999): 137–150.

6. A.L. Pastore, and K. Maguire. *The sourcebook of criminal justice statistics.* Washington, DC: U.S. Bureau of Justice Statistics, 1999.

7. U.S. Department of Health and Human Services (USDHHS), *Mental health.*

8. U.S. Department of Health and Human Services (USDHHS). *Mental health: A report of the Surgeon General-Exectutive Summary.* Rockville, MD: Substance Abuse and Mental Health Services Administration, Center for Mental Health Services, National Institute of Health, National Institute of Mental Health, 1999.

9. K.J. Pottick and L.A. Warner. *Children's use of mental health services doubles, new research-policy partnership reports. Updates: Latest findings in Children's Mental Health.* New Brunswick, NJ: Institute for Health, Health Care Policy, and Aging Research, Rutgers University, 2002.

10. Ibid.

11. E.J. Costello, E.M. Farmer, A. Angold, B.J. Burns, and A. Erkanli. "Psychiatric disorders among American Indian and white youth in Appalachia: The Great Smoky Mountains study." *American Journal of Public Health* 87 (1997): 827–832.

12. S.P. Cuffe, J.L. Waller, M.L. Cuccaro, A.J. Pumariega, and C.Z. Garrison. "Race and gender differences in the treatment of psychiatric disorders in young adolescents." *Journal of the American Academy of Child and Adolescent Psychiatry* 34 (1995): 1536–1543.

13. P.J. Cunningham, and M.P. Freiman, "Determinants of ambulatory mental health service use for school-age children and adolescence."

14. G.E. Zahner and C. Daskalakis. "Factors associated with mental health, general health, and school-based service use for child psychopathology." *American Journal of Public Health* 87 (1997): 1440–1448.

15. E.R. Brown, V.D. Ojeda, R. Win, and R. Levan. *Racial and ethnic disparities in access to health insurance and health care.* Los Angeles, CA: UCLA Center for Health Policy Research and the Henry J. Kaiser Family Foundation, 2000.

16. Substance Abuse and Mental Health Services Administration. *Mental health, United States 1998.* Rockville, MD: Center for Mental Health Services, 1998.

17. U.S. Department of Health and Human Services (USDHHS), *Mental health.*

18. D.K. Padgett, E.L. Struening, H. Andrews, and J. Pittman. "Predictors of emergency room use by homeless adults in New York City: The predisposing, enabling, and need factors." *Social Science and Medicine* 41 (1995): 547–556.

19. P.L. Owens, K. Hoagwood, S.M. Horwitz, P.J. Leaf, J.M. Poduska, , S.G. Kellam, and N.S. Ialongo. "Barriers to children's mental health services." *Journal of the American Academy of Child and Adolescent Psychiatry* 41 (2002): 731–738.

20. L.A. Richardson. "Seeking and obtaining mental health services: What do parents expect?" *Archives of Psychiatric Nursing* 15 (2001): 223–231.

21. C. Diala, C. Muntaner, C. Walrath, K.J. Nickerson, T.A. LaVeist, and P.J. Leaf. "Racial differences in attitudes toward professional mental health care and in the use of services." *American Journal of Orthopsychiatry* 70 (2000): 455–464.

22. J. Keller and K. McDade. "Attitudes of low-income parents toward seeking help parenting: Implications for practice." *Child Welfare* 79 (2000): 285–312.

23. L.R. Snowden. "Racial differences in informal help seeking for mental health problems." *Journal of Community Psychology* 26 (1998): 429–438.

24. Ibid.

25. L. Cooper-Patrick, N.R. Powe, M.W. Jenckes, J.J. Gonzales, D.M. Levine, and D.E. Ford. "Identification of patient attitudes and preferences regarding treatment of depression." *Journal of General Internal Medicine* 12 (1997): 431–438.

26. L.R. Snowden. "African American folk idiom and mental health services use." *Cultural Diversity & Ethnic Minority Psychology* 5 (1999): 364–370.

27. A.L. Strauss and J. Corbin. *Basics of qualitative research: techniques and procedures for developing grounded theory.* Thousand Oaks: Sage, 1998.

28. M.S. Spencer, L.P. Kohn, and J.R. Woods. "Early identification versus stigmatization: The dilemma of early screening for children's mental health problems among African Americans." *African American Perspectives* 8 (2003): 1–14.

29. D. Baumrind. "The influence of parenting style on adolescent competence and sub-stance use." *Journal of Early Adolescence* 11(1) (1991): 56–95.

30. E.E. Maccoby, and J.A. Martin. *Socialization in the context of the family: Parent–child interaction.* In P. H. Mussen (Ed.) and E. M. Hetherington (Vol. Ed.), *Handbook of child psychology: Vol. 4. Socialization, personality, and social development* (4th ed., pp. 1–101). New York: Wiley, 1983.

31. U.S. Department of Health and Human Services (USDHHS). *Community Health Advisors: Models, Research, and Practice.* USDHHS, Public Health Services, Centers for Disease Control and Prevention, Atlanta, GA: September, 1994.

CHAPTER 8

IMMIGRANT STATUS, POVERTY, AND CHILD HEALTH

Magdalena Szaflarski and Jun Ying

Children of immigrants are growing in numbers and face greater economic hardships than children of U.S. natives.[1,2] In 2000, one in five children in the United States had a foreign-born parent, and one in four low-income children was an immigrant's child.[3] While, in the past, poverty rates among children of immigrants were lower than among children of natives, the situation has been reversed. Currently, 22 percent of children of immigrants under the age of 18 live in poverty compared to 15 percent of children of natives and 10 percent of non-Hispanic white children.[4] This substantial economic disadvantage would be expected to produce corresponding health and healthcare disparities, considering a well-documented relationship between poverty and poor health.[5,6] However, the picture is mixed. Overall mortality and morbidity risks are lower among immigrant children and adults than among their native counterparts.[7–12] On the other hand, children of immigrants fare worse on some measures of well-being such as parent-reported health status,[13,14] and they have lower healthcare utilization rates.[15]

Despite growing interest in the well-being of children in immigrant families, the literature is still limited. A prior in-depth assessment of health status and adjustment of children of immigrants[16] relied on data from the mid-1990s, and a more current study is now needed. Recent health comparisons of children of immigrants and children of natives focus on access to health care and/or include only a single indicator of physical health and a few indicators of mental and social well-being, for example, negative behaviors and school and extracurricular activities.[17,18] A comprehensive immigrant–native comparison including multiple indicators of health and health care use has recently been conducted only for adults;[19] a similar study on children is warranted. Furthermore, little attention has been given to diversity of the immigrant population. Even treatment of the large, and the most economically vulnerable,

Hispanic/Latino population is sparse and lacking systematic research.[20,21] Finally, past studies might have underestimated immigrant disadvantage by including in the definition of "immigrant" children with one foreign-born and one U.S.-born parent. Children with both parents foreign-born may be more vulnerable than those whose at least one parent is a U.S. native.

The goal of this study was to examine the relationship between child health, immigrant status, and poverty. Specifically, we aimed to compare the extent of health-related disadvantage among poor children based on immigrant vs. native status. We defined immigrant children as having both foreign-born parents and native children as having at least one U.S.-born parent. Our analysis is based on a nationally representative sample of U.S. children. We include multiple health/health-care indicators and examine the role of immigrant background by racial/ethnic status as well as parental region of origin.

THEORETICAL FRAMEWORK

It is clear that poverty and health are strongly related.[22,23] Poverty leads to poor health outcomes, and it can also result from poor health. In general, access to health care, which may depend on socioeconomic resources, plays a relatively small role in population health, but medical care saves individual lives, decreases suffering, and improves functioning. Poverty can put children at risk of poor health regardless of family native background. However, the intersection of two or more kinds of social disadvantage (e.g., poverty and minority status) is likely to exacerbate the situation. To what extent children from immigrant families experience the burden of minority and socioeconomic disadvantage in health is yet to be shown. Several perspectives should be considered.

Economic and Political Migration

Many immigrants seek economic opportunities in the United States and a chance to attain higher standards of living. Some immigrants were economically disadvantaged before entry to the United States and their disadvantage continues in the United States because of low-pay employment, discrimination, and segregation.[24] This group tends to consist of emigrants from less developed and/or economically troubled countries (e.g., Mexico). In the United States, they face economic, legal, and linguistic barriers to health care, resulting in under-utilization of medical services and reducing their chances for optimal health. Refugees are another highly vulnerable population. Coming from conflict and poverty stricken regions of the world (e.g., Africa), they may have special health needs (e.g., dietary, mental health) which are often not adequately addressed because of access-related and communication barriers.[25,26] That said, economic and political immigrants are often better off in the United States than they would have been in their home countries, and, thus, relative poverty may not affect them as much as U.S. natives.

Immigrant Selection and Assimilation

A potential advantage that immigrants have vis-à-vis U.S. natives, at least at baseline or time of entry to the United States, is their relatively low prevalence of disease and disability.[27] People who migrate tend to be healthy based on logistic (e.g., travel, employment) and legal requirements of immigration (e.g., health screening component of visa application). However, the health status of immigrants is likely to change with length of stay and each new generation born in the United States.[28,29] Some immigrants may be able to attain higher health status during their stay in the United States due to the advanced American health-care system or their assimilation into the "health" culture of American society. For example, families may take advantage of availability of vaccinations and get children protected against disease. Other immigrants' health may worsen in the course of assimilation because of the health risks embedded in the American culture (e.g., fast food consumption, inactive lifestyles) or because of limited access to health-care.

Cultural Diversity

Finally, it is important to keep in mind that immigrants come from various cultures, which continue to shape their health-related attitudes and behaviors.[30] Health consciousness may be high in some immigrants and they will seek health services and/or pursue healthy lifestyles despite their limited resources and barriers faced within the healthcare system (e.g., communication). For example, Cubans, who come from a system of socialized medicine, which has made great strides toward disease eradication and health promotion, may have good health habits and use medical services on a regular basis. Asians may practice holistic health and use complementary/alternative medicine, following their traditional cultures. As noted above, these attitudes may change during the assimilation process—with positive or negative consequences for health.

HYPOTHESES

Our central goal was to assess how poor children of immigrants fare in terms of health and use of healthcare vis-à-vis their native counterparts. We expected that overall health and health-care use would be lower among children of immigrants than among the natives because of the additional burden/barriers associated with immigrant and minority status. However, this relationship was expected to be moderated by racial/ethnic status; that is, racial/ethnic minority natives were expected to have the same or worse outcomes than children of immigrants. Also, we expected some variation within the immigrant population based on length of U.S. stay and parental place of origin. The effects of length of stay were thought to be positive and negative, as explained above, and thus, possibly balance each other out. Children of immigrants from less developed countries were expected to fare worse than children of immigrants from advanced societies. The former group was expected to fare worse while the latter group was expected to fare better than U.S.-native children.

METHODS

Data

In this study, we used data from the National Health Interview Survey (NHIS), a multipurpose health survey conducted annually by the National Center for Health Statistics (NCHS), Center for Disease Control and Prevention.[31] The survey is based on a probability sample and personal household interviews. Using appropriate weighting procedures, results based on these data are generalizable to the U.S. population. The weights were calculated by NCHS staff to produce estimates consistent with the population estimates by age, sex, and race or ethnicity, based on projections from the 2000 U.S. Census. In addition to basic sociodemographics and an extensive health component, the NHIS contains information on the respondent's place of birth by region. This information is more detailed than in any other national health survey.

We used 3 years of data, 2001, 2002, and 2003, in the study. A preliminary study showed no significant changes of the study variables over time. We combined the 3 years of data to increase the reliability of estimates and the power of tests for some of the smaller population subgroups.

Data were derived from two NHIS files. Sociodemographic infomation, health insurance status, and general health status were derived from the Person File (household head report) while data regarding specific health conditions were derived from the Sample Child File. A total of 80,400 children under 18 years of age were identified based on the Person File. There were 54,596 children (68.2%) whose parents had valid birthplaces and who, hence, were eligible for the study. For most of the variables from the Person File, the overall percentage of unknown values was small, usually less than 1 percent. However, 25.4 percent of the cases had missing family income information or the respondents stated that their combined family income was either less than $20,000 or $20,000 or more without providing additional detail. Therefore, poverty status, which is based on family income, also has a high nonresponse rate. Also, 3.5 percent of cases were missing parental education data.

A total of 38,477 children were obtained from the Sample Child File, with 25,741 (66.9%) children whose parents had valid birthplace and who, hence, were eligible for the study. The unknown or missing rates for learning disability, and attention deficit-hyperactivity disorder/attention deficit disorder (ADHD/ADD) were 19.1 percent and 12.9 percent, respectively. Cases with missing values were excluded from computation.

Measures

Our dependent variables included health status, health insurance, and health-care use indicators. Our main independent variables were immigrant status and poverty status. Other covariates included age, gender, race/ethnicity, and parent education.

Health Status

General health status is parent-reported health status based on a question in the survey that asked respondents, "Would you say (child's name)'s health in general is excellent, very good, good, fair, or poor?" Parents also reported change in child's health status by responding to the question, "Compared with 12 months ago, would you say (child's name)'s health is now better, worse, or about the same?" In addition, we examined indicators of the most common childhood health problems: asthma, allergies (hay fever, other allergies), a learning disability, and ADHD/ADD.[32,33] If they were ever told their child had asthma, a learning disability, or ADHD/ADD was indicated with an affirmative response to the question, "Has a doctor or other health professional ever told you that {child's name} had {condition}?" Had asthma attack in past 12 months is based on the question, "During the past 12 months, has {child's name} had an episode of asthma or an asthma attack?" A similar question was asked about hay fever and other types of allergies. In addition to general health status and specific conditions, we examined prescription medication use based on the question, "Does {child's name} now have a problem for which he/she has regularly taken prescription medication for at least 3 months?" and for school-aged children (5–17 years), number of missing school days in the past 12 months.

Health Insurance

NHIS respondents were asked about their health insurance coverage at the time of interview. For children, types of insurance were classified as follows: private (obtained directly through employer or workplace, purchased directly, or through a local or community program), Medicaid (and/or other State-sponsored health plans including State Children's Health Insurance Program, or SCHIP), other coverage (e.g., military or other government programs), and uninsured (including persons only covered by Indian Health Service, or IHS, or a plan that pays for one type of service such as accidents or dental care).

Health Care Use

We used several indicators of health-care utilization: usual source of health care, last health-care visit, number of emergency room (ER) visits, and last dental visit. Respondents were asked about the place where they go most often when the child is sick, with the following response categories: clinic or health center, doctor's office or HMO, hospital ER, hospital outpatient department, "some other place," and "doesn't go to one place most often"; we used a dummy-coded variable indicating lack of usual source of healthcare (the last response category). Respondents were also asked if the child saw a health professional and had two or more ER visits in the past 12 months. In addition, respondents were asked about the child's last dental visit using a question, "About how long has it been since (child's name) last saw or talked to a dentist? Include all types of dentists, such as orthodontists, oral surgeons, and all other dental specialists, as well as dental hygienists." Responses were categorized as follows: "6 months or less," "more than 6 months but not more than 1 year ago," "more than

1 year, but not more than 2 years ago," "more than 2 yrs, but not more than 5 years ago," and "more than 5 years ago." We dichotomized the variable as "in the past 12 months" vs. "more than 1 year ago."

Immigrant Status and Length of Stay

Immigrant status is measured by parental place of birth: U.S. versus foreign-born. Immigrant children are defined as having both foreign-born parents; native children are defined as having at least one U.S.-born parent. We also use a detailed parental region of birth variable. The NHIS region of birth variable categorizes all respondents into one of 12 categories according to the CIA online World Factbook.[34] Due to a small number of cases in some categories available for our analysis, we combined some regions and used the following five categories of detailed parental region of birth: (1) United States, (2) Mexico, Central America, Caribbean Islands, and South America, (3) Europe and the former USSR, (4) Asia, and (5) "Elsewhere." In addition to parental place of birth, we examined length of stay in the United States, which is measured in NHIS using the following time intervals: "less than 1 year," "1 year, less than 5 years," "5 years, less than 10 years," "10 years, less than 15 years," and "15 years or more." We combined these categories into: "less than 5 years," "5 to 10 years," and "11 or more years."

Poverty Status

The poverty status variable is based on adult respondents report of family's income (total combined income before taxes from all sources for the previous calendar year), information supplied either as a dollar amount or as an interval estimate. This variable is the ratio of family's income to the corresponding year's poverty threshold defined by the U.S. Census Bureau, considering the family's size and number of children. In our study, we dichotomized poverty status as "less than 200 percent of the poverty threshold" and "equal or more than 200 percent of the poverty threshold." We will refer to the former group as "poor" or "near poor" and to the latter group as "not poor"[35] (or, sometimes, "higher income"). For the demographics table, we list the original four levels of poverty status: "less than 100 percent of the poverty threshold," "100–199 percent," "200–299 percent," and "equal or more than 300 percent."

Sociodemographic Covariates

Demographic variables include age, gender, race/ethnicity, Hispanic heritage, and education. Race/ethnicity is categorized as follows: non-Hispanic white, non-Hispanic black, Hispanic, and other. Hispanic ethnicity is classified as: Mexican/Mexican-American; Puerto Rican, Cuban/Cuban American, and Dominican (Republic); Central/or South American; and "other." Parent education is defined as the highest level of school completed for the parent with the higher level of education.

Analysis

We computed percentage distributions with standard errors for all of the categorical variables. Estimates with relative standard errors of greater than 30 percent were considered unreliable[36] and were identified and indicated with an asterisk (*) in the tables. For binary outcomes, logistic regression models were used to assess the effects of independent variables, adjusted for other sociodemographic covariates. For categorical and ordinal outcomes, multinomial and cumulative logistic regression models were used instead. Outcomes in subpopulations were assessed using the same statistical models.

All analyses were performed using SAS-callable SUDAAN Version 9.0.1 (Research Triangle Institute, NC). All estimates were weighted using the U.S. Census-based weights derived by the NHIS. Specifically, the data in 2001 and 2002 used weights derived from the 1990 U.S. Census-based postcensal population estimates, and the data in 2003 used weights derived from the 2000 U.S. Census-based postcensal population estimates.[37]

FINDINGS

Sample

Table 8.1 shows the distribution of sociodemographic variables for the total sample and for the native and immigrant children subsamples. The sample consisted of 54,596 children including 13,100 (23.9%) children from immigrant families. The children of immigrants were somewhat younger than the native children. The majority of the native children were non-Hispanic white (80%) whereas the majority of the immigrant children were Hispanic (60%). Many more immigrant children (56%) than native children (23%) were "poor" or "near poor" (family poverty level, or FPL < 200%), which is consistent with other recent reports.[38–40] Parents of the native children tended to have higher education levels than those of the immigrant children. Over 75 percent of parents of the native children completed more than high school/GED education, compared to only 45 percent in the immigrant group. Only 4 percent of parents of the native children had below high school education, compared to 36 percent in the immigrant group. These differences may be due, in part, to differences between the U.S. and foreign systems of education (e.g., vocational training opportunities in lieu of high school in other countries).

We also examined the distribution of the immigrant children by parental region of birth and of all children by Hispanic ethnicity. About 60 percent of the immigrant children had parents who were born in Mexico, Central America, or the Caribbean Islands. Children of South East Asians were the second largest group (10%). Single-digit percentages were observed for all other regions of birth. In regard to Hispanic ethnicity, over 70 percent of the native and the immigrant children were Mexican/Mexican American. More native (16%) than immigrant (7%) children were Puerto Rican, Cuban/Cuban American, and Dominican (Republic), whereas more immigrant (18%) than native (7%) children were Central or South American.

Table 8.1
Sociodemographic Characteristics of US Children by Immigrant Status, 2001–2003

	Percent (standard error)		
Selected Characteristic	All ($n = 54,596$)	US Native Children[a] ($n = 41,696$)	Immigrant Children[b] ($n = 13,100$)
Age			
0–4 years	28.47 (.27)	28.04 (.31)	30.70 (.49)
5–11 years	39.04 (.25)	38.78 (.28)	40.37 (.47)
12–17 years	32.49 (.27)	33.18 (.30)	28.93 (.46)
Gender			
Male	51.44 (.23)	51.48 (.26)	51.19 (.51)
Female	48.56 (.23)	48.52 (.26)	48.81 (.51)
Race/ethnicity			
Hispanic	16.55 (.42)	8.20 (.28)	59.51 (1.20)
Non-Hispanic white	69.46 (.54)	80.37 (.47)	13.23 (.80)
Non-Hispanic black	8.76 (.32)	9.36 (.36)	5.66 (.46)
Non-Hispanic other	5.23 (.21)	2.07 (.13)	21.60 (.94)
Family's federal poverty level			
<100%	9.25 (.31)	6.60 (.28)	23.73 (.98)
100–199%	18.42 (.38)	15.88 (.41)	32.41 (.87)
200–299%	19.60 (.35)	20.00 (.38)	17.57 (.64)
≥300%	52.73 (.57)	57.52 (.59)	26.30 (1.05)
Parents' education			
Less than high school or GED	9.53 (.30)	4.32 (.19)	36.31 (1.04)
High school or GED	20.14 (.33)	20.44 (.38)	18.36 (.62)
More than high school or GED	70.34 (.43)	75.24 (.41)	45.33 (1.05)
Child's living status			
Lives with single parent	1.93 (.08)	1.87 (.09)	2.23 (.17)
Lives with both parent	96.37 (.12)	96.36 (.14)	96.37 (.23)
Does not live with parent(s)	1.70 (.08)	1.77 (.09)	1.40 (.14)
Family size			
≤4	54.07 (.41)	56.44 (.45)	41.68 (.81)
>4	45.93 (.41)	43.56 (.45)	58.32 (.81)
US region of residence			
Northeast	17.95 (.36)	18.00 (.39)	17.78 (.86)
Midwest	23.97 (.48)	26.48 (.54)	10.95 (.84)
South	35.12 (.52)	36.38 (.59)	28.60 (1.06)
West	22.96 (.51)	19.13 (.54)	42.67 (1.25)

Note: (1) Values in the cell are weighted mean (standard error) of frequency in percent. (2) SUDAAN Proc Descript was used in estimation. Estimates were adjusted for age based on the 2000 U.S. standard population.
[a] At least one parent is US-born.
[b] Both parents are foreign-born or a single parent is foreign-born.

Poverty, Immigrant Status, and Health

Our main findings are presented in Tables 8.2–8.5. A preliminary analysis showed that immigrant length of stay was not associated with any of the key variables; therefore, we excluded it from further analyses.

Immigrant-Native Status

In Table 8.2, we compare the health and health-care indicators by immigrant-native and poverty status. As expected, the vast majority of children in both groups were in good, very good, or excellent health; less than 2 percent of children were reported to have fair or poor health. Health status was associated with poverty status. In particular, the children from "not poor" families (FPL ≥ 200%) showed better health than those from "poor" or "near poor" families, regardless of immigrant status. Among the natives, 51 percent of the children who were "poor" or "near poor" reported excellent health compared with 63 percent of the higher income children, and 1.6 percent of the children who were "poor" or "near poor" reported poor or fair health versus 1 percent of the higher income children. The native children were reported to have better health than the immigrant children in "not poor" families. However, immigrant status had no effect on health status in the "poor" or "near poor" families. Interestingly, the health advantage due to higher incomes was smaller among the immigrants than among the natives. On the other hand, the immigrant children, regardless of poverty status, were less likely than the native children to report worse health and more likely to report better health than a year ago. For example, among children who were "poor" or "near poor," 27 percent of the immigrant children reported better health than a year ago compared with only 22 percent of the native children.

In terms of chronic health conditions, the native children were roughly twice as likely as the immigrant children to have been told they had asthma (~12% vs. ~6%) and to report an asthma attack in the past 12 months (~5% vs. ~2%). A similar native disadvantage vis-à-vis the immigrant children was observed for prevalence of hay fever and respiratory allergy. Poverty status was associated with a higher likelihood of having asthma only in the native children; about 13 percent of the children who were "poor" or "near poor" reported having asthma compared with 11 percent of the children who were "not poor." In the immigrant children, poverty status was associated with a *lower* likelihood of having an asthma episode, respiratory allergy, or food or skin allergies. For example, 6 percent of the immigrant children who were "poor" or "near poor" reported respiratory allergy compared with 9 percent of their higher income counterparts.

A learning disability and ADHD/ADD were the most prevalent in the native children who were "poor" or "near poor" (9% and 5%, respectively for a learning disability and ADHD/ADD) compared with the other native and immigrant children (e.g., 3% and 1% in the immigrant children who were "poor" or "near poor"). Poverty status was not associated with having a learning disability or ADHD/ADD in the immigrant children.

Table 8.2
Health and Health Care of US Children by Immigrant Status and Federal Poverty Level (FPL

Variable	US Native Children		Immigrant Children	
	FPL < 200%	FPL ≥ 200%	FPL < 200%	FPL ≥ 200%
General health status				
Excellent	51.00 (.99)A	63.23 (.53)aB	50.81 (1.66)A	58.22 (1.35)bB
Very good	32.26 (.58)A	25.92 (.43)aB	32.34 (.81)A	28.72 (.79)bB
Good	15.17 (.51)A	9.89 (.23)aB	15.27 (.85)A	11.88 (.59)bB
Fair	1.37 (.09)A	.84 (.05)aB	1.38 (.12)A	1.03 (.08)bB
Poor	.20 (.03)A	.12 (.02)aB	.20 (.03)A	.15 (.02)bB
Health better, about the same, or worse than 12 months ago				
Better	21.38 (.83)a	20.81 (.40)a	26.55 (1.32)b	25.15 (1.33)b
About the same	77.02 (.77)a	77.53 (.42)a	72.23 (1.24)b	73.54 (1.25)b
Worse	1.61 (.12)a	1.66 (.10)a	1.21 (.11)b	1.30 (.12)b
Ever been told that had asthma	12.81 (.65)aA	11.03 (.32)aB	5.86 (.67)b	6.95 (.79)b
Had an asthma episode in past 12 months	5.54 (.44)a	5.27 (.23)a	1.73 (.33)bA	3.07 (.49)bB
Had hay fever in past 12 months	9.66 (.56)a	9.84 (.35)a	6.51 (.77)b	7.65 (.79)b
Had respiratory allergy in past 12 months	13.12 (.74)a	13.37 (.35)a	5.71 (.70)bA	8.50 (.94)bB
Had food/digestive or eczema/skin allergy in past 12 months	12.54 (.75)a	12.31 (.32)	6.09 (.73)bA	10.58 (.88)B
Ever told had a learning disability	8.82 (.63)aA	5.93 (.28)aB	3.01 (.46)b	2.06 (.39)b
Ever told had ADHD/ADD	5.43 (.55)aA	4.08 (.25)aB	1.01 (.24)b	1.16 (.30)b
≤5 missing school days in past 12 months (age 5–17)	77.55 (1.08)aA	82.81 (.45)aB	89.84 (1.10)b	87.57 (1.34)b

Table 8.2
(continued)

Variable	US Native Children		Immigrant Children	
	FPL < 200%	FPL ≥ 200%	FPL < 200%	FPL ≥ 200%
Prescription medication for 3+ months for a current health problem	15.17 (.76)aA	13.29 (.35)aB	4.78 (.63)b	6.21 (.77)b
Health insurance coverage	61.21 (1.17)A	93.50 (.31)aB	56.72 (2.21)A	89.93 (.87)bB
Private coverage	11.61 (.79)A	.69 (.12)B	10.34 (1.68)A	1.06 (.28)B
Medicaid	5.77 (.71)aA	2.47 (.23)aB	1.37 (.31)bA	.46 (.15)bB
Other coverage	21.41 (.95)aA	3.33 (.19)aB	31.57 (1.75)bA	8.55 (.80)bB
Uninsured				
Saw/spoke to health professional in past 12 months	91.36 (.60)aA	94.01 (.22)aB	87.26 (1.05)bA	92.25 (.74)bB
Has usual place of health care when sick	95.66 (.39)aA	98.21 (.14)aB	92.47 (.91)bA	96.71 (.51)bB
Two or more ER visits in 12 months	91.63 (.52)aA	94.53 (.23)B	93.71 (.72)b	94.18 (.75)
Saw/talked to dentist in past 12 months (age 5–17 years)	78.80 (1.24)A	88.28 (.57)B	78.86 (1.96)A	87.04 (1.50)B

Note: (1) Values in the cell are mean (standard error) of frequency of "yes" (event) in percent. (2) SUDAAN Proc Rlogist and Proc Multilog were used in computation of logistic, cumulative logistic, and multinomial regression models. Estimates were adjusted for age, gender, race/ethnicity, and parents' education. P values < .05 are considered statistically significant. (3) Different lower-case letters in the same FPL group in a row indicate means are statistically different between two immigrant status groups. (4) Different upper-case letters in the same immigrant status group in a row indicate means are statistically different between two FPLs.

* indicates the estimate has a relative standard error of greater than 30% and should be used with caution as they do not meet the standard of reliability or precision.

Disparities were also observed for school attendance and prescription medication use. The native children who were "poor" or "near poor" had the lowest school attendance: 78 percent missed five or fewer school days in the past 12 months, compared to 83 percent of the native children who were "not poor," and 88–90 percent of the immigrant children. Furthermore, the native children who were "poor" or "near poor" were most likely of all the groups to have taken prescription medication for 3 months or longer: 15 percent of those children reported using prescription medication compared to 13 percent of the native children who were "not poor" and 5–6 percent of the immigrant children. No differences were observed among the immigrant children's prescription medication use based on poverty status.

In regard to health insurance coverage, disparities were even more striking than for health indicators, with the immigrant children who were "poor" or "near poor" experiencing the greatest disadvantage. About a third of immigrant children who were "poor" or "near poor" were uninsured, compared with a fifth of their native counterparts, and only 9 percent and 3 percent, respectively, of the immigrant and the native children who were "not poor." Medicaid coverage rates were similar between the immigrant status groups, though, of course, they differed based on poverty level; e.g., 12 percent of the native children who were "poor" or "near poor" had Medicaid versus less than 1 percent of their "not poor" counterparts. While the rates of private insurance coverage were similar for the native and the immigrant children who were "poor" or "near poor," the rate was somewhat lower for the immigrant children who were "not poor" (90%) versus their native counterparts (94%).

Despite the varying rates of health insurance coverage across the study groups, the vast majority of children saw or spoke to a health professional in the past 12 months and reported having a regular source of health care (vs. not going to the same place most of the time). The immigrant children who were "poor" or "near poor" reported the lowest rate of a medical encounter and a regular source of healthcare (87% and 93%, respectively), followed by their native counterparts (91% and 96%), and their "not poor" immigrant (92% and 97%) and native (94% and 98%) counterparts. Two or more ER visits in the past 12 months were also reported for the vast majority of children. Although the immigrant children who were "poor" or "near poor" had a somewhat higher rate of reporting two or more ER visits (94%) than their native counterparts (92%), their rate was not different from the rates for the immigrant and the native children who were "not poor." Finally, the rates of a dental visit in the past 12 months varied by poverty level but not by immigrant status. About 79 percent of the native and the immigrant children who were "poor" or "near poor" reported a dental visit within the past year compared with more than 87 percent of their "not poor" counterparts.

Region of Birth Comparisons

Table 8.3 shows a comparison of the health status and health-care indicators based on parental region of birth. We refrained from including poverty status as a stratification variable, as we expected few observations in some variable categories. Also, some of the estimates do not meet our reliability standard (see Methods) and should

Table 8.3
Health and Health Care of US Children by Parental Region of Birth

| | US Native Children | Immigrant Children | | | |
| | | Mexico and CA/CI/SA[a] | Europe[b] | Asia[c] | Else[d] |
Variable					
General health status					
Excellent	60.05 (.47)	58.60 (1.54)	51.13 (3.11)#	53.07 (3.32)#	62.06 (4.62)
Very good	27.76 (.41)	28.55 (.86)	32.34 (1.42)#	31.35 (1.63)#	26.63 (2.67)
Good	11.10 (.23)	11.69 (.68)	15.07 (1.55)#	14.14 (1.55)#	10.31 (1.78)
Fair	.96 (.06)	1.01 (.08)	1.37 (.18)#	1.27 (.18)#	.88 (.18)
Poor	.13 (.02)	.14 (.02)	.19 (.04)#	.18 (.03)#	.12 (.03)
Health better, about the same, or worse than 12 months ago					
Better	20.90 (.39)	24.37 (1.22)#	22.29 (3.19)	30.53 (3.27)#	28.78 (3.91)#
About the same	77.45 (.41)	74.27 (1.13)#	76.19 (2.91)	68.47 (3.12)#	70.13 (3.71)#
Worse	1.66 (.10)	1.36 (.13)#	1.53 (.30)	1.00 (.17)#	1.09 (.21)#
Ever been told that had asthma	11.43 (.30)	5.67 (.61)#	6.89 (2.19)#	6.21 (1.28)#	9.44 (2.41)
Had an asthma episode in past 12 months	5.30 (.21)	2.43 (.48)#	*2.13 (1.17)#	2.71 (.80)#	*2.89 (1.30)
Had hay fever in past 12 months	9.77 (.31)	6.99 (.77)#	*4.74 (1.89)#	8.23 (1.65)	*7.09 (2.26)
Had respiratory allergy in past 12 months	13.26 (.33)	7.19 (.71)#	8.52 (2.32)#	7.61 (2.02)#	*6.25 (2.25)#
Had food/digestive or eczema/skin allergy in past 12 months	12.24 (.30)	7.97 (.79)#	7.71 (1.83)#	11.99 (2.14)	*5.70 (1.99)#

Ever told_had a learning disability	6.50 (.27)	2.93 (.42)#	*1.87 (1.12)#	*.55 (.35)#	*1.67 (1.19)#
Ever told_had ADHD/ADD	4.34 (.26)	1.17 (.25)#	*.79 (.56)#	*.61 (.39)#	*1.39 (1.08)#
≤5 missing school days in past 12 months (age 5–17)	81.66 (.43)	90.57 (1.06)#	85.04 (3.37)	92.50 (1.71)#	86.03 (4.35)
Prescription medication for 3+ months for current health problem	13.69 (.31)	5.24 (.55)#	5.51 (1.93)#	5.29 (1.14)#	5.57 (2.04)#
Health insurance coverage					
Private coverage	88.84 (.40)	85.00 (1.19)#	90.56 (2.73)	89.92 (2.30)	83.81 (3.32)
Medicaid	1.69 (.18)	1.23 (.19)#	*3.44 (1.49)	*.98 (.41)	*2.60 (1.24)
Other coverage	3.29 (.29)	1.13 (.24)#	*.36 (.30)#	*.26 (.12)#	*1.23 (.74)#
Uninsured	6.18 (.25)	12.65 (1.10)#	5.64 (1.85)	8.84 (2.16)	12.36 (2.94)#
Saw/spoke to health professional in past 12 months	93.52 (.22)	90.49 (.81)#	91.13 (2.40)	89.52 (2.06)	93.79 (1.94)
Has usual place of health care when sick	97.80 (.14)	96.25 (.52)#	94.71 (1.86)	96.83 (.0087)	95.44 (1.69)
Two or more ER visits in 12 months	93.97 (.22)	94.27 (.69)	95.00 (1.51)	95.13 (1.50)	95.83 (1.67)
Saw/talked to dentist in past 12 months (age 5–17 years)	86.51 (.54)	85.62 (1.54)	89.88 (4.17)	81.87 (4.01)	95.11 (2.72)#

Note: (1) Values in the cell are mean (standard error) of frequency of "yes" (event) in percent. (2) SUDAAN Proc Rlogist and Proc Multilog were used in computation of logistic, cumulative logistic, and multinomial regression models. Estimates were adjusted for age, gender, race/ethnicity, and parents' education. *P*-values < .05 are considered statistically significant.

[a] includes Mexico, Central America, the Caribbean Islands, and South America.

[b] includes Europe and Russia and other former USSR areas.

[c] includes East Asia South–East Asia and the Indian Subcontinent.

[d] includes the Middle East, Africa, and other countries and regions.

* indicates the estimate has a relative standard error of greater than 30% and should be used with caution as they do not meet the standard of reliability or precision.

# indicates the mean under a specific foreign born region is significantly different from that in the US native group.

119

be interpreted with caution. Generally, the results indicate similarities among the immigrant groups in how they compare to the native children. For example, for specific health conditions and use of prescription medication, the immigrant children from the various regional backgrounds had a similarly low prevalence compared to the children of natives—roughly a half of the native rate or lower. However, the immigrant children from European and Asian backgrounds had worse health than the native children, while the children who had parents from Mexico, Central and South America, and the Caribbean Islands had the same health status as the native children. When change in health status was considered, more immigrant children who had parents from Mexico, Central and South America, the Caribbean Islands, and Asia reported better health than the native children, while the children of European parents had the same improvement in health as the native children. The immigrant children who had parents from Mexico, Central and South America, and the Caribbean Islands were less likely than the native children to have health insurance and a regular place of health care and to have seen/talked to a health professional in the past 12 months; other immigrant groups did not differ from the natives on these indicators. On the other hand, school attendance (missing 5 or fewer school days) was higher among the children who had parents from Mexico, Central and South America, and the Caribbean Islands (91%) and from Asia (93%), compared with the native children (82%).

Immigrant versus Native Black Children

Table 8.4 compares the native white and black non-Hispanic children to the immigrant children. Estimates for all children as well as children who were "poor" and "near poor" are shown for each racial group. The results again indicate that the native children had a higher prevalence of various health problems and worse school attendance than the immigrant children. However, there were significant racial disparities among the native children. The prevalence of asthma, asthma attacks, food/skin allergies, and prescription medication use was higher among the black children than among the white children. General health status was also lower among the black children, and especially low among the black children who were "poor" or "near poor." On the other hand, hay fever, respiratory allergies, and ADHD/ADD were more prevalent among the white children. Interestingly, the native white children were somewhat more likely to report worse health and less likely to report better health than a year ago compared with both the native black children and the immigrant children.

In contrast to health status, the immigrant children were less likely to have health insurance than the white or the black children. The percentage of children who were uninsured was especially high among the immigrant children who were "poor" or "near poor"—35 percent versus 21 percent among their native white and black counterparts. A similar immigrant disadvantage was noted for medical encounter, regular place of health care, and ER and dental visits. That is, the immigrant poor children were less likely than their native white and black counterparts to have seen/talked to a health professional in the past 12 months, to have a regular place of health care, to have two or more ER visits in the past 12 months, and to have

Table 8.4
Health and Health Care of US Children by Immigrant Status and Race

| | Immigrant Children | | US Native Children | | | |
| | | | Non-Hispanic White | | Non-Hispanic Black | |
Variable	Total	FPL < 200%	Total	FPL < 200%	Total	FPL < 200%
General health status						
Excellent	54.72 (.96)	48.04 (1.53)	62.04 (.52)#	53.32 (1.21)#	49.17 (1.42)#&	40.56 (1.74)#&
Very good	30.52 (.59)	33.72 (.75)	26.61 (.43)#	31.38 (.69)#	33.04 (.71)#&	36.23 (.82)#&
Good	13.41 (.47)	16.50 (.83)	10.35 (.23)#	13.88 (.59)#	16.10 (.75)#&	20.87 (1.65)#&
Fair	1.19 (.08)	1.51 (.12)	.88 (.05)#	1.23 (.09)#	1.47 (.12)#&	2.03 (.25)#&
Poor	.17 (.02)	.23 (.04)	.13 (.02)#	.18 (.03)#	.21 (.03)#&	.31 (.05)#&
Health better, about the same, or worse than 12 months ago						
Better	27.78 (.87)	28.72 (1.20)	19.88 (.43)#	20.55 (1.03)#	26.81 (1.19)&	22.76 (2.11)#
About the same	71.08 (.82)	70.20 (1.14)	78.37 (.44)#	77.78 (.95)#	71.99 (1.13)&	75.77 (1.95)#
Worse	1.14 (.09)	1.08 (.10)	1.76 (.11)#	1.67 (.14)#	1.20 (.10)&	1.47 (.20)#
Ever been told that __ had asthma	6.99 (.56)	6.53 (.70)	10.66 (.33)#	12.63 (.79)#	15.11 (.97)#&	14.22 (1.76)#
Had an asthma episode in past 12 months	2.58 (.33)	1.66 (.30)	5.11 (.23)#	5.25 (.53)#	7.30 (.69)#&	7.54 (1.30)#
Had hay fever in past 12 months	6.66 (.52)	5.96 (.65)	10.42 (.34)#	10.34 (.70)#	7.89 (.78)&	7.81 (1.43)
Had respiratory allergy in past 12 months	6.65 (.54)	5.11 (.59)	13.94 (.37)#	14.23 (.91)#	11.87 (.92)#&	8.00 (1.38)#&
Had food/digestive or eczema/skin allergy in past 12 months	8.80 (.61)	5.73 (.67)	12.17 (.35)#	12.81 (.93)#	15.30 (1.02)#&	13.22 (1.81)#
Ever told __ had a learning disability	2.01 (.23)	2.73 (.38)	6.74 (.31)#	9.10 (.78)#	6.20 (.58)#	10.97 (1.51)#
Ever told __ had ADHD/ADD	.79 (.15)	.78 (.19)	4.87 (.30)#	5.94 (.72)#	3.25 (.45)#&	4.43 (.92)#

(continued)

Table 8.4
(continued)

Variable	Immigrant Children		US Native Children			
			Non-Hispanic White		Non-Hispanic Black	
	Total	FPL < 200%	Total	FPL < 200%	Total	FPL < 200%
≤5 missing school days in past 12 months (age 5–17)	91.29 (.73)	91.57 (.89)	80.31 (.50)[#]	76.01 (1.39)[#]	86.41 (1.15)[#&]	80.81 (2.28)[#]
Prescription medication for 3+ months for a current health problem	4.46 (.39)	3.79 (.47)	14.70 (.36)[#]	15.98 (.97)[#]	12.29 (.90)[#]	15.38 (1.61)[#]
Health insurance coverage						
Private coverage	83.84 (.85)	51.76 (1.74)	89.91 (.41)[#]	63.40 (1.44)[#]	86.65 (1.21)[#&]	58.13 (2.86)
Medicaid	1.99 (.30)	11.01 (1.29)	1.48 (.16)[#]	10.80 (.87)	2.05 (.38)	13.14 (1.88)
Other coverage	1.13 (.20)	1.72 (.34)	2.82 (.28)[#]	5.04 (.73)[#]	5.05 (.83)[#&]	7.68 (1.73)[#]
Uninsured	13.04 (.74)	35.50 (1.63)	5.79 (.29)[#]	20.76 (1.21)[#]	6.25 (.69)[#]	21.05 (3.09)[#]
Saw/spoke to health professional in past 12 months	88.91 (.59)	83.82 (1.15)	93.98 (.24)[#]	91.76 (.70)[#]	92.79 (.67)[#]	92.11 (1.25)[#]
Has usual place of healthcare when sick	94.25 (.47)	88.44 (1.05)	98.16 (.14)[#]	96.31 (.40)[#]	97.08 (.38)[#&]	94.87 (.97)[#]
Two or more ER visits in 12 months	95.11 (.43)	94.33 (.61)	93.89 (.25)[#]	91.62 (.68)[#]	92.59 (.75)[#]	93.31 (.90)[#]
Saw/talked to dentist in past 12 months (age 5–17 years)	82.87 (1.19)	73.77 (2.05)	87.82 (.55)[#]	79.56 (1.45)[#]	83.90 (1.74)[&]	81.34 (2.85)[#]

Note: (1) Values in the cell are mean (standard error) of frequency of "yes" (event) in percent. (2) SUDAAN Proc Rlogist and Proc Multilog were used in computation of logistic, cumulative logistic, and multinomial regression models. Estimates were adjusted for age, gender, race/ethnicity, and parents' education. P-values < .05 are considered statistically significant.

[#] indicates the mean of a native parent subgroup (non–Hispanic white or non–Hispanic black) is significantly different from that in the immigrant group.

[&] indicates the means of two native groups (non–Hispanic white and non–Hispanic black) are significantly different.

[*] indicates the estimate has a relative standard error of greater than 30% and should be used with caution as they do not meet the standard of reliability or precision.

seen/talked to a dentist in the past 12 months. Although the black children generally fared worse in terms of health care than the white children, the black and the white children who were "poor" or "near poor" appeared equally disadvantaged.

Hispanic Ethnicity

Finally, we compared children of various Hispanic backgrounds based on native-immigrant status (Table 8.5). We found that despite lower prevalence of various health problems, the Mexican/Mexican American immigrant children had lower general health and more limited access to health care than their native counterparts. For example, 45 percent of the Mexican/Mexican American immigrant children were uninsured versus 21 percent of their native counterparts. They were also less likely to have seen/spoken to a health professional and dentist in the past 12 months and to have a regular place of health care than the Mexican/Mexican American children from native families. Similar patterns but fewer differences were noted between the immigrant and the native Puerto Rican, Cuban/Cuban American, and Dominican children. Interestingly, the immigrant children of Central/South American heritage were more likely to report better health now than 12 months ago than their native counterparts. However, they were more likely than the natives to be uninsured and less likely to have a regular source of health care.

DISCUSSION

Our findings complement the current literature on the health and health care of children of immigrants in the United States. Notably, our findings are consistent with a 1998 report, which showed that children of immigrants generally have better health status and fewer health problems than U.S.-born children.[41] Our results, thus, do not support the immigrant disadvantage in health status that is reported in two recent studies.[42,43] While those studies focused on mental and social well-being, our emphasis was on specific medical conditions and overall health. It is possible that children of immigrants are still "protected" by immigrant selection (process in which the healthy individuals migrate), and thus show fewer specific health problems. On the other hand, children of immigrants are less likely to see medical providers and, therefore, may be less likely to be diagnosed with a certain medical condition. Future longitudinal studies that assess children of immigrants at baseline, or entry to the United States, and follow them over time, in terms of both health and health-care assessment, may be able to show the effects of immigrant selection versus health-care utilization on the health status of children of immigrants.

Our results also support previous studies which showed that children of immigrants are more likely to lack health insurance[44–47] and access to health and dental services.[48,49] We were able to take a step further by looking more closely at the contribution of poverty, parental region of birth, and racial/ethnic background to the health status and health care of children from native and immigrant families. Our study provides more evidence that the intersection of two or more types of disadvantage, for example, poverty and immigrant or racial and/or ethnic minority status,

Table 8.5
Health and Health Care of US Children by Immigrant Status and Hispanic Ethnicity

	US Native Children				Immigrant Children			
Variable	(A)	(B)	(C)	(D)	(A)	(B)	(C)	(D)
General health status								
Excellent	49.26 (1.43)	53.07 (2.45)	59.00 (4.11)	52.94 (3.44)	40.86 (1.17)$^{#}$	53.68 (2.87)	53.78 (2.19)	46.27 (5.23)
Very good	29.73 (.83)	28.34 (1.11)	25.79 (2.00)	28.39 (1.47)	31.93 (.73)$^{#}$	28.10 (1.29)	28.06 (1.02)	30.66 (1.64)
Good	19.13 (.86)	16.97 (1.39)	13.94 (1.99)	17.04 (1.90)	24.58 (.98)$^{#}$	16.64 (1.57)	16.59 (1.27)	20.95 (3.29)
Fair	1.67 (.16)	1.43 (.18)	1.13 (.20)	1.44 (.23)	2.32 (.20)$^{#}$	1.40 (.19)	1.39 (.16)	1.87 (.42)
Poor	.22 (.04)	.19 (.04)	.15 (.03)	.19 (.04)	.30 (.05)$^{#}$	.18 (.04)	.18 (.03)	.24 (.07)
Health better, about the same, or worse than 12 months ago								
Better	24.36 (1.23)	27.36 (2.29)	18.66 (3.18)	22.95 (2.65)	26.99 (.94)	28.09 (2.61)	32.49 (2.11)$^{#}$	24.96 (5.08)
About the same	73.64 (1.15)	70.93 (2.10)	78.56 (2.63)	74.89 (2.37)	71.26 (.89)	70.25 (2.40)	66.16 (1.98)$^{#}$	73.10 (4.58)
Worse	2.00 (.22)	1.71 (.26)	2.78 (.63)	2.16 (.37)	1.75 (.19)	1.65 (.28)	1.35 (.20)$^{#}$	1.94 (.54)
Ever been told that had asthma	10.20 (.81)	17.83 (2.01)	11.60 (2.43)	10.43 (2.13)	4.55 (.47)$^{#}$	15.96 (1.90)	7.07 (1.00)	*5.32 (1.76)
Had an asthma episode in past 12 months	3.74 (.48)	8.83 (1.76)	*2.61 (1.14)	*4.26 (1.29)	1.33 (.26)$^{#}$	4.61 (1.19)	1.74 (.40)	*3.66 (1.57)
Had hay fever in past 12 months	8.07 (.75)	5.36 (1.18)	*4.67 (1.44)	12.56 (2.46)	5.66 (.57)$^{#}$	4.18 (1.13)	6.28 (.96)	*5.64 (1.97)$^{#}$
Had respiratory allergy in past 12 months	9.85 (.88)	9.24 (1.53)	7.77 (2.19)	7.90 (1.73)	5.59 (.52)$^{#}$	5.63 (1.37)	5.30 (.86)	*3.03 (1.38)$^{#}$
Had food/digestive or eczema/skin allergy in past 12 months	8.69 (.67)	12.40 (1.84)	10.53 (2.58)	15.32 (2.68)	5.14 (.45)$^{#}$	5.01 (1.29)$^{#}$	7.58 (1.14)	7.42 (2.29)$^{#}$

Ever told_had a learning disability							
5.68 (.72)	10.06 (2.01)	*4.30 (1.87)	*3.84 (1.61)	2.69 (.41)#	5.10 (1.32)#	2.90 (.75)	*4.22 (2.48)
Ever told_had ADHD/ADD							
3.13 (.52)	5.25 (1.17)	*4.09 (1.78)	*1.27 (.73)	.69 (.15)#	*2.19 (.96)#	*1.45 (.54)	*3.13 (1.91)
≤5 missing school days in past 12 months (age 5–17)							
82.61 (1.25)	77.37 (3.26)	89.69 (3.46)	74.37 (4.09)	90.11 (.77)#	88.59 (2.33)#	88.92 (1.66)	83.63 (4.83)
Prescription medication for 3+ months for a current health problem							
8.10 (.66)	14.17 (1.86)	7.32 (1.94)	7.98 (2.19)	3.65 (.33)#	5.52 (1.77)#	4.78 (.93)	*6.23 (2.66)
Health insurance coverage							
Private coverage							
66.95 (1.33)	76.96 (3.84)	79.25 (3.25)		44.02 (1.47)#	64.54 (3.16)#	56.06 (2.38)#	62.54 (5.54)#
Medicaid							
9.38 (.97)	9.00 (1.35)	*3.76 (1.56)	*5.54 (1.77)	9.64 (.82)	13.19 (2.48)	7.68 (1.07)#	5.62 (2.55)
Other coverage							
3.21 (.49)	4.15 (1.10)	*3.96 (1.94)	*4.08 (1.44)	1.39 (.26)#	*4.26 (1.38)#	1.42 (.36)	*.38 (.41)
Uninsured							
20.46 (1.34)	11.96 (1.92)	15.33 (3.25)	11.13 (2.29)	44.95 (1.40)#	18.00 (2.43)#	34.84 (2.32)#	31.45 (5.35)#
Saw/spoke to health professional in past 12 months							
88.90 (.73)	92.69 (1.37)	90.77 (2.96)	94.55 (1.53)	80.57 (1.00)#	88.26 (1.92)	88.36 (1.25)	88.50 (3.05)
Has usual place of healthcare when sick							
93.24 (.68)	98.08 (.80)	96.37 (1.65)	96.75 (1.24)	88.62 (.85)#	92.78 (1.29)#	88.33 (1.49)#	91.77 (3.49)
Two or more ER visits in 12 months							
94.54 (.56)	91.44 (1.53)	95.04 (1.86)	93.83 (1.51)	95.22 (.52)	92.04 (1.61)	93.43 (.93)	88.28 (2.97)
Saw/talked to dentist in past 12 months (age 5–17)							
74.89 (1.76)	72.22 (4.11)	74.24 (6.93)	81.55 (5.80)	68.50 (1.52)#	80.25 (4.52)	74.35 (2.97)	81.86 (5.26)

Note: (1) Values in the cell are mean (standard error) of frequency of "yes" (event) in percent. (2) SUDAAN Proc Rlogist and Proc Multilog were used in computation of logistic, cumulative logistic, and multinomial regression models. Estimates were adjusted for age, gender, race/ethnicity, and parents' eductation. P-values < .05 are considered statistically significant. (3) Column headings are as follows: (A) Mexican & Mexican American; (B) Puerto Rican, Cuban/Cuban American & Dominican (Republic); (C) Central or South American; and (D) Others.

# indicates two means under the same ethnic subgroups are significantly different.

* indicates the estimate has a relative standard error of greater than 30% and should be used with caution as they do not meet the standard of reliability or precision.

is associated with an especially high risk of having poor health and limited access to health care. However, considering specific constellations of statuses is crucial to identify the most vulnerable groups on various health-related outcomes. For example, children from low-income and Mexican/Mexican American immigrant families are the most vulnerable among U.S. children in regard to health care, while black children from low-income native families have the lowest health status. These findings provide specific direction for public policy and interventions as to which groups to target to improve the health status and health-care access among U.S. children.

There are some methodological differences between our study and the previous studies, which may have contributed to some variation in findings. First, the studies use different data sources and samples. Our estimates of health and health-care indicators are consistent with other reports using recent NHIS data, including any variations by racial/ethnic status.[50] Thus, we have confidence in our analyses. A second source of variation among the current studies (including our findings) is the definition of immigrant status. Some of the previous studies have defined immigrant status of children based on parental U.S. citizenship status or have considered an immigrant family one in which at least one parent was foreign-born.[51,52] We used parental place of birth as an indication of immigrant status and defined immigrant family as one where both parents are foreign-born, and thus be potentially most vulnerable.

Interestingly, while focusing on the potentially most vulnerable group, we found that group showing relatively few health problems. At the same time, a more in-depth analysis by parental region of birth and by race and ethnicity showed considerably more variation in health status among children from immigrant families. This leads us to believe that specific ethnicity and culture play an important role in how health is assessed. That is, ratings of health may be higher in some cultures and lower in other cultures. Culturally based somatization of health and illness is widely discussed in the literature; for example, Hispanic adults have been shown to provide lower self-rated health scores than Anglo adults with similar objective measures of health.[53]

Our study has several limitations. The data are cross-sectional providing only a snapshot of the health situation of U.S. children at one point in time. A longitudinal design would be more powerful to observe the effects of poverty and immigration on the health of U.S. children. At least, our data are based on 3 survey years, and, as such, reflect a broader time span. We are also concerned about possible selection bias—that due to the sampling procedures, illegal immigrants and individuals with the lowest income and the poorest health are likely to be excluded from the survey. Thus, the data probably under-represent the two populations of most interest in this study: poor children and children of immigrants. In addition, the foreign-born population is confined to a limited number of regional categories, which may contain little to a great deal of cultural variation (e.g., Mexico, Central America, and the Caribbean Islands). Although more data are needed to describe this variation, some general patterns emerge from this study based on the broader immigrant categories. Finally, our study was limited in scope and focused on several variables of interest. Additional analyses are possible with these data. For example, other indicators of health and health care can be examined (e.g., other health conditions, immunizations, health behaviors, or specialist visits).

All in all, our study provides additional evidence regarding the health status and health care among U.S. children based on immigrant status, family income, and racial/ethnic background. Future work should continue focusing on multiple health and health-care indicators and on various subpopulations of children to pinpoint more precisely where the greatest disparities exist and to design appropriate interventions. Cultural diversity and generational changes in the immigrant population must also be considered in further research, public policy, and clinical work.

NOTES

1. Jennifer Van Hook. "Poverty Grows among Children of Immigrants in US." Washington, DC: Migration Policy Institute, 2004.

2. Yuval Elmelech, Katie McCaskie, Mary Clare Lemon, and Hsien-Hen Lu. "Children of Immigrants: A Statistical Profile (September 2002)." New York: National Center for Children in Poverty, 2002.

3. Michael E. Fix, Wendy Zimmerman, and Jeffrey S. Passel. *The Integration of Immigrant Families in the United States.* Washington, DC: The Urban Institute, 2001.

4. Van Hook, op. cit.

5. Richard G. Wilkinson. *Unhealthy Societies: The Afflictions of Inequality.* London; New York: Routledge, 1996.

6. Richard G. Wilkinson. *The Impact of Inequality: How to Make Sick Societies Healthier.* New York: New Press: Distributed by W.W. Norton, 2005.

7. G. K. Singh and B. A. Miller. "Health, Life Expectancy and Mortality Patterns among Immigrant Populations in the United States." *Can J Public Health* 95(3) (2004): 114–121.

8. G. K. Singh and M. Siahpush. "All-Cause and Cause-Specific Mortality of Immigrants and Native Born in the United States." *Am J Public Health* 91(3) (2001): 392–399.

9. G. K. Singh and M. Siahpush. "Ethnic-Immigrant Differentials in Health Behaviors, Morbidity, and Cause-Specific Mortality in the United States: An Analysis of Two National Data Bases." *Hum Biol* 74(1) (2002): 83–109.

10. G. K. Singh and Stella M. Yu. "Infant Mortality in the United States: Trends, Differentials, and Projections, 1950 through 2010." *Am J Public Health* 85(7) (1995): 957–964.

11. G. K. Singh and Stella M. Yu. "Adverse Pregnancy Outcomes: Differences between US- and Foreign-Born Women in Major US Racial and Ethnic Groups." *Am J Public Health* 86(6) (1996): 837–843.

12. Donald J. Hernandez and Evan Charney, eds. *From Generation to Generation: The Health and Well-Being of Children in Immigrant Families.* Washington, DC: National Academy Press, 1998.

13. Zhihuan J. Huang, Stella M. Yu, and Rebecca Ledsky. "Health Status and Health Service Access and Use among Children in U.S. Immigrant Families." *Am J Public Health* 96(4) (2006): 634–640.

14. Jane Reardon-Anderson, Randy Capps, and Michael Fix. "The Health and Well-Being of Children in Immigrant Families." *New Federalism: National Survey of America's Families* Vol. Series B, no. No. B-52 (2002).

15. Huang, Yu, and Ledsky, op. cit.

16. Hernandez and Charney, op. cit.

17. Huang, Yu, and Ledsky, op. cit.

18. Reardon-Anderson, Capps, and Fix, op. cit.

19. Achintya N. Dey and Jacqueline Wilson Lucas. "Physical and Mental Health Characteristics of U.S.- and Foreign-Born Adults: United States, 1998–2003. Advance Data from Vital Health Statistics; no. 369." Hyatsville, MD: National Center for Health Statistics 2006.

20. G. Flores, E. Fuentes-Afflick, O. Barbor, O. Carter-Pokras, L. Claudio, M. Lara, J. A. McLaurin, L. Pachter, F. J. Ramos-Gomez, F. Mendoza, R. B. Valdez, A. M. Villarruel, R. E. Zambrana, R. Greenberg, and M. Weitzman. "The Health of Latino Children: Urgent Priorities, Unanswered Questions, and a Research Agenda." *JAMA* 288(1) (2002): 82–90.

21. Michael Seid, Donna Castaneda, Ronald Mize, Mirjana Zivkovic, and James W. Varni. "Crossing the Border for Health Care: Access and Primary Care Characteristics for Young Children of Latino Farm Workers Along the US-Mexico Border." *Ambul Pediatr* 3(3) (2003): 121–130.

22. Wilkinson, 1996, op. cit.

23. Wilkinson, 2005, op. cit.

24. Van Hook, op. cit.

25. Hernandez and Charney, op. cit.

26. I. Harry Minas and Susan M. Sawyer. "The Mental Health of Immigrant and Refugee Children and Adolescents." *Med J Aust* 177(8) (2002): 404–405.

27. Hernandez and Charney, op. cit.

28. Hernandez and Charney, op. cit.

29. Lauren Clark and Lisa Hofsess. "Acculturation." In *Handbook of Immigrant Health,* edited by Sana Loue, 37–59. New York, NY: Plenum Press, 1998.

30. Hernandez and Charney, op. cit.

31. National Center for Health Statistics. "Data File Documentation, National Interview Survey, 2003 (Machine Readable Data File and Documentation)." Hyattsville, Maryland: National Center for Health Statistics, Centers for Disease Control and Prevention, 2004.

32. B. Bloom and A. N. Dey. "Summary Health Statistics." Hyattsville, MD: National Center for Health Statistics, 2006.

33. Agency for Healthcare Research and Quality. "Child Health Research Findings. Program Brief." Rockville, MD: Agency for Healthcare Research and Quality, April 2005.

34. National Center for Health Statistics. "Data File Documentation, National Health Interview Surveys, 2001 (Machine Readable Data Files and Documentation)." Hyattsville, MD: National Center for Health Statistics, 2002.

35. Bloom and Dey, op. cit.

36. Dey and Lucas, op. cit.

37. Bloom and Dey, op. cit.

38. Van Hook, op. cit.

39. Elmelech et al., op. cit.

40. Reardon-Anderson et al., op. cit.

41. Hernandez and Charney, op. cit.

42. Huang, Yu, and Ledsky, op. cit.

43. Reardon-Anderson et al., op. cit.

44. Huang, Yu, and Ledsky, op. cit.

45. Michael E. Fix and Jeffrey S. Passel. "Trends in Noncitizens' and Citizens' Use of Public Benefits Following Welfare Reform: 1994–97." Washington, DC: Urban Institute, 1999.

46. Kaiser Commission on Medicaid and Uninsured. "Immigrants' Health Care: Coverage and Access." Washington, DC: Kaiser Commission on Medicaid and the Uninsured, 2000.

47. Wendy Zimmerman and Michael E. Fix. "Declining Immigrant Applications for Medical and Welfare Benefits in Los Angeles County." Washington, DC: Urban Institute, 1998.

48. S. M. Yu, H. A. Bellamy, M. D. Kogan, J. L. Dunbar, R. H. Schwalberg, and M. A. Schuster. "Factors That Influence Receipt of Recommended Preventive Pediatric Health and Dental Care." *Pediatrics* 110(6) (2002): e73.

49. S. M. Yu, H. A. Bellamy, R. H. Schwalberg, and M. A. Drum. "Factors Associated with Use of Preventive Dental and Health Services among U.S. Adolescents." *J Adolesc Health* 29(6) (2001): 395–405.

50. Bloom and Dey, op. cit.

51. Huang, Yu, and Ledsky, op. cit.

52. Reardon-Anderson et al., op. cit.

53. S. M. Shetterly, J. Baxter, L. D. Mason, and R. F. Hamman. "Self-Rated Health among Hispanic vs. Non-Hispanic White Adults: The San Luis Valley Health and Aging Study." *Am J Public Health* 86(12) (1996): 1798–1801.

CHAPTER 9

IMMIGRANT CHILDREN
IN POVERTY

Uma A. Segal, Zubin N. Segal,
and Anu R. Diwakaran

Census 2000 indicates that one of four people in the United States was born outside its borders, with substantial numbers having entered after the liberalization of immigration laws in 1965, consequently, U.S. society is becoming increasingly aware of ethnic and cultural differences between immigrants, particularly those of color, and the native-born populations. Interest in understanding attitudes, values, religions, and behaviors is reflected in the burgeoning literature on immigrants and refugees. Social service agencies have often had to mediate between immigrants and U.S. institutions as newcomers learn to adapt to their new environments. In the process, the environment has begun to become sensitized to the diversity of the new arrivals.

Less focus has been placed on the systematic understanding of the socioeconomic levels of these immigrant groups and their implications for adaptation and achievement. Based on the allocation of immigration visas, there have been a variety of legal immigrant streams that have entered the United States in the last few decades. While earlier immigrants of the 1960s were, primarily of a professional stream, current streams are more likely to include large numbers entering through family reunification processes. These individuals and groups may not have the human capital and skills that are readily transferable into the fast-paced technological society. Consequently, the promised "land of milk and honey" may not be so for them.

Two additional populations to the United States, refugees and undocumented immigrants, may find that they are frequently on the fringes of society—the former for a significant portion of their lives, and the latter, almost for their entire stay in the United States. Thus, a large segment of the immigrant group, particularly the newer immigrants of the last decade, is likely to be marginalized. Without the requisite English language competencies, education, and usable job skills, many hover at poverty levels.

The census data and the records of the continuing inflow of newcomers, furthermore, suggest that a large number of immigrant families are entering with dependent children.[1] Although the importance of cultural competence cannot be overemphasized and is relevant for understanding these populations, as significant is recognition that immigrants in poverty face unique difficulties—perhaps distinct from those of the native-born population—and their children may be especially vulnerable.

This chapter explores implications of immigrant child poverty for academic success, mental health, and health-care access. Following institutional review board approval, elementary quantitative data from a local pediatric health clinic, Glennon Care Pediatrics, provide examples of the current and relevant experience of immigrant families in poverty. Guidelines for intervention are presented.

FOREIGN-BORN POPULATION

The 2003 population survey of the U.S. Census[2] indicates that of the 286 million residents in the United States, approximately 34 million (12%) are foreign born. Of the foreign born, 4.6 million are from Europe, 8.4 million from Asia, 17.8 million from Latin America, and 2.7 million from other regions, including Africa. Estimates suggest that approximately 9.3 million, in addition, are in the nation without the requisite papers.[3] Newcomers to the United States enter under a variety of conditions. Early migrants of the nineteenth and early twentieth centuries came as volunteer immigrants, indentured laborers, or as slaves. Most however, were considered "legal immigrants," particularly in the absence of any legislation. Present-day immigrants may be categorized as voluntary immigrants (legal or undocumented) or as refugees (and asylees). Several legal voluntary immigrants or refugees, after a minimum length of residence in the country, choose to apply for U.S. citizenship.

The 1965 Immigration and Nationality Act (INA), despite minor modifications, continues to set the guidelines for annual quotas of immigrants into the country, with a family-sponsored preference limit of 226,000 and for employment-based preference immigrants of at least 140,000. The 2006 quota for family-sponsored preference, however, is 480,000. The INA, furthermore, allocates another 55,000 diversity visas for individuals from countries not represented by the above quotas.[4] A substantial number of legal immigrants include those not subject to these numerical limits—relatives of U.S. citizens and children born abroad to permanent residents. In 2004, this number was approximately 407,000.[5]

Among those who voluntarily migrate to the United States are immigrants without the requisite papers, the undocumented population. While there is no valid method of counting undocumented immigrants, estimates suggest a number as high as 9.2 million,[6] and it is believed that this number grows at a rate of 500,000 individuals annually.[7] Even more recent estimates report numbers as high as 12 million.[8] These are people who are in the United States without governmental approval and are often described as economic refugees, but are not so recognized by the United Nations High Commissioner for Refugees. Although undocumented immigrants lack the legal documentation to be residing in the United States, they may have entered the country legally or illegally. Despite perceptions of undocumented immigrants being those who slip across borders without appropriate documentation, the Immigration and Naturalization Service stated that a large proportion (about 41%) of all undocumented immigrants, particularly from Asian countries, are "overstays" who fail to return to their homelands when the period of their visas expires.[9]

Refugees and asylees, unlike immigrants, are usually involuntary migrants. The United States has always been a refuge for those fleeing from persecution and, traditionally, has the largest number of the world's refugees.[10] According to the definition presented in the 1951 convention and the 1967 protocol setting forth the mandate of the United Nations High Commissioner for Refugees, refugees are persons who are outside their homelands and are unable to return because of fear of persecution. The U.S. president, in consultation with Congress, can establish annual numbers and allocations of refugees based on the current political climate of the world. In recent years, these annual numbers have been as high as 91,000 in 1999 and as low as 70,000 in 2005 and 2006.[11] Asylees differ from refugees in that they usually enter the United States on their own volition without prior approval. Once within the United States, they apply for asylum, which may or may not result in an admission under refugee status. They are detained until a determination is made, at which time, they are either legally admitted into the country as refugees or are repatriated to their homelands. Refugees may apply to adjust their status to permanent resident after a year.

In throwback fashion to earlier migration periods of the early twentieth century, the nation is beginning to see three more groups of migrants—victims of human smuggling, victims of human trafficking, and mail-order brides. Those smuggled into the country pay a substantial price to enter the country clandestinely, and once in the United States find they are burdened with debt and have few employment opportunities. Victims of human trafficking, on the other hand, continue to be exploited for illicit reasons and are enslaved to those who bring them into the country.[12] Finally, the mail-order bride market is burgeoning, with 590,000 Web sites catering to a growing clientele.[13] Mail-order brides are usually women from developing countries who register with a catalogue or Web site their intent to marry foreign men. Usually there is no period of courtship, and marriages take place in absentia, with the man having "shopped" for the wife who fits his needs. These women, then, enter the country legally as the wives of U.S. citizens.

CHILDREN OF IMMIGRANTS

Children of immigrants, either by birth or by migration, are the fastest growing segment of the children population in the United States. While most immigrant families include both citizen and noncitizen parents, more than 70 percent of the children of immigrants are citizens. Immigrants compose approximately 11 percent of the total population in the country; however, immigrant children under the age of 6 years are 22 percent of the child population, and, overall, one in five children under the age of 18 years is in an immigrant family. Furthermore, 4.7 million of these children have undocumented immigrant parents, and about 1.6 are, themselves, undocumented.[14] Census data indicate that of the 36 million and 37 million people living below the poverty line in 2003 and 2004 respectively, 20 percent were foreign born; 80 percent of the foreign born in poverty was not naturalized.[15] Thus, children of immigrants, particularly of recent immigrants and of undocumented immigrants are more likely to be living in poverty than are children of native-born parents. Furthermore, immigrant children more likely than native-born children to (1) be poor, (2) be at risk for poverty even if their parents work full time, (3) be in poverty even with parents with high school degrees, and (4) be poor despite living in two-parent homes.[16]

The American Psychological Association (APA) in 1998 adopted the APA Resolution on Immigrant Children, Youth, and Families, continues in 2006 to recognize the unique issues faced by this group in the United States.[17] Research cited in the document supports its statements that

- the experience of immigration is especially intense for the psychological and social well-being of children
- the unique stresses, prejudice, and poverty experienced by immigrants places their children at risk not only for health, emotional, and behavioral problems but also for learning and academic difficulties
- children of service workers from Asia and Haiti and migrant farm workers from Mexico and Central or South America often enter the migrant stream to work with their parents; few states set minimum age for farm labor
- health prevention, mental health, and social services are infrequently used, and
- executive and legislative initiatives periodically limit immigrants' civil rights and access to public benefits.

In addition, children of immigrants must early learn to become bicultural, for they must successfully function in the dominant American culture during the day, yet return to the cultural norms of their parents in the evening. Most must learn to negotiate their surroundings in a language that is not spoken in their homes.[18] Despite these difficulties many children face, immigrant families often come with significant strengths that enable them to navigate the morass of barriers. Children of immigrants, more often than children of native-born parents, are likely to live in two-parent families and are more likely to be born healthier.[19] Further, as most immigrant families come to the United States to pursue the *American Dream* and experience a second lease on life, they imbue their children with the importance of hard work and the significance of education. In fact, at least until adolescence, most tend to do better in school than the children of native-born parents.[20]

ACADEMIC SUCCESS

A 2001 issue of the *Harvard Educational Review* focused specifically on immigrant children, and studies revealed much that is generally understood, that low English language proficiency, difficulties associated with adaptation, discrimination, poverty, and low teacher expectations can have significant influence on academic achievement.[21] On the other hand, children in various immigrant groups differ in their levels of achievement; with children of Mexican immigrants frequently performing more poorly than do children of Asian or European immigrants. However, many of the former are highly resilient, and many overcome tremendous hurdles in order to succeed.[22]

MENTAL HEALTH

The experience of many immigrants and almost all refugees has been fraught with turmoil. Stereotypes about immigrants abound and range from the negative to the overwhelmingly positive, often ascribing to immigrants characteristics they do not possess. Furthermore, those who are political refugees bring with them a burden of horrendous experiences that others cannot begin to fathom and that may have resulted in major depressive and post traumatic stress disorders.[23] Many have been left with psychosocial problems that are compounded by the social, economic, and cultural distance between them and the U.S. society. This combination of difficulties has not only affected their personal adjustment but has wreaked havoc with long-established family roles and traditional patterns of interaction.

Studies of the mental health of immigrant children provide mixed results. While a number of studies suggest that children in immigrant families are at higher risk for mental health problems than are the children of U.S.-born parents[24] another has found that although foreign-born children were twice as likely as the native-born counterparts to be in poverty, the mental health and behavioral problems they evidenced were significantly lower.[25]

HEALTH AND HEALTH-CARE ACCESS

Concomitant with poverty is lack of adequate health insurance, and, hence, health-care access. The uninsured rate of immigrants (33.7%) is about 2.5 times that of native-born residents (13.3%); however, when broken further, it is clear that newer immigrants are highly vulnerable, with those who are not naturalized having an uninsured rate of 44.1 percent.[26] Socioeconomic status is a strong determinant of child well-being and is related to physical and mental health development, and frequently children of low-income immigrant families face substantial health disparities from those of their more affluent counterparts.[27]

U.S. health policy, which allows health coverage for many, but not for all, has particular implications for those in poverty, those who are near poverty, and those of low socioeconomic status and income, and those who are self-employed as are many immigrants. The last group is least likely to be able to afford private insurance coverage, yet it is ineligible for means-tested coverage, such as Medicaid. In addition, most immigrants are ineligible for public benefits in the first five years of their residence in the United States, making them more likely to leave curable illnesses untreated. Implications of health policy for immigrants are not limited to issues of coverage A number of other cultural and educational concerns confound their access to health-care services. Health policy must focus not only on who is covered but also on how services are utilized. Currently, general access to health-care services is fraught with problems for many immigrant groups, and the access problems are exacerbated by the implementation of the 1996 Federal Welfare Reform law (H.R. 3734). Responsibility and financial risk for immigrants have moved from the top level of government (federal) to the lowest level (county).[28] Under this structure, each county must ensure that its policies in delivering services reflect awareness of the unique needs of immigrant groups. Another essential component of effective health-care policy is research effort that recognizes the interaction of race, ethnicity, nativity, and health.[29] Health policy must also be driven by how, when, and why health services are used—or not used—because of a mix of cultural effects.

Invariably, the most vulnerable and dependent members of any group have access to the least resources. Policy makers must take into account the particular needs of children, the elderly, and those with disabilities among the immigrant populations. Multicultural awareness and policies that address the diversity of issues must be integrated into health-care policy so that not only is lack of insurance removed as a barrier to health service access, but so are cultural factors. In California, for example, many low-income women are unaware of their eligibility for Medi-Cal (California's equivalent of national Medicaid) and healthy-family programs, and an even larger proportion of immigrant women are unaware of, or intimated by, the system. Not only is there a high uninsured rate among immigrants in California, but even those who are eligible for public health care do not seek it because of the morass of paperwork required to qualify for eligibility and the unfounded fear of deportation. Women and children, more often than men, are likely to deprive themselves of health-care services under such conditions.[30] In addition, immigrants may be more suspicious of different treatment methods, uncomfortable with interaction patters with health-care providers. It is most important that those who are responsible for providing these services understand culturally based perceptions of medical care and physicians as well as the role of traditional medicine and how it dovetails with modern medicine. It is essential, further that translators be bicultural, for they must be able to adequately translate not only the language but also the meanings of events and communication, for a number of phenomena are unique to specific immigrant groups and their experience of illness and treatment must be understood within the cultural context.

EXPLORATORY STUDY OF PARENTAL PERCEPTIONS

To explore the experience of low-income immigrant families and to compare them with that of low-income U.S. native families, a pilot study sought responses from parents regarding their perceptions of their needs. The study began after it received Institutional Review Board approval from the two collaborating organizations—the University of Missouri-St. Louis and St. Joseph's Hospital in St. Charles, Missouri.

All parents who brought their children to a public pediatric health clinic (Glennon Care Pediatrics at St. Joseph's Hospital) over a 1-month period, were invited to participate in the study by anonymously completing a 15-minute, Likert-type questionnaire regarding their economic, social, physical, psychological, and health needs. Parents were recruited while they and their children were awaiting the physician in the examination room. After giving informed consent, they anonymously placed completed questionnaires in a sealed box. In the event that parents were unable to read or needed a translator, the questionnaire was read to them. It was estimated that approximately 20 percent of the patient pool of the clinic is of an immigrant group, and an average of 125 families are seen in the clinic on a weekly basis. Thus, 500 subjects were anticipated for inclusion in the study, however, only 289 subjects were treated at the clinic in the month of February 2006. Of the 289 potential subjects, 235 completed the questionnaire for a response rate of 81.3 percent.

Demographic information can be found in Table 9.1 which is presented based on immigrant status: 170 subjects self-identified as American (whose parents were born in the United States), 17 are second generation (who were born in the United States but whose parents are immigrants), and 30 are immigrants.

While there is a wide range in the ages, the highest concentration in age is from 21–30 years for all backgrounds. In addition, female respondents far outnumber male respondents in each group. Among the American subjects, the majority of respondents had some college education. The majority of second generation respondents had a high school diploma, and the majority of immigrants had less than a high school education. Most American subjects were from single households (never married), second generation subjects had more respondents that were married than were single (8:5), and immigrant subjects also had a greater ratio of married to single (10:8) families. The majority of American subjects had household with one child, while second generation subjects were more likely to have two children in their households, and immigrants had an equal number of respondents with one and two children in the family. Most American subjects earned $10,000 a year or less, the largest number of second generation respondents earned either $10,000 or between $21,000 and $30,000, and the majority of immigrants reported an annual income of between $11,000 and $20,000.

Data from the 35 item Likert-type questionnaire were coded and, when the factor analysis method of data reduction was applied, resulted in four underlying perceptual dimensions (factors) that could be identified as reflecting (1) antisocial behavior, (2) perceptions of helplessness, (3) perceptions of low levels of belongingness, and (4) poor financial resources. The three subject groups—Americans, second generation, and immigrants—were compared across the four dimensions. The analysis of variance procedure (ANOVA) was applied to the factor scores to statistically assess intergroup differences along the four factors that emerged. Using average perceptual dimension scores, a relative index was created for each dimension and for each group (Figure 9.1). These results are also supported by descriptive measures of surrogate variables for each of the perceptual dimensions.

Although the results of the ANOVA revealed that only Helplessness was statistically significant at $p \leq 05$, with the second generation evidencing more such feelings than either the American or the immigrant groups, because of the pilot nature of the study, it was considered important to also present the direction of other observed differences. A review of the directionality, rather than the magnitude, of the findings indicates

Table 9.1
Ethnicity $N = 235^a$

Demographics	American	2nd Generation	Immigrants	Total
Ethnicity				
White	151	11	9	170
African American	15	1	5	21
Hispanic	2	3	9	14
Asian	0	0	6	6
Middle Eastern	0	2	0	2
Other	3	0	1	2
Total	170	17	30	217^a
Age				
Less than 18 years	3	0	1	4
18–20 years	18	1	2	21
21–30 years	92	10	15	115
31–40 years	41	3	9	53
40 and above	19	3	2	24
Total	171	17	29	217^a
Gender				
Male	17	6	5	28
Female	153	9	23	185
Total	170	15	28	213^a
Education				
Less than high school	29	4	10	43
High school diploma	53	10	6	69
Some college	63	3	5	71
College diploma	26	0	7	33
Total	171	17	28	216^a
Family Income				
$10,000 or under	49	6	4	59
$11,000–$20,000	41	2	10	53
$21,000–$30,000	35	6	4	45
$31,000–$40,000	20	1	1	22
$41,000 and above	19	1	3	23
Total	164	16	22	202^a
Marital status				
Single, never married	75	5	9	89
Married	47	8	11	66
Partnered	14	1	2	17
Separated	7	1	6	14
Divorced	25	2	2	27
Widowed	3	0	0	3
Total	169	17	30	216^a
Number of children				
0	1	0	0	1
1	67	3	7	77
2	48	5	10	63
3	29	3	7	39
4 or more	12	4	3	19
Total	157	15	27	199^a

^{a}Missing data when totals do not equal 235.

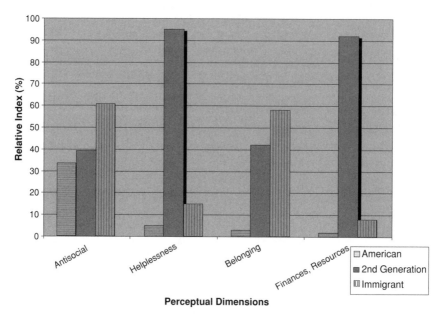

Figure 9.1
Latent Perceptual Demensions: A Relative Assessment

that self reported perceptions of Helplessness (95%) and poor Finances/Resources (92%) are evidenced most often by second generation Americans. In addition reports of Antisocial Behaviors (61%) and low levels of feelings of Belonging (58%) are felt the greatest by immigrants in the study.

Statistically, second generation Americans in this sample evidence a much greater degree of helplessness than either Americans or immigrants. This could be a result of the pressures associated with trying to maintain a bicultural identity. Coping with pressures and prejudices of not truly belonging to either group may force these subjects to feel incapable of fulfilling both sets of expectations. In contrast, regardless of their economic status, both immigrants and Americans may have clearly defined backgrounds, traditions, and support systems to negotiate daily stresses. In addition, the second generation American may not be aware of available supports or available societal resources. This seems to be reflected, also, in the direction of the financial concerns, as the second generation perceives this to be a greater problem than do members of the other groups. That the direction of the antisocial behaviors and low levels of feelings of belonging is greater for the immigrant group than for the others should not be surprising. Literature suggests that the stresses of acculturation and/or adaptation can take their toll and express themselves in behaviors that are less than acceptable (such as domestic violence, substance abuse, or gambling) and perceived social distance from the members of the host country, particularly those living in the neighborhood, may result in feelings of isolation.

Clearly this pilot study is limited by the size and selectivity of the sample, as well as by the self-report data and the results should be viewed with extreme caution. However, it is interesting to note that, in general, despite differences in immigrant status, subjects in poverty report similar types of experience.

SUMMARY AND CONCLUDING REMARKS

With President George Bush's proposal for a temporary worker program for undocumented immigrants, which as of the Friday, June 2, 2006 preceding the writing of this paper, found disagreement between the House and the Senate, the fate of many immigrants and immigrant children is in the forefront of the U.S. public's consciousness. A number of options are proposed to handle the issue of illegal immigration. Specifically, they can be put on a route to citizenship, they should leave the country and reapply to enter legally, or they and their employers would be subjected to greater penalties than currently exist.

Recent estimates suggest there are approximately 12 million undocumented immigrants, the majority who come from Mexico and most who live in poverty. However, with the increased current focus on this group of immigrants, it is easy to forget that this is not the only immigrant population in poverty. Seven and a half million documented immigrants are also living in poverty; their children, who are not identified as immigrants as most (80%) are born in the United States and are citizens, are also poor, increasing the numbers exponentially. The social services must be especially aware that although this group of immigrants and their children is underrepresented in the client pool, this is not because of an absence of need or a private trough of resources.

Traditionally people of countries outside the borders of the United States have either believed it unacceptable to utilize resources outside their personal networks or the societies from which they have come have no services and supports to offer them. Thus, the concept of seeking assistance is alien to them, and many suffer without approaching social services for the help for which they are eligible. While the social services must be applauded for their increasing focus on learning about cultural differences and their effects on the client-worker relationship, they must also recognize that a disproportionately low number of immigrants in poverty actually seek their services. The profession must proactively reach out to immigrant populations in poverty to prevent longer-term difficulties in adaptation among the second generation such as those evidenced in the pilot study undertaken for this chapter.

NOTES

1. U.S. Census. Immigrants Admitted by Major Class of Admission and Selected Demographic Characteristics: Fiscal Year 2004. Available at http://uscis.gov/graphics/shared/statistics/yearbook/2004 (January 25, 2006).

2. U.S. Census. Current Population Survey, Annual Social and Economic Supplement, 2003. http://www.census.gov/population/www/socdemo/foreign/ppl-174.html#cit (January 25, 2006).

3. J.S. Passel, R. Capps, and M. Fix. Undocumented Immigrants: Facts and Figures. Washington, DC: Urban Institute (2004). Available at http://www.urban.org/1000587_undoc_immigrants_facts.pdf(January 25, 2006).

4. U.S. Department of State. Immigrant Numbers for February 2006. Visa Bulletin, VIII (90). Washington, DC: Department of State (2006). Available at http://travel.state.gov/visa/frvi/bulletin/bulletin_2771.html (January 25, 2006).

5. U.S. Census. Immigrants Admitted by Major Class of Admission and Selected Demographic Characteristics.

6. Passel, Capps, and Fix. Undocumented Immigrants.

7. Passel, Undocumented Immigrants, 10.

8. John M. Broder. Immigrants and the Economics of Hard Work, *The New York Times*, p. 3 (April 2, 2002).

9. Immigration and Naturalization Service (INS). Illegal Alien Resident Population. (2000). Available at http://www.cestim.it/14clandestino_usa.htm> (January 25, 2006).

10. Nazneen S. Mayadas and Uma A. Segal. Refugees in the 1990s: A U.S. Perspective. In Pallassana R. Balgopal (ed), *Social Work Practice with Immigrants and Refugees* (New York: Columbia University Press, 2000), 198.

11. U.S. Department of State. Proposed Refugee Admissions for Fiscal Year 2006 Report to the Congress. (2005). Available at http://www.state.gov/g/prm/refadm/rls/rpts/52366.htm#proposed (January 26, 2006).

12. U.S. Department of State. Smuggling? Trafficking? What's the Difference. *East Asia and the Pacific*. (2004). Available at http://usinfo.state.gov/eap/east_asia_pacific/chinese_human_smuggling/difference.html (January 26, 2006).

13. Sexuality Information and Education Council of the United States. The International Mail-Order Bride Industry: An Increasing Threat to Women, *Making the Connection—News and Views on Sexuality: Education, Health and Rights*, 3(2) (2004). Available at http://www.siecus.org/inter/connection/conn0048.htm (January 22, 2006).

14. Kinsey A. Dinan. *Federal Policies Restrict Immigrant Children's Access to Key Public Benefits*, (New York: Columbia University, 2005), 4.

15. U.S. Census Bureau. Current Population Survey, 2004 and 2005 Annual Social and Economic Supplements (2005).

16. National Center for Children in Poverty. *Children of Immigrants: A Statistical Profile* (New York: National Center for Children in Poverty, 2002).

17. American Psychological Association. APA Resolution on Immigrant Children, Youth, and Families (1998). Available at http://apa.org/pi/cyf/res_imm.html (February 10, 2006).

18. Uma A. Segal. *A Framework for Immigration: Asians in the United States* (New York: Columbia University Press, 2002).

19. Margie K. Shields and Richard E. Behrman. Children of Immigrant Families: Analysis and Recommendations, *The Future of Children*, 14(2) (2004): 4–16.

20. Cynthia C. Coll and Laura A. Szalacha. The Multiple Contexts of Middle Childhood, *The Future of Children*, 14(2) (2004): 79–97.

21. The Immigration Project at Harvard University. *Harvard Educational Review Special Issue: Immigration and Education*. Available at http://gseweb.harvard.edu/~hepg/si/(February 21, 2006).

22. N.F. Chavkin and J. Gonzalez. *Mexican Immigrant Youth and Resiliency: Research and Promising Programs*. ERIC Clearinghouse on Rural Education and Small Schools Charleston, WV. Available at http://www.ericdigests.org/2001-3/mexican.htm (February 21, 2006).

23. Lin & Shen 1991; Mitra, 1995)

24. S.M. Yu, Z.J. Huang, R.H. Schwalberg, M. Overpeck, and M.D. Kogan. Acculturation and the Health and Well-Being of U.S. Immigrant Adolescents. *Journal of Adolescent Health*, 33(6) (2003): 479–488; A.J. Pumariega, E. Rothe, and J.B. Pumariege. Mental Health of Immigrants and Refugees. *Community Mental Health Journal*, 41(5) (2005): 581–597.

25. M. Beiser, F. Hou, I. Hyman and M. Tousignant. Poverty, Family Process, and the Mental Health of Immigrant Children in Canada. *American Journal of Public Health*, 92(2) (2002): 220–227.

26. Carmen DeNavas-Walt, Bernadette D. Proctor and Cheryl H. Lee. Income, Poverty, and Health Insurance Coverage in 2004, Current Population Reports: Consumer Income (Washington, DC: Government Printing Office, 2005), 26.

27. Committee on Community Health Services. Providing Care For Immigrant, Homeless, and Migrant Children. *Pediatrics*, 115 (2005): 1095–1100.

28. R.L. Riedel. Access to Health Care. In W. Loue (ed.), *Handbook of Immigrant Health* (New York: Plenum, 1998), 101–123.

29. R.A. Hummer, R.G. Rogers, C.B. Nam and F.R. LeClere. Race/Ethnicity, Nativity, and U.S. Adult Mortality. *Social Science Quarterly*, 80(1) (1999), 136–153.

30. E. Dutt. Many Asian Indians in California Lack Health Coverage. *India Abroad* (November 5, 1999): 52.

INDEX

AAP. *See* American Academy of Pediatrics

ADHD. *See* Attention Deficit Hyperactivity Disorder

AEA. *See* Area Education Agency

African Americans: asthma among, 33–38, 41–43, 45; folic acid use in, 13; health insurance of, 76–77, 82; IMR in, vii, 2, 4–7; income of, 76; maternal mortality rates of, vii; mental health care in, xii, 74, 76–77, 93–97, 99–103; poverty in, 3, 76; pregnancy/childbirth complications in, 4–5; SIDs intervention for, 9–11

Air pollution, 36

Alaimo, Katherine, viii, xi

The Alliance to End Hunger, x

Amaro, Hortensia, 78

American Academy of Pediatrics (AAP), 9–10

American dream, the, 133

American Indian/Alaska Natives, 9; IMR in, 2, 4–5, 7; poverty and health among, 76

American Lung Association, 40

American Psychological Association (APA), 133

Americans, 2nd generation: education of, 136–37; household status of, 136–37; income of, 136–37; self-perception of, 136, 138

Andersen, Ronald M., 77–78

Anencephaly, 6, 12

Anglin, Trina M., 84

Anyon, J., 23

APA. *See* American Psychological Association

Area Education Agency (AEA), 68, 71

Asian/Pacific Islanders: child's health in, 3; folic acid use in, 13; IMR in, 1, 4–5, 7; SIDs intervention for, 10

Assured ability, 23

Asthma: in Baltimore, 36; causes and treatment of, 34–45; child's experience of, 42–45; cigarette smoking and, 37; depression and, 43; hospitalization for, 38; obesity and, 37–38; during Olympics, 36; poverty and, xi, 3, 33, 36; race/ethnicity and, xi, 3, 33–38, 41–43, 45; SES and, 41–42; stress and, 42–44

Asylees. *See* Refugees

Attention Deficit Hyperactivity Disorder (ADHD), xii, 3, 56, 78, 109

Autism, 66–69

National Health Interview Survey (NHIS), xii, 3, 109
National Heart, Lung and Blood Institute (NHBLI), 38
National Institute of Child Health and Human Development (NICHD), 9
National Survey of Early Childhood Health, 2000, 82
National Vital Statistics System, 1
Native Americans. *See* American Indian/Alaska Natives
NCHS. *See* National Center for Health Statistics
NCPP. *See* National Collaborative Perinatal Project
Netherlands, the, 13
Neural tube defects (NTD), xi, 2, 6, 9; folic acid and, 12; IMR and, 6–7
New Zealand, SIDs in, 6
NHANES. *See* National Health and Nutrition Examination Survey
NHBLI. *See* National Heart, Lung and Blood Institute
NHIS. *See* National Health Interview Survey
NICHD. *See* National Institute of Child Health and Human Development
Nord, M., 19
North Dakota, 63
NTD. *See* Neural tube defects
Nyugen, Uyen-Sa, 76

Oberg, Charles, x–xi
Obesity, xi, 37–38
Ohio Supreme Court, viii
Olympics, 36
Owens, P.L., 94

Person File, 109
Pescosolido, Bernice A., 79
Pickett, K.E., 10–11
Portability, job, 56
Poverty: asthma and, xi, 3, 33, 36; birthweight, intelligence and, 2; disabilities and, xi–xii, 50–52; extreme, 3; health and, 33, 50, 107; in immigrants, xi, 106, 114, 117, 130,

133, 139; IMR and, x–xi, 4–7, 9; international rates of, 17; in Iowa, 63–71; race/ethnicity and, x–xi, 3–7, 9, 76, 81, 121–22; rural, 63; status, 111; in United States, 17, 33
Poverty line, 20
Pregnancy, complications of, 4–5
Prenatal care, vii–viii, 4
Proctor and Gamble, x
Proposition 187, 82
Prozac, 67, 71
Psychological distress, 2
Puerto Ricans: asthma among, 33; health care in, 75–76; IMR in, 7; mental health care in, 76–77

Race/ethnicity: asthma and, xi, 3, 33–38, 41–43, 45; child's health and, 3; health and, 3, 76, 121–22; health care and, 3, 75–78, 81, 106–7, 121–22; health insurance and, 76–77, 81–82, 122; immigrants and, xii, 120, 139; IMR and, vii, x–xi, 1–2, 4–7, 9; income and, 76; mental health and, xii, 74–86, 93–97, 99–103; poverty and, x–xi, 3–7, 9, 76, 81, 121–22; SIDs and, 9–11
Radimer, K., 18
Refugees, 107, 130–32
Relton, C.L., 12
Richardson, L.A., 94
Rich, Michael, 44
Rinaldi, Maria, x–xi
Rogers, Everett, 6–7
Rural areas, xii; health care in, 64–68, 72; poverty in, 63. *See also* Iowa, poverty in

Sample Child File, 109
San Antonio, 54
SBHCs. *See* School-based health centers
SCHIP. *See* State Children's Health Insurance Program
School-based health centers (SBHCs), 84–86
School Lunch Program, 17
School systems, health care and, 69–70
Segal, Uma A., xiii
Segal, Zubin N., xiii

About the Editors
and Contributors

Barbara A. Arrighi is associate professor of sociology at Northern Kentucky University. Her research interests include work and family, as well as issues related to race, class, and sexism. Her books include: *America's Shame: Women and Children in Shelter and the Degradation of Family Roles* and *Understanding Inequality: The Intersection of Race/Ethnicity, Class, and Gender*. Professor Arrighi has published in the *Journal of Family Issues* and elsewhere.

David J. Maume is professor of sociology, and Director, Kunz Center for the Study of Work and Family, at the University of Cincinnati. His teaching and research interests are in labor market inequality and work-family issues, with recent publications appearing in the *Journal of Marriage and Family*, *Work and Occupations*, and *Social Problems*. He is currently researching gender differences in providing urgent child care in dual-earner families, gender differences in the effects of supervisor characteristics on subordinates' job attitudes, and the effects of shift work on the work and family lives of retail food workers (funded by the *National Science Foundation*).

Katherine Alaimo, PhD, is an assistant professor in the Department of Food Science and Human Nutrition at Michigan State University. Her research interests are in the areas of U.S. hunger and its consequences for children, community food security, urban agriculture, policy and environmental supports for promoting healthy eating and physical activity, and community-based participatory research. She has published several research articles on the prevalence and consequences of food insufficiency in the United States. Dr. Alaimo's current community-based research projects include an evaluation of an urban gardening program in Detroit, Michigan, and the development and evaluation of the Michigan Promoting Active Communities Award and *Design Guidelines for Active Michigan Communities*. Dr. Alaimo has worked as an antihunger researcher, as a W.K. Kellogg Community Health Scholar at the University of Michigan, as Associate Evaluation Director with the Prevention Research Center of Michigan, and as a nutritionist for the National Center for Health Statistics, U.S. Centers for Disease Control and Prevention. Dr. Alaimo holds a PhD in Community Nutrition from Cornell University.

Linda Burton is professor in the Sociology Department at Duke University. Her program of research is conceptually grounded in life course, developmental, and ecological perspectives and focuses on three themes concerning the lives of America's poorest urban, small town, and rural families: (1) intergenerational family structures, processes, and role transitions; (2) the meaning of context and place in the daily lives of families; and, (3) childhood adultification and the accelerated life course. Her methodological approach to exploring these issues is comparative, longitudinal, and multimethod. The comparative dimension of her research comprises in-depth within group analysis of low-income African American, white, and, Hispanic/Latino families, as well as systematic examinations of similarities and differences across groups. She employs longitudinal designs in her studies to identify distinct and often nuanced contextual and ethnic/racial features of development that shape the family structures, processes (e.g., intergenerational care-giving) and life course transitions (e.g., grandparenthood, marriage) families experience over time. She is principally an ethnographer, but integrates survey and geographic and spatial analysis in her work. She is currently one of six principal investigators involved in a multisite, multimethod collaborative study of the impact of welfare reform on families and children (Welfare, Children, and Families: A Three-City Study). She directs the ethnographic component of the Three-City Study and is also principal investigator of an ethnographic study of rural poverty and child development (The Family Life Project).

Cindy Dell Clark is associate professor of Human Development and Family Studies at Pennsylvania State University. Her research belongs to the interdisciplinary field of Childhood Studies, with a focus on children's own perspectives and cultural contributions. She has studied chronic illnesses (childhood asthma and diabetes) as well as the role of play, imagination, and ritual in children's social worlds.

Anu R. Diwakaran, MD, is a board certified pediatrician at Glennon Care Pediatrics in St Charles, MO, a clinic of SSM Cardinal Glennon Children's Hospital in St Louis, MO. She received her pediatric training at the Children's Hospital of Michigan, Wayne State University in Detroit, MI. She is a Fellow of the American Academy of Pediatrics and in 1999 received the "Child Advocate of the Year" award by the Kiwanis Club in Michigan for her commitment to prevention of child abuse and neglect. She serves as a clinical preceptor for family nurse practitioner programs in the St Charles area.

Ricardo B. Eiraldi, PhD, is assistant professor of Clinical Psychology in the Department of Pediatrics at the University of Pennsylvania, and serves as the Program Director of the Behavioral Health in Urban Schools program at The Children's Hospital of Philadelphia.

Dr. Eiraldi's research interests and areas of expertise include the development and application of models of help-seeking behavior to study disparities in the delivery of mental health services, and the evaluation of diagnostic strategies for girls and ethnic minority children with symptoms of attention-deficit/hyperactivity disorder (ADHD). Dr. Eiraldi was supported for the writing of this chapter by grant MH64080 from the National Institute of Mental Health.

Cynthia Needles Fletcher is professor and Extension Specialist in the Department of Human Development and Family Studies, Iowa State University. Her research addresses economic well-being and family/consumer policy issues, especially among low-income families. Recent studies have focused on welfare reform and transportation barriers facing poor families. She has authored many extension publications and policy briefs for general audiences and has published in *Journal of Consumer Affairs*, *Journal of Family and Economic Issues*, *Family Relations*, *Social Indicators Research*, and *Journal of Public Service and Outreach*.

Stacey Lyn Grant served as the project manager for the Family Development Project until 2003. Currently, she resides in Germany and is working toward earning her master's degree in Human Relations and International Relations from the University of Oklahoma. Her research interests include interdisciplinary collaboration and nonprofit management aimed toward community building and the advancement of less developed countries.

Rachael D. Jankowski currently is a Government Affairs Associate with the AIDS Alliance for Children, Youth, and Families in Washington, DC. She served as a research assistant with the Family Development Project until her graduation from the University of Michigan, School of Public Health, in 2006 with her MPH degree. Her interests are in poverty and health, HIV/AIDS, and international public health.

Laura P. Kohn-Wood is an associate professor of Clinical Psychology. Her research program focuses on the development and expression of psychopathology among African Americans. She has studied factors related to risk for mental illness including mood disorders, the relationship between mental health and violent behavior, and ethnic and gender differences in the experience of illness and mental health service utilization.

William Lachicotte, PhD, is research assistant professor of Social Medicine, adjunct assistant professor of Anthropology, and research associate, FPG Child Development Institute, at the University of North Carolina at Chapel Hill. His research explores, through the lens of personal and social identity, the effects of institutional and professional conditions on the production of medical care and, consequently, on the health and lives of individuals, families and communities in the United States.

Laurie B. Mazzuca, PhD, is program coordinator of the Behavioral Health in Urban Schools Program and staff clinical psychologist at The Children's Hospital of Philadelphia. Dr. Mazzuca's research interests and areas of expertise center in the development and implementation of strategies for addressing service disparities in school settings.

Jennifer Elizabeth Mccall served as a research assistant for the Family Development Project. Her research interests center on depression, body distortions, and eating disorders and how these disorders vary in terms of gender and ethnic backgrounds. Her interests also include community-based psychology and how it may serve as a bridge to helping low-income families receive mental health services.

Charles N. Oberg, MD, is Chair of Maternal & Child Health at the University of Minnesota School of Public Health. In addition, he is an associate professor of Pediatrics and Public Health.

Dr. Oberg's work in the area of childhood poverty and public policy began in the early 1980s as a Special Legislative Assistant on Health in the United States Senate as a Congressional Fellow through the American Association for the Advancement of Science (AAAS). He has helped to conceptualize and implement numerous programs addressing health-care access needs for the poor and underserved at both the Federal and State level. For example, he was a member of the Minnesota Health Care Access Commission, the legislative advisory committee that created the framework for MinnesotaCare, a health plan to address the uninsured in Minnesota. In addition, he served as the initial Medical Director of the Hennepin County Health Care for the Homeless, a federal grant program operated under the Stewart B. McKinney Act from 1988 to 1995. He has maintained his involvement in public policy affecting children at both the federal and state level by serving as a member and/or chairing several national committees dealing with public policy, ethics, and children's issues.

Dr. Oberg's research interests lay particularly in the domain of access to care and health disparities for underserved populations. This includes numerous papers and reports including the book entitled, *America's Children-Triumph or Tragedy*, published by the American Public Health Association.

Maria C. Rinaldi is a PhD candidate in the Department of Epidemiology at the University of Minnesota School of Public Health. Maria received a bachelor's and master's degree from Tufts University in Human Factors Engineering and a master's in public health from the University of Minnesota School of Public Health. In addition to her PhD studies, Maria works as a teaching and research assistant in the Department of Epidemiology and Community Health. Ms. Rinaldi's research focuses on maternal and child health. In particular, she studies reproductive, psychiatric, and infant/child health.

Uma A. Segal, PhD is professor and director of the baccalaureate program in the School of Social Work at the University of Missouri-St. Louis, MO, and she holds a research fellow position in its Center for International Studies. Uma is editor of the *Journal of Immigrant and Refugee Studies* and has moved toward making it a premier journal on international and interdisciplinary studies in migration. Her areas of research interest and publication are immigrant and refugee concerns, Asian American acculturation, and cross-national issues in family violence—focusing primarily on Asian countries and, particularly, Japan and India. Two current research projects are an assessment of health and mental health issues of immigrant children in poverty and a cross-national collaborative and comparative analysis of immigration policies through the Hellenic Foundation for European and Foreign Policy in Athens, Greece.

Zubin N. Segal graduated from Northwestern University with a Bachelor of Arts in Biology and a minor in Spanish. After a tenure with Americorps and assisting with research in both neuroscience and neonatology, Zubin is enrolled at the University of Texas at Houston School of Public Health. In addition to having laboratory and academic experience, Zubin has worked closely with coauthor Dr. Anu Diwakaran, assisting in data collection and analysis and database management. Zubin's plans are to work in the public and nonprofit sectors, specifically in the field of health policy and epidemiology.

Debra Skinner, PhD, is a senior scientist at FPG Child Development Institute, and an adjunct associate professor in the Department of Anthropology at the University of North Carolina at Chapel Hill. She is a cultural anthropologist with postdoctoral training and research in Nepal and the United States on interdisciplinary and cross-cultural approaches to the study of child and human development. She has developed theoretical models and qualitative methods to examine the cultural production of identity and agency; and worked to integrate qualitative and quantitative methods on large interdisciplinary and longitudinal projects focused on issues related to families, culture, poverty, and disability. She is currently involved in a number of ethnographic and multimethod longitudinal studies on families' understandings of and responses to childhood disability and genetic disorders, including fragile X syndrome, and the broader cultural, economic, and political contexts of these beliefs and practices. She has published extensively on these topics. Her publications can be found athttp://www.fpg.unc.edu/people/search_people.cfm?staffID=87

Michael S. Spencer is an associate professor whose research focuses on the physical and mental health and service use of populations of color. Dr Spencer is the principal investigator of the Family Development Project, a University of Michigan/Detroit Head Start community-based research partnership, whose goal is to improve mental health service use and delivery among families enrolled in the Detroit Head Start Program.

Magdalena Szaflarski, PhD, is a research assistant professor in the Department of Family Medicine and a research scientist in the Institute for the Study of Health at the University of Cincinnati. Dr. Szaflarski's research interests include health disparities, immigrant health, comparative health research, and health-related quality of life in neurological diseases and HIV/AIDS. In 2003, Dr. Szaflarski received a research award from the Peter F. McManus Charitable Trust to study alcohol use and health in the U.S. immigrant population. Dr. Szaflarski's recent publications include a study of individual and area-level effects on self-reported health in the United States and Poland (*International Review of Modern Sociology*) and a study of health-related quality of life in patients with epilepsy (*Epilepsy and Behavior*).

Mary Winter is professor emerita, Human Development and Family Studies. Her research interests focus on the responses of ordinary families to extraordinary circumstances. She examined the responses of families in Mexico and Poland to changes in their country's economy, and resource development, and allocation among U. S. families with a family business. Recent work has focused on the effects of welfare reform on low-income families and adaptation by immigrants to their new environment in rural Iowa. Her work has been published in *Social Science and Medicine, Urban Anthropology, Journal of Marriage and the Family, Journal of Consumer Affairs, International Labour Review, Women's Policy Journal of Harvard, John F. Kennedy School of Government, Family Business Review, Journal of Family and Economic Issues, Financial Counseling and Planning, Journal of Research in Science Teaching*, and *Marriage and Family Review*.

Jun Ying, PhD, is a research assistant professor in the Department of Internal Medicine and a research scientist in the Institute for the Study of Health at the University of Cincinnati. Dr. Ying's research interests include longitudinal and cross sectional data analysis. He is also interested in statistical methods in hierarchical Bayesian computation and diagnostic medicine (e.g., ROC curve, agreement). Dr. Ying has published articles in *Journal of Forecasting, Journal of Nuclear Medicine*, and *American Journal of Roentgenology*.